Industrial Organization:
Theory and Practice

D

Industrial Organization: Theory and Practice

Second Edition

JOAN WOODWARD

Oxford University Press

Oxford University Press, Walton Street, Oxford OX2 6DP
London Glasgow New York Toronto
Delhi Bombay Calcutta Madras Karachi
Kuala Lumpur Singapore Hong Kong Tokyo
Nairobi Dar es Salaam Cape Town
Melbourne Auckland
and associates in
Beirut Berlin Ibadan Mexico City Nicosia

Published in the United States by
Oxford University Press, New York

First published 1965
Second edition 1980
Reprinted 1982

British Library Cataloguing in Publication Data

Woodward, Joan
    Industrial organization.—2nd ed.
    1. Industrial organization
    I. Title
    658.1   HD38   80-41051

    ISBN 0-19-874122-7 Pbk
    ISBN 0-19-874123-5

Printed offset and bound in Great Britain at
The Camelot Press Ltd, Southampton

Preface to the First Edition

This book presents chronologically the results of nearly ten years' empirical study of management organization in British industry. The story starts at the South East Essex College of Technology in 1953. At that time there was a growing awareness that our ability to make the most of the technological advances of recent years depended upon how far and how fast we could solve the social and economic problems that would inevitably result from these advances. But only a very small part of the resources of the universities was being expended in this field; even less was being done by the technical colleges. In an attempt to make good this deficiency, a small Human Relations Research Unit was set up at the College in September 1953 on the initiative of the Principal, Dr F. Heathcoat; the Joint Committee on Human Relations in Industry of the Department of Scientific and Industrial Research and the Medical Research Council, agreeing to sponsor a research project in the management organization field and finance it for four years from Counterpart Funds derived from U.S. Economic Aid, under the Conditional Aid Scheme.

The project formed part of this Committee's wider programme aimed at speeding up the development of the analytical social sciences in industry and commerce. It was felt that part of the resources available should go to the technical colleges, as owing to their close working relationship with local industry, adequate facilities for field research would readily be available to them.

The research project carried out by the Unit took the form of a broad survey of the organizational structure of a hundred firms in the catchment area of the College, supplemented by some more detailed case studies. The main part of the field work of the original study was completed early in 1958, and after the findings had been discussed with representatives of the firms that had participated, a short account of the investigations was published by the Department of Scientific and Industrial Research (Joan Woodward (1958) *Management and Technology*, London, H.M.S.O. *Problems and Progress in Industry* 3).

The research had shown not only that the firms studied varied considerably in their organizational structure, but also that similar administrative expedients could lead to wide variations in results. Firms in which organizational structure reflected an implicit acceptance of what has come to be known as classical management theory were not always the most successful from a commercial point of view. This theory did not therefore appear to be adequate as a practical guide to those responsible for the organization of industry.

Many of the variations found in the organizational structure of the firms studied did, however, appear to be closely linked with differences in manufacturing techniques. Different technologies imposed different kinds of demands on individuals and organizations, and these demands had to be met through an appropriate structure. Commercially successful firms seemed to be those in which function and form were complementary.

These ideas have become so much a part of management thinking that it is now difficult to understand why the booklet created so much controversy at the time it was published. The reason for this was that the conclusions reached were interpreted by some of the reviewers as undermining completely the principles and concepts of classical management theory, and by teachers of management subjects as an attack on management education.

The discussions held with participating firms illustrated the fact that in the social science field, the feeding back of research results often marks not so much the completion of a project as the beginning of a new phase in it. The reaction to the research findings and, in particular, the extent to which their implications were accepted and absorbed into the thought processes of those concerned with organizational problems was interesting in itself and enabled the research workers to reach a deeper understanding of the situation and to identify the areas in which further and more intensive work was needed.

Circumstances made it difficult to continue with the research at the South East Essex College of Technology: there was no reluctance on the part of the College but there were difficulties in obtaining adequate staff and resources, the original team having disintegrated by 1958. At about this time, however, industrial sociology was introduced into the syllabus of the post-graduate courses offered by the Production Engineering and Management Studies Section, of the Imperial College of Science and Technology, under the direction of Professor S. Eilon. The research material was therefore taken there and worked on for a further period. As a corollary to the teaching it was also possible to follow up some of the ideas that had emerged from the earlier research and to carry on the work on a more limited scale.

This book not only contains a fuller report than has yet been published of the original research with more supporting evidence for the conclusions reached but also takes the story further. Part III describes the additional work undertaken at the Imperial College of Science and Technology, and discusses the theoretical implications of the research findings, in particular their relevance to the problem of how far and how fast we can proceed to a valid theory of management based on solid research.

Contents

PART ONE: THE SURVEY

PART TWO: THE CASE STUDIES

Acknowledgements

As far as the original studies were concerned, the members of the Human Relations Research Unit at the South East Essex College of Technology who worked with Miss Woodward were Mr R. S. Webster, Miss J. Batstone, and Mrs M. Sanderson.

They are extremely grateful to all who made the research possible and, in particular, to the management of the manufacturing firms in South Essex who co-operated in a way that was unprecedented in a study of this kind. A hundred firms (91 per cent of the firms located in the catchment area of the College) employing a hundred people or more participated; this high percentage supporting the view that technical colleges are particularly well placed to secure research facilities. Indeed, the interest aroused locally, the involvement of so many firms in a project of this kind, and the resultant generation of energy may in themselves have made the research worth while.

More co-operation was sought from some firms than from others. Participation in the broader survey involved a senior member of the management in approximately an hour and a half's discussion with a research worker, and subsequent completion of a questionnaire. Some of these firms will now remember little about the investigations or the part they played in them. At the other end of the scale, where the research no doubt had a more lasting impact, there were firms which had members of the research team on their premises for as long as six months, co-operating with them in an intensive interviewing programme. But all the firms approached, once they had agreed to participate, gave as much co-operation as was sought from them.

Thanks are also due to Mr H. Silcock, of the Department of Social Science of the University of Liverpool, who advised the research workers how to set about the analysis of the background survey information; Mr R. G. Stansfield and later Mr A. Cherns of the Department of Scientific and Industrial Research, who gave help and guidance throughout; Mr H. Hickling, Head of the Department of Business Studies and Management at the College, and members of the teaching staff, in particular, Mr H. Lucas, Mr D. Foulkes, and Dr H. Haskey, with whom the project was discussed and who made useful comments and criticisms as the work developed.

In the subsequent stages of the research several more people became involved. Reference is made in Part III to the work done by Mr R. C. Brewer and some of the students of the Production Engineering and Management Studies Section at Imperial College. A number of post-graduate students of the Department of Social and Administrative Studies of the University of Oxford also participated in the follow-up investigations. Finally, reference must be made to Mr P. G. Combey, also of Imperial College, who was extremely helpful in the production of the diagrams and tables for the book.

INTRODUCTION

Joan Woodward and the Development of Organization Theory

SANDRA DAWSON AND DOROTHY WEDDERBURN

The main thesis of this book is well known. It is that industrial organizations which design their formal organizational structures to fit the type of production technology they employ are likely to be commercially successful. To quote Joan Woodward's preface: 'Commercially successful firms seemed to be those in which function and form were complementary.'

However, this is a book where to know its main thesis is no substitute for reading the book itself. It lives up to its title *Industrial Organization: Theory and Practice* possessing, as it does, interest and relevance both for intending students of organizations, as well as for anyone who is practically involved in industry as manager or employer. To appreciate the full significance of the work, it is necessary to understand something of its place in history, both in terms of why it was that Woodward embarked upon the research which forms the basis of the book in the first place, as well as in terms of its contribution to subsequent developments in organization theory. This introductory essay aims to do three things: the first is to summarize the development of Joan Woodward's thinking, both as displayed in this book and in her subsequent work; secondly to summarize and examine the major criticisms levelled at her work; and finally to provide a brief account of how organization theory has developed in the post Woodward era.

I. JOAN WOODWARD'S WORK

The reason Joan Woodward embarked on the research from which she developed her thesis was that in the early fifties she was teaching management courses at what was then the South East Essex

College of Technology. At that time the view which dominated management education was that there was 'one best way to organize' although there were at least two competing traditions on which this 'one best way' was founded. On the one hand students and managers were taught how to design formal structures by applying principles of Scientific Management, derived from the work of people like Fayol, Urwick, Follett, and Taylor (summarized in Massie, 1965). On the other hand a great deal of emphasis was placed on achieving the best management style in accordance with the work of Mayo and his associates in the Human Relations tradition. Woodward was uncomfortable in propagating such definite principles of management without putting them to some sort of empirical test. Furthermore her contacts with local industry showed her that a common and complex problem facing many organizations was the relationship of staff and line personnel. So she decided to test the current theories of organization which lay behind these prevailing principles and to examine systematically 'the dichotomy between executive and advisory responsibilities, and the resultant relationship between line supervision at different levels, and the various technical and administrative specialists being introduced in increasing number into industry' (p. 5, 1965).

In general then she addressed herself to the following questions: how and why do industrial organizations vary in structure and why do some structures appear to be associated with greater success for the organization than others ? These questions are still uppermost in the minds of those who work in industry and this book offers them important insights into the problem although it does not pretend to offer any ready-made solutions. However, the partialness of the solutions proposed has in itself stimulated a whole range of further research which has deepened our understanding of the processes which influence the structure and functioning of complex organizations. Thus for the student of organization theory the work remains an essential starting-point for the exploration of most other contributions in the field since the mid-sixties. But because Joan Woodward was unashamedly concerned with understanding the management task and helping those who worked in industry, be they managers, trade unionists, or workers, to appreciate that there were regularities and patterns underlying the often apparently random problems associated with behaviour in organizations, it provides a framework which is still of practical value.

Having decided on a study of organization structure, with special reference to line and staff relationships, Woodward chose a two-stage research strategy. The first stage involved a broad survey of industrial plants located in South East Essex and thus easily available to the researchers from their base at the local College of Technology. Firms employing less than 100 people were excluded and of the remaining 110 firms in the area 91 per cent (i.e. 100) agreed to co-operate. General trends which emerged in this first stage were then explored in depth through detailed case studies of just a few of these firms in the second stage of the research. In the first stage the following information was collected from all larger firms in the area:

1. History, background, and objectives.
2. Description of the manufacturing processes and methods.
3. Forms and routines through which the firm was organized and operated.
4. Facts and figures that could be used to make an assessment of the firms' commercial success. (p. 11, 1965)

Part I of this book deals with the method of collection and analysis of the data. The presentation follows the researchers own exciting path of discovery and documents how it was that, having looked in vain for a single general pattern of organization, they proceeded to an analysis of technical variables. Only then did they hit upon the relationship between technology and organizational characteristics as the key to making sense of their material. Thus each firm was placed on Woodward's eleven point scale of production systems (p. 39, 1965), itself an elaboration of a division normally used by production engineers, which reflected the complexity of the technology in terms of the degree to which the production process was inherently controllable and predictable. The scale ranged from the production of unit articles to customers' individual requirements through an intermediate stage of the mass production of standardized goods, to the most technically complex stage, that is, the continuous flow production of dimensional products.

Subsequent analysis relating organization variables to this scale showed three definite trends. Firstly it established a linear relationship between a firm's technical complexity and aspects of its organization chart and personnel ratios, for example the length of line of command; the span and control of the chief executive and the ratio of managers to total personnel (p. 51, 1965). Secondly, it revealed a curvilinear relationship between a firm's technical complexity and its place on an implied 'social structural continuum', which had been originally developed by Burns (1958) and which ran from organic, informal adaptable management systems to mechanistic formal systems of management (pp. 69 ff., 1965). Finally it was found that firms were more successful financially when they conformed to the median organizational form for their 'technology group' than when they diverged from it. The classical principles of management with their emphasis on clear formal definitions of responsibility seemed to be appropriate to large batch and mass technology, but to be detrimental to success in both unit and process production.

These findings which were fully documented when the present book was published in 1965 were first briefly summarized in a DSIR pamphlet in 1958. Even in this abbreviated form their effect on practitioners and theorists alike was profound. At last practitioners had definite and descriptive criteria rather than mere exhortation on which to begin to base decisions about the design of their organization. Indeed, in demonstrating the importance of systematic comparative empirical studies as a basis for management thinking, Woodward was charting new territory in a world where most study had previously been highly prescriptive.

> The demonstration of a link between technology, organization and success has practical significance for the industrial manager; it can lead not only to the development of techniques helpful in the appraisal of organization structure, but also make it possible to plan organization change simultaneously with technical change. (p. 72, 1965)

Far from feeling, however, that she had found the complete solution to problems of organizational design, Woodward quite rightly realized that she was just at the beginning of understanding the complexities of organization. Thus she turned from stage one and the broad survey to stage two of the research—the case studies of particular firms which are described in Parts 2 and 3 of this book. The rich detail of the case studies deals with such important and topical issues as relations between departments and between levels in the hierarchy, and provides some guidelines on the successful management of change in organizations. They demonstrate that what Joan Woodward called the 'analysis of situational demands' could lead

> . . . not only to the development of better techniques for appraising organizational structure and for conscious planning, but also to an increased understanding of the personal qualities and skills required in different industrial situations, and to improved methods of training directed towards giving those concerned a better understanding of the strains and stresses associated with the roles they are likely to occupy. (p. 80, 1965)

For example she explained why unit production firms were more successful if they had short lines of command in terms of their heavy reliance on interpersonal and direct communication between managers of different functions. Long hierarchies led to unnecessarily complex communications systems. On the other hand she found that in large batch and mass production firms

> The independence of functions meant that end results did not depend on the establishment of a close operational relationship between the people responsible for development, production, and sales respectively. This tended to encourage sectional interests and exaggerate departmental loyalties. (p. 137, 1965)

She commented that these differences were especially acute between production and development and therefore advised that these functional groups should be kept as separate as possible whilst ensuring that adequate communications were maintained between them. Such separation she noted, however, would be counter-productive when new products were being launched and in these circumstances she recommended the formation of product development teams. Such ideas as these have been developed by other writers who have variously discussed the appropriateness of product, functional, and matrix structures to different levels and types of technology (cf., for example, Lorsch and Lawrence (1970), Kingdom (1973), Galbraith (1973)).

At the same time as Woodward was documenting these relationships between technology and structure, other theorists in the UK and USA, notably Burns and Stalker (1961), Thompson (1967), Lawrence and Lorsch (1967), and Perrow (1967) were exploring similar relationships between technology, certain characteristics of the environment of organizations and features of organization structure. Together with Joan Woodward they can be credited with the foundation of the school known as the contingency theory of organizations. The common theme underlying this theory is that if an organization is to maintain good performance its structure in particular, must be designed to fit the situational demands which stem from the technology being used, its market position, its product diversity and rate of change, and its size. The common focus is that these contingent factors—technology, market situation, diversity, size—generate varying degrees of uncertainty and complexity which have to be 'coped with' by the development of appropriate structures and the encouragement of appropriate behaviour and attitudes on the part of management and workers.

Woodward continued the rest of her work within this paradigm although she by no means accepted organizations as static totally determined systems. Indeed her subsequent work paid increasing attention to the effects of a variety of social and economic factors in organization design which had been identified through the case studies documented in the present volume. These investigations had confirmed Woodward's suspicions that the relationships between technology and structure were not quite as straightforward as might have been supposed from the first stage of her research. Indeed they presented a puzzle which was to engage Woodward and her fellow researchers until her untimely death in 1971. The puzzle derived from the detailed analysis of organizations with technologies in the middle ranges of large batch and mass production where it was found that the fit between technology, structure, and performance was less good than at other points of her scale of technology. To quote Joan Woodward, the

> physical work flow did not impose such rigid restrictions, with the result that technology did not so much determine organisation as define the limits within which it could be determined. The separation of production administration from production operations, rationalisation of production processes, and attempts to push back the physical limitations of production resulted in the emergence of a control system that depended in part on the physical work flow and in part on top management policy. (p. 185, 1965)

Here we find a first hint that there is something which might be called 'managerial choice'.

Woodward took this conclusion as the basis for developing her next programme of research, this time at Imperial College, where she had become senior lecturer in 1962 and subsequently Professor of Industrial Sociology in 1969. Her research team approached the problem of the relations between technology and structure in batch production firms by concentrating on the definition, measurement, and operation of two sets of variables—one relating to the technology, the other to management control systems, which by now had been identified as important features of the design of organizations. In the case of technical variables the search was for a means of characterizing production systems in terms of uncertainty and complexity. A certain amount of progress was made in measuring technical variables, for example through the degree of variation in product range, the extent of standardization of components and the number of separate assembly or conversion stages in a manufacturing process (Rackham, Woodward, 1970).

But it was the analysis of the second set of variables relating to control systems which proved to be theoretically and practically more exciting. The findings of this part of the research are reported in detail in Reeves (1967), Woodward (1970a), Reeves and Turner (1972), Wedderburn and Crompton (1972). In approaching the definition and comparison of control systems the research team was influenced by Eilon's (1962) recognition that any production system based on division of labour requires systems to plan, co-ordinate, monitor, and provide feedback about progress in achieving the task of the organization. The detailed examination of control systems, which had already begun in the case studies presented in this book, resulted in the development of a typology based on two parameters: the degree to which control was exercised personally or indirectly; and the degree to which control systems were integrated or fragmented.

(i) *The degree of personal control.* At one end of this scale the researchers identified completely personal, hierarchical control, such as that exercised by an 'owner–employer deciding what he wants done and seeing that it is done' (p. 44, 1970a). In her inaugural lecture Woodward described how

traditionally and historically the successful achievement of the goals of any organisation depends on the exercise of one man's influence and authority over others. With increases in size and technical complexity, however, the exercise of personal hierarchical control becomes more difficult and leadership skills become less directly relevant to the organisational success. Line management can no longer have an intimate knowledge of all the various specialised and complex processes intrinsic to the production task and impersonal processes of control are built into the organisation to influence and regulate the work behaviour of those employed. (p. 119, 1970b)

These impersonal controls may be administrative—for example complex programmes for production planning and cost control which effectively control behaviour through formal standardized procedures. But alternatively impersonal controls may be built into the production process and operate through mechanical or electronic devices such as in 'the automatic control of machine tools or continuous flow production plant' (p. 45, 1970a).

(ii) *The degree to which control systems were integrated or fragmented.* At the integrated end of this scale were firms where great effort was devoted to relating 'the standards set for various departments by the different functional specialists and the performance and adjustment mechanisms associated with them, into a single integrated system of managerial control' (p. 50, 1970a).

At the other end of the scale were firms where 'either because different departments make different products and for different markets, or because departmental standards related to such factors as cost, quality and time were set independently and never related to each other, control was fragmented' (p. 50, 1970a).

Putting these two scales together, Reeves and Woodward identified four categories of control and suggested that the normal processes of industrial and technical development would move a firm in the direction indicated by the arrows in Fig. 1 (Fig. 4 in 1970a, p. 53).

It was decided to re-analyse the data gathered in the South East Essex study and presented in this book (1965) in order to allocate each of the one hundred firms to one of these four categories of control. Clear links then emerged between control categories and technology as is demonstrated in Table I (Table III in 1970a, p. 54). These relationships are discussed fully in 'Industrial Organization. Behaviour and Control' (1970a).

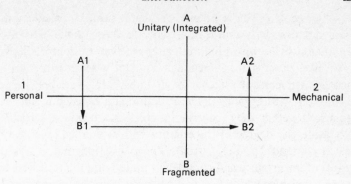

Fig. I. The categorization of control systems

From this it seemed, firstly, that the similarities in structure already noted in this book between firms utilizing unit and process technology could be explained by the fact that both groups tended

Table I. *Relationship between Type of Technology and Control System in South East Essex Survey*

Technology	Control system Categories as in Fig. I			
	A1 %	B1 %	B2 %	A2 %
Unit and small batch	75	25	–	–
Large batch and mass	15	35	40	10
Process	–	–	5	95
TOTAL FIRMS	28	21	18	33

to operate with integrated control systems, although in one group the integration was achieved by personal administration while in the other it was achieved by means of mechanically integrated data processing computer systems or by control mechanisms built into the hardware of the production systems. Secondly,

the heterogeneity in structure and organizational behaviour associated in the South Essex study with the batch and mass production group may be linked with the fact that they spread across the whole of the control processes spectrum. (p. 55, 1970a)

Large batch and mass production firms with predominantly

personal controls were found to share similar organizational characteristics with unit firms, whereas large batch and mass production firms with predominantly mechanical controls looked more like process organizations. Thus it was possible to see management control systems as an intervening variable, linking technology with organizational structure and behaviour not least because 'together they (control variables and technical variables) determine the degree of uncertainty with which an organization has to contend' (p. 237, 1970a). The realization that it was the degree of uncertainty and complexity underlying the technical and control variables which was so important in influencing structure and behaviour in organizations encouraged Woodward and her colleagues at Imperial College

> to apply the conceptual framework and methodology we have developed to organisations other than manufacturing firms. A quasi-government organisation like the N.B.P.I. (National Board of Prices and Incomes) producing reports on a one-off basis has a number of behavioral characteristics in common with a manufacturing firm making one off products. Uncertainty in the Industrial Division of N.E.D.O. (National Economic Development Office) arises from the fact that the work of the E.D.Cs (Economic Development Councils) is self-generated . . . (1970b)

Just as the case study material in this book illuminates and deepens our understanding of Woodward's earlier theoretical position, so the case material in the second book about industrial organizations enriches her statements about control systems and we see her beginning to raise questions about the range of choice available to management in its design of control systems. This led to the emergence of a concern with such issues as conflicts of interest and beliefs of powerful individuals and groups within the organization. Thus, Woodward acknowledged the importance of social, psychological, and economic as well as technical factors as inputs into managerial decisions about structure and control. This was particularly demonstrated in the two unpublished studies of the NBPI and NEDO which she made in the last years of her life and in the research she sponsored in hospitals (Davies, Francis, 1976) and prison industries (Dawson, 1975).

Thus when Joan Woodward died the seeds were already firmly sown for the Imperial College research team to extend its concerns from manufacturing to include service organizations as well as to examine political processes within organizations with a view to establishing the extent to which structure and behaviour can be seen as the outcome of material constraints on the one hand and the product of psychological, social, and economic factors on the other. This transition period is described briefly in Davies *et al.* (1973) and its fruits are more fully documented in the collection of essays edited by Abell (1975) where his own model of organization as technically constrained bargaining and influence systems (OCBIS) is elaborated. As Abell himself later claimed 'It is one of the claims of the OCBIS model that it is able to elucidate the relative importance of "constraint" and "choice" in determining organizational outcomes within a systematic theoretical framework' (Abell, 1978).

II. AN EVALUATION OF WOODWARD AND CONTINGENCY THEORY

Moving now from an account of Woodward's work to an evaluation of its significance for the development of organization theory as a whole, it is important to distinguish criticism of two kinds. First there have been those who basically accept the usefulness of a contingency framework but disagree about the relative weight to be assigned to various contingencies. Secondly there are those who not only criticize Woodward but the contingency framework generally, and are concerned to ensure that concepts of power and ideology are made more central to the analysis of complex organizations.

   With regard to the first set of criticism, the problem is that whilst at an intuitive level many people believe that the physical nature of the production system (technology) is an important factor which must be borne in mind in the design of organization structure, no one, apart from Zwerman (1970), has claimed to have had much success in replicating Woodward's survey findings, although several leading researchers have conducted studies which have attempted, at least partially, to do so (*inter alia* Hage and Aitken (1969), Hickson, Pugh, and Pheysey (1969), Mohr (1971), Child and Mansfield (1972), Blau, McKinley, and Tracey (1976)). Thus as the reviews by Aldrich (1972), Mohr (1971), and Donaldson

(1976) indicate, we cannot accept a simple thesis which relates technology, structure, and performance. Nor can we regard technology as an easily operational concept. For example Mohr, after his review and his own study of 144 work groups in 13 local US health departments, concludes that 'technology may be related to structure but not as a magical package. Neither is it unidimensional nor even a relatively homogeneous concept' (p. 454). He and other scholars have variously highlighted the importance of such things as size, market factors, government policy, and trade unions as influences on performance and/or structure, whilst at the same time pointing out that all these 'external factors' have to be reviewed and acted on by people, who in turn have their own ideas and power bases from which to pursue them.

Woodward herself would not have been surprised by the confusion which has surrounded attempts to reconcile the findings of various studies into relationships between technology and structure. Indeed contrary to several statements about her views, she never said that technology determines structure. Her claims even in the midst of the initial excitement which accompanied publication of the findings of her first research programme were far more circumspect:

> Therefore the main conclusion reached through this research project was that the existence of the link between technology and social structure first postulated by Thorstein Veblen (1904) can be demonstrated empirically. It is not suggested that the research proved technology to be the only important variable in determining organizational structure or that such factors as the history and background of the firm and the personalities of the people who built it up and subsequently managed it were unimportant. (p. 50, 1965)

Furthermore, as we have shown, her subsequent work demonstrates that she was fully aware of the need to explore other influences on structure as well as to develop techniques for the definition and measurement of technology, although this, in fact, largely eluded both her and others who have attempted comparable exercises. Indeed a recurrent theme in most of the replication attempts has been that both technology and structure are complex multi-dimensional concepts that cannot be expected to be related in a simple manner and need themselves to be subject to finer definition. A principal confusion arises because although most measures of technology attempt to encapsulate some notion of the extent of predictability of operations, some researchers (e.g. Hickson *et al.*, 1969) have followed Woodward in considering the predictability of the whole system, including the work done by machines, whereas others, e.g. Perrow (1967) and, Hage and Aiken (1969), have concentrated upon the predictability of the work actually done by people within the production system.

Hickson *et al.* (1969) go further than most of Woodward's critics in offering an explanation of discrepant findings. They claim that there is considerable evidence to support the view that technology is especially important in influencing structural features at the level of shop-floor organization, for example in the numbers of people in inspection and maintenance functions, but that it is far less important in influencing patterns of organization and management higher up the hierarchy. The view that technology is a major influence upon production operations is consistent with the long socio-technical tradition of analysis associated with the Tavistock Institute of Human Relations (p. 36, 1965). Thus one explanation for the apparent incompatability of some empirical findings relates to size, for especially by today's standards Woodward's firms were fairly small, and thus all parts of the organization were 'nearer' to the technical core. Towards the end of her life, Joan Woodward began to study strategic decision making at headquarters level in conglomerate industrial enterprises. There she recognized that her technological scale had to be supplemented and whilst still preoccupied with the importance of uncertainty and complexity, she utilized concepts such as the degree of inter-dependency derived from Thompson (1967) and Allen (1970).

Whilst these battles raged about causality and the relative and prior importance of different contingencies, notably technology and size, a number of publications at the turn of the decade (Silverman, 1968, 1971, Child, 1972) began to call in question what were seen as the essentially mechanistic assumptions of the contingency theorists. Coincidentally they emphasized the need for an approach to organizational analysis which acknowledged process over time, as well as the role of purposive human action in situations where assumptions about consensus between groups and individuals within organizations were deemed inappropriate.

It is the case that each of the contingency theorists in some way, and to varying degrees, acknowledged the importance of power, choice, and values within organizations, although with a few exceptions the tendency was for those features of organizational life to be regarded as interesting but residual. Burns is the outstanding exception. Whilst working within a type of contingency theory he developed the idea of a plurality of social systems within organizations (1966) and emphasized the importance of micropolitical activity in organizational change (1961). Woodward never went as far as Burns in this matter but in this present book (1965) she does acknowledge the importance of departmental divisions of interest and explores the implications of this for organization structure. We have also seen how the possibility that managerial choice might be influenced by beliefs and values was acknowledged in her later work. But Woodward saw different interests in organizations as deriving mainly from the nature of the demands imposed by the production system and she regarded the acceptance of the over-all goals and objectives of the organization as essentially non-problematic. Organizations, in her eyes, were systems for collective action which develop a structure and pattern of functioning which equips them, more or less well, for coping with externally given constraints and uncertainties in order to achieve objectives. Her view of control was essentially apolitical and defined as independent of the social factors she wanted to explain; the problem facing the organization was how to control the technology 'for the good' of 'the organization'. Paradoxically it was her strong and worthy concern to say something practically useful and relevant which prevented her from exploring the wider implication of some of her findings. For her, it was in the interests of all parties—different levels of management, shop-floor workers and trade unionists alike—that industrial organizations should work efficiently. Thus she concentrated on those elements of her theoretical analysis which appeared to lie both within managerial control and not to conflict strongly with a managerial view of the world.

A summary (Dawson, 1979) of the criticisms made of contingency theory as a whole suggests that there are four main issues which merit serious attention. Three of them relate to conceptualization and these will be discussed in some detail. The fourth, which will be mentioned now, highlights the essentially mechanistic nature of contingency models of organizations and concerns its failure to give adequate emphasis to the unanticipated consequences of 'planned' change. The pedigree of debate in this area is long and distinguished (see, for example, Selznick, 1949, Gouldner, 1954, Merton, 1957), but a recent example of it is provided by a fascinating discussion of changes which had taken place in the BBC over a ten-year period (Burns, 1977):

> The biggest change in the BBC between 1963 and 1973 was not, I believe, the reconstruction of top management, the institution of stricter financial budgeting and surveillance, the increase of the powers of Managing Directors and the Controllers over them, or the depletion of the 'baronial' powers of heads of group and heads of department, nor was it the increase in size or increased union militancy or the appearance of a 'radical underground'. What did make the differences was the breakdown of the ordinary institutions of social interaction between the variety of people engaged in programme production—i.e. the unanticipated consequence of these changes, which did more to alter the internal working of the organization than the intentional changes effected by management.
> (p. 272)

These unanticipated consequences were such that they so increased the segmentation between already traditionally rival groups that they seriously under-mined the over-all commitment of employees to shared objectives and exacerbated feelings of insecurity and anxiety. Given Woodward's own perceptive description of her case studies, one feels that she would have had great sympathy with this analysis.

Turning now to the conceptual problems identified by the critics of contingency theory, the first one arises in relation to organizational performance—the dependent variable in the schema of Joan Woodward and her fellow contingency theorists. Implicit in the notion of aspects of organizational life adjusting to meet constraints inherent in technology, environment, size, etc., is the notion that the 'fit' between the parts will be made in order to maximize performance criteria. However, a variety of goals are pursued by different interests involved in organizations and we may legitimately ask 'performance' for whom? Furthermore organizational performance, even in respect of one group of objectives, is multi-facted in aspects of efficiency and effectiveness. For example economists like Marris (1964) have debated the objectives of profit maximization versus growth. Thus it is impossible to derive a single utility function which can be treated as the criterion of the goodness of 'fit' between various organizational features. The question then arises of understanding why one utility function prevails over another. This brings the analysis back to questions of perceptions of interest, or the basis of different interests and the way in which the distribution of power and influence affect their pursuit. This type of question possesses a distinguished ancestry in Weber's analysis of power and the different types of rationality underlying purposive social action. Certain of Joan Woodward's contemporary organization theorists, such as March and Simon (1958), Thompson (1967), and Cyert and March (1963) had underlined the limited and variable nature of the concept of rationality, as applied to organizational behaviour, because people are always operating in organizations with less than complete information about the full range of alternatives and of consequences. An understanding of the limits to the rationalities of individuals and groups becomes even more important if it is acknowledged that organizations are collections of groups of people with different interests, stratified along a number of important, but not necessarily congruent dimensions such as function, level, and occupational reference group. Then the mechanisms by which these groups are held together and through which they pursue their own interests become critically important to the understanding of organizational processes and outcomes. Thus an analysis of the access which different interest groups have to a range of power resources, such as information, skill, expertise, and ability to offer rewards and sanctions emerges as an important subject of study as in the work of, *inter alia*, Emerson (1962), French and Raven (1959), Mechanic (1962), Crozier (1964), Hickson *et al.* (1971). This focus on power, choice, purpose, action, and change within and between organizations has resulted in a rich picture of what life is like for participants in complex organizations (see for example Pettigrew (1973), Burns (1977), Warmington (1977)).

The second conceptual problem concerns the causal patterns implied in most contingency theories, wherein performance is seen as a dependent variable and structure as an intervening variable. It is of course probable that some factors influence performance quite independently of structure. For example, as Sayles wrote in a letter, forming part of an exchange of views about Woodward's work in OMEGA (1978), 'no matter what the structure, incompetence is incompetence and it is deadly' (p. 110). Personal characteristics of management and workforce apart, there will also be changes in labour and product markets equally 'deadly' to organizational performance and which cannot be coped with merely by changes in structure. Furthermore there is potential for multi-way relationships between all organizational variables. Thus it is conceivable that levels of present performance precipitate change in other organizational characteristics. For example Child (1972) has cited studies showing a relationship between poor performance in profit and growth terms and tight cost controls (such as manpower budgets), where it is at least as plausible that poor performance leads to the tightening of controls as vice versa.

The third conceptual problem concerns the supposed status of the independent 'contingent' variables of technology, nature of the market, diversity and size as being 'given', and beyond the control of organizational members. Many writers have now taken issue with such a view. For example, Galbraith (1967) and Perrow (1972) have suggested that large corporations can, in fact, exert considerable control over sectors of their environment. Advertising may be effective in controlling consumers and influencing the size or stability of the market, while pressure group politics can influence the formulation of government legislation. Nor can production technology necessarily be taken as 'given'. The experiments with car assembly plants in Scandinavia show that there may be the possibility of choice concerning the type of technology to be employed to manufacture a given product (Aguven *et al.*, 1976). Yet another body of research suggests that national systems of training and education have a profound effect upon dominant forms of organization structure within countries—see Brossard and Maurice (1976), Sorge and Warner (1978).

Furthermore Elgar (1975) has commented on the need to see the administrative structure of organizations as the outcome of negotiation between different organizational participants. In making this point he is emphasizing a need echoed by many critics of contingency theory that organizational analysis should be more processual in approach, rather than operating within the sort of static framework which is implied by a straightforward contingency theory of organizations:

> this processual viewpoint implies that 'organisation structure' as a pattern of social relations and social constraints, should be seen as the ongoing product of social processes enacted by organisation members rather than as some form of 'given' which furnishes automatic constraints on lines of actions of these members . . . (this) perspective . . . emphasises the humanly created and sustained character of social institutions and attends to the conflicts of interest generated by the typical social relations of industrial concerns, together with those social processes which mitigate, conceal, contain, organise and intensify these conflicts. (p. 91)

In summary then, contingency theory has been justly criticized for its deterministic assumptions about the nature of change in organizations, its inadequate appreciation of the role of strategic choice, beliefs, and power, its simplistic assumptions about organizational performance and effectiveness and its neglect, among other things, of unanticipated consequences and the fact that organizations are collections of diverse interests.

And yet, do these criticisms require us to jettison completely the idea that there are environmental, technological and other factors which influence organizational outcomes? If we read Joan Woodward's contribution to this analysis fifteen years later the answer must be emphatically: no. For it depends first upon the time-scale with which the analysis is concerned. In the short run, for example, production technology must be given. Second it depends upon the perspective of the analysis. Joan Woodward always saw herself as contributing to the development of 'middle range' theory and to bridging the gulf between practising managers and academics in the management field:

> academics must recognise that in the present limited state of knowledge, management needs a system of beliefs, and that the propagation of this system of beliefs is a legitimate part of management education, and management must recognise that a system of beliefs becomes less necessary as factual knowledge is extended and must be prepared to modify or relinquish their assumptions as soon as evidence is produced to show that they are no longer tenable. (p. 257, 1965)

Looking forward from Woodward to see in what directions our knowledge about organizations has been extended, one finds a bewildering array of empirical and theoretical work, but the contribution of Woodward is not obliterated. It may be the case that concern with technology has been to some extent over-shadowed by broader considerations of the environment. Perrow (1979), for instance, reviewing trends in organization theory, documents the development of contingency theory which, he says, in the late 60s and early 70s:

> stimulated a wave of theorising and research which is now rapidly being absorbed. It has left its mark, as did the human relations tradition, but it has lost its handsome crest of frothy promise. Task, or technology, prove to be important variables, but not of the over-riding importance we first claimed for them. The new wave gathering force appears to be the environment. (p. 200)

A growing concern with 'interorganizational relations' and the recent publication of a number of 'textbooks' on the environment (e.g. Aldrich, 1978, Pfeffer and Salancik, 1978) have occasioned the consolidation of these developments. Interestingly, however, the issues which are raised in relation to the definition, measurement, and theoretical place for 'the environment' in organizational analysis are very similar to those which have been discussed in relation to the use of technology as an explanatory variable.

III. ALTERNATIVE PERSPECTIVES

However varied these criticisms of contingency theory, and how-ever much emphasis is currently placed upon the importance of the study of political processes within and between organizations, the underlying framework has none the less remained essentially a pluralist one, which assumes that conflicts of interest within organi-zations and indeed within societies can ultimately be accommo-dated. An introduction to *Industrial Organization: Theory and Practice* is not the place to attempt a fully comprehensive review of all of contemporary organization theory: nevertheless, in conclusion, and in order to provide signposts to possible future developments, reference should be made to a very different approach to organiza-tional analysis. This is one which rejects this pluralist paradigm as irrelevant since it maintains that organizations are but reflections of the wider social structures in which they operate.

Here we refer to two developments. First, to the relevance for
organization theory of the renewed interest in the nature of power
contained in the work of contemporary political scientists and
philosophers. Secondly, to what has been called a 'radical' approach to the study of organizations, which maintains that in the
capitalist world they are above all else arenas for, and tools in,
class conflict.

The first development owes a great deal to the seminal analysis
of poverty programmes in the USA produced by Bachrach and
Baratz (1970), in which they demonstrated the ability of powerful
groups so to manipulate the political debate that some issues were
never even raised. In this way they drew attention to the importance of 'non decision-making' and the 'mobilization of bias' as
aspects of the political process. The moral of this story for students
of organization was clear—they too had hitherto overemphasized
the more overt manifestations of power to the neglect of an intensive analysis of less obvious but more far reaching differences
of interest. The uneasiness engendered amongst organization
theorists by the parallels which could be drawn between studies of
power in communities and in organizations has been exacerbated
by the philosophical analysis of the nature of power produced by
Lukes (1974), in which he identified what he called three dimensions of power. The first dimension—the decision-making view—
involves a focus on behaviour in the making of decisions on issues
over which there is observable conflict of (subjective) interests,
seen as express policy preferences (p. 15).

Such a focus can be found in several studies of organizations. For
example, Heller (1971) focused attention on managerial decision-
making in relation to leadership styles and in the department Joan
Woodward founded at Imperial College researchers have carried
out detailed studies of power through an analysis of decision-
making—see, for example, Edwards and Harper (1975), Abell
(1978).

Lukes described his second dimension as involving:

a qualified critique of the behavioural focus . . . and . . . [allowing]
for consideration of the way in which decisions are prevented from
being taken on potential issues over which there is an observable
conflict of [subjective] interests, seen as embodied in express policy
preferences and subpolitical grievances. (p. 20)

Such an approach has been little used in studies of organizations despite its fuller treatment in a wider social context in Bachrach and Baratz's own work and in Crenson's (1971) comparative study of air pollution in two American cities. In a theoretical article, Abell (1977) has argued that developing concepts of manipulation and autonomy alongside those of power and influence should provide a base from which to study non decision-making in organizations.

Lukes's third dimension of power takes the critique of behavioural approaches to a different level, arguing that the first two dimensions are still 'too individualistic'. His third dimension

> allows for consideration of the many ways in which potential issues are kept out of politics, whether through the operation of social forces and institutional practices or through individuals' decisions. This moreover can occur in the absence of actual, observable conflict, which may have been successfully averted. . . . What one may have here is latent conflict.   (p. 24)

As Lukes recognizes, there are serious methodological problems (except possibly for the historian) in empirically uncovering this process.

Concern with these sort of theoretical and methodological problems has undoubtedly influenced the development of various strands of 'radical' or 'critical' organization theory. These approaches are predicated on a conviction that power relations in society are such that a wider societal frame of reference must be adopted. Attention in such theory is focused on two fronts: firstly upon deeper and more unobtrusive structures of power and domination which underly the epiphenomena of organization; and secondly on the phenomenology of the social construction of reality through the interplay of individuals and groups. Thus Benson (1977a) calls for a dialectical approach to the study of organizations which is: 'fundamentally committed to the concept of process. The social world is in a continuous state of becoming . . . (while) . . . organisations constitute important instruments of domination in the advanced industrial societies' (Benson, 1977a).

To date there has been little empirical work in this genre, although Clegg's study of a building site developed similar concepts of power, rule, and domination in a specific setting (Clegg, 1975) and Heydebrand's account of organizational contradictions in public service bureaucracies, with special reference to the American courts of law, shows how Marxian categories and propositions may be used to explicate the processes and outcomes of organizing (Heydebrand, 1977).

Developing his theme in another publication, Benson (1977b) argues that theory must be developed to cope with the four analytical problems of 'action, power, levels and process'.

> an adequate approach to organisational analysis must deal with (1) (action) the social production of organisational reality, including the reality—constructing activity of the organisation scientist (2) (power) the political bases of organisational realities, including the ties of theorists to power structures (3) (levels) the connection of organisations to the larger set of structural arrangements in the society (4) (process) the continuously emergent character of organisational patterns.   (p. 16)

The collection of readings which this statement of aims introduces shows however that, with the exception of Heydebrand (1977), although the questions and problems confronting these theorists are well formulated the answers and indeed the methodology for generating the answers are still relatively undeveloped. Hence these writers may more appropriately be said to be working as 'critical' rather than 'radical' theorists.

The semantics of the debate are confusing since at one level most contemporary organizations theorists are concerned with Benson's four problems of action, power, levels and process, but many of them are prepared to adopt a more 'revisionist' approach in terms of their assumptions. Indeed the differences between what we might call conventional and critical theory relate to two very important characteristics. First, what it is that theorists are prepared to take for granted as given constraints on action and secondly, and closely related, what is it they are seeking to explain. In terms of preparedness to accept material conditions as constraints on action and hence essentially non-negotiable, one finds curiously that Woodward has more in common with the critical theorists, albeit for different reasons, than with those who have emphasized choice and negotiation. Woodward developed a model in this present book in which the nature of technological and environmental factors were largely taken as given and as constraints on action. The critical theorists also lay great stress on material

constraints but there any similarity ceases for they see these
constraints not as features of organization, but as characteristics of
society revealed in organizations. The immanent laws of socio-
political-economic systems are thus the mainspring of action and
hence it is largely irrelevant to consider determinants of action
within organizations.

The use of the word 'irrelevant' highlights the second important
difference—namely what it is that various theorists are in fact
trying to explain, and here one finds wide diversity. Woodward
wished to explain patterns of formal structure and the structural
basis of efficiency and effectiveness. Critics of contingency theory
with their emphasis on choice have been more concerned with
strategic and operational decision-making and with how organizations maintain their supplies of necessary resources. Finally critical
theorists concentrate on the role of organizations in social control
and social change. Thus one is bound to admit that although
phrases like 'organization theory', 'organization behaviour', or
'organizational analysis' appear to signify a body of common
knowledge such commonality, hinged around a shared use of the
word 'organization' is largely illusory. But this very diversity means
that Woodward's work is as relevant today as it was fifteen years
ago. Organization theory is not yet a discipline in which earlier
work becomes superseded and irrelevant as later research findings
are published. Theorists, albeit all concerned with understanding
aspects of organization, work with different models, different
assumptions, and different objectives and in doing so shed light on
different problems.

Woodward, one suspects, would have had little patience with
those preoccupied exclusively with the issues of critical theory, not
least because by definition it precludes practical application within
the organization, and as she said in her inaugural lecture the
ultimate objective (of her research) was: 'to enable those concerned
with industrial organisations, at whatever level they may be working, to refine their models and to deal in a more sophisticated way
with the problems of organisational structure and behaviour they
encounter' (p. 122, 1970b).

In this present book Woodward heralded the foundation of
contingency theory in this country and as such it has made a
significant and lasting contribution to our understanding of life in

industrial organizations. For practitioners it is still as fruitful a source of perceptive guidelines for action today as it was when it was first published. For students it is essential reading if they wish to understand the development of ideas about complex organizations in modern society, while for empirical researchers, few would fail at least to consider the role of technology as an important influence on life in organizations. Subsequent developments, as we have seen, have not justified Woodward's hopes for a single path for organization theory in which 'factual knowledge' would gradually accumulate thereby providing an increasingly unambiguous basis for the re-evaluation of managerial assumptions. Indeed, as we have seen, unverified assumptions abound still, not least among academics and different sets of assumptions beget different theories. Joan Woodward's ideas may have been variously denied, criticized, and embellished but they still remain one of the corner-stones of our knowledge of organizations.

Bibliography

ABELL, P. (1975) (ed.), *Organisations as Bargaining and Influence Systems*, Heinemann, London.

ABELL, P. (1977), 'The Many Faces of Power and Liberty: revealed preference, autonomy and teleological explanation', *Sociology*, Vol. 11, No. 1.

ABELL, P. (1978), 'The Task and Power Determinants of Decentralisation Between Headquarters and U.K. Subsidiaries of International Corporations', in (ed.) Wilpert B. and Negandhi, A., *Work Organisation Research: European and American Perspectives*, Kent State University (1978).

AGUVEN, S., HANSSON, R., KARLSON, K. G. (1976), *The Volvo Kalmar Plant Rationalisation Council*, SAF-LO, Sweden.

ALDRICH, H. (1972), 'Technology and Organisational Structure: a Reexamination of the Findings of the Aston Group', *Administrative Science Quarterly*, Vol. 17, 1.

ALDRICH, H. (1978), *Organisations and Environments*, Prentice-Hall, New Jersey.

ALLEN, S. C. (1970), *Corporate-Divisional Relationships in Highly Diversified Firms*, in Lorsch, J. R., Lawrence, P. R. (ed.), 1970.

BACHRACH, P., BARATZ, M. S. (1970), *Power and Poverty*, Oxford University Press.

BENSON, J. K. (1977a), 'Organisations: a Dialectical View,' *Administrative Science Quarterly*, Vol. 22, 1.

BENSON (1977b) (ed.), *Organisational Analysis: Critique and Innovation*, Sage Publications, London.

BLAU, P. M., FALBE, C. M., MCKINLEY, W., TRACEY, K. (1976), 'Technology and Organisation in Manufacturing', *Administrative Science Quarterly*, March, Vol. 21, 1, 20–41.

BROSSARD, M., MAURICE, M., 'Is there a Universal Model of Organisation Structure?', *International Studies of Management and Organisations*, No. 6, 1976, 11–45.

BURNS, T. (1958), *Management in the Electronics Industry—a study of eight English Companies*, Social Science Research Centre, University of Edinburgh, subsequently elaborated in T. Burns and G. Stalker, 1961.

BURNS, T. (1961), 'Micropolitics: Mechanisms of Institutional Change', *Administrative Science Quarterly*, Vol. 6.

BURNS, T., STALKER, G. (1961), *The Management of Innovation*, Tavistock, London.

BURNS, T. (1966), On the Plurality of Social Systems, in Lawrence, J. R. (ed.), *Operational Research and the Social Sciences*, Tavistock, London.

BURNS, T. (1977), *The BBC*, Macmillan, London.

CHILD, J. (1972), 'Organisational Structure, Environment and Performance: The role of strategic choice', *Sociology*, 6.

CLEGG, S. (1975), *Power, Rule and Domination*, Routledge & Kegan Paul.

CRENSON, M. A. (1971), *The Un-politics of Air Pollution: A study of Non-decision making in the Cities*, The Johns Hopkins Press, Baltimore.

CROZIER, H. (1964), *The Bureaucratic Phenomenon*, Tavistock, London.

CYERT, R. M., MARCH, J. G. (1963), *A Behavioral Theory of the Firm*, Prentice-Hall, New Jersey.

DAWSON, S. (1975), *Power and Influence in Prison Workshops*, in Abell, P. (ed.), 1975.

DAWSON, S. (1979), 'Organisational Analysis and the Study of Policy Formulation and Implementation', *Public Administration Bulletin*, No. 31, December.

DAVIES, C., DAWSON, S., FRANCIS, A. (1973), 'Technology and other variables', in (ed.) Warner, M. (1973), *Sociology of the Workplace*, Allen & Unwin.

DAVIES, C., FRANCIS, A. (1976), 'Perceptions of the Structure in NHS Hospitals', in (ed.) Stacey, M. (1976), *The Sociology of the NHS*, Sociological Review Monograph 22, University of Keele.

DONALDSON, L. (1976), 'Woodward, technology, organisational structure and performance—a critique of the universal generalisation', *Journal of Management Studies*, October.

EDWARDS, C., HARPER, D. G. (1975), *Bargaining at the Trade Union-Management Interface*, in Abell, P. (ed.), 1975.

ELGER, H. J. (1975), 'Industrial Organisations', in McKinley, J. B. (ed.), *Processing People*, Holt, Rhinehart & Winston, New York, 91–149.

EILON, S. (1962), 'Problems in Studying Management Control', *International Journal of Production Research*, I, 13–20.

EMERSON, R. M. (1962), 'Power-Dependence Relations', *American Sociological Review*, 2, 31–41.

FRENCH, J. R. P., RAVEN, B. (1959), 'The Basis of Social Power', in (ed.) Cartwright, D., *Studies in Social Power*, Michigan Ann Arbor Institute for Social Research.

GALBRAITH, J. K. (1967), *The New Industrial State*, Hamish Hamilton, London.

GALBRAITH, J. (1973), *Designing Complex Organisations*, Addison-Wesley.

GOULDNER, A. W. (1954), *Patterns of Industrial Bureaucracy*, Free Press, New York.

HAGE, J., AIKEN, M. (1969), 'Routine Technology, Social Structure and Organisation Goals', *Administrative Science Quarterly*, Vol. 14, 366–76.

HELLER, F. A. (1971), *Managerial Decision Making*, Tavistock, London.

HEYDEBRAND, W. (1977), 'Organizational Contradictions in Public Bureaucracies: Toward a Marxian Theory of Organizations', *Sociological Quarterly*, 18.

HICKSON, D., PUGH, H. D., PHEYSEY, D. (1969), 'Operations Technology and organisational structure: an empirical reappraisal', *Administrative Science Quarterly*, Vol. 14, 3.

HICKSON, D. J., HININGS, C. R., LEE, C. A., SCHNECK, R. E., PENNINGS, J. M. (1971), 'A Strategic Contingencies Theory of Intra-Organisational Power', *Administrative Science Quarterly*, Vol. 16, 2, 216–89.

KINGDOM, O. R. (1973), *Matrix Organisation*, Tavistock.

LAWRENCE, P. R., LORSCH, J. W. (1967), *Organisation and Environment*, Harvard Business School, Boston.

LORSCH, J. W., LAWRENCE, P. R. (ed.) (1970), *Studies in Organisational Design*, Irwin Dorsey.

LUKES, S. (1974), *Power, a Radical View*, Macmillan.

MARCH, J., SIMON, H. (1958), *Organisations*, Wiley, New York.

MARRIS, R. (1964), *The Economic Theory of Managerial Capitalism*, Macmillan, London.

MASSIE, J. L. (1965), 'Management Theory', in (ed.) March, J., *Handbook of Organisations*, 1965.

MECHANIC, D. C. (1962), 'Sources of Power of Lower Participants in Complex Organisations', *Administrative Science Quarterly*, Vol. 7, 3.

MERTON, R. K. (1957), *Social Theory and Social Structure*, Free Press, Glencoe, Illinois.

MOHR, L. B. (1971), 'Organisational technology and organisational structure', *Administrative Science Quarterly*, Vol. 16, 4, 444–59.

OMEGA, (1978), *Feedback: letters on structural determinism*, 109–15.

PETTIGREW, A. (1973), *The Politics of Organisational Decision Making*, Tavistock, London.

PERROW, C. (1967), 'A Framework for the Comparative Analysis of Organisations', *American Sociological Review*, 32, (2).

PERROW, C. (1970), *Organisational Analysis*, Tavistock.

PERROW, C. (1972), *Complex Organisations, A Critical Essay*, Scott, Foresman & Co., Illinois.

PERROW, C. (1979), *Complex Organisations, A Critical Essay*, 2nd Edition, Scott, Foresman & Co., Illinois.

PFEFFER, J., SALANCIK, G. R. (1978), *The External Control of Organisations*, Harper & Row, New York.

RACKHAM, J., WOODWARD, J. (1970), *The Measurement of Technical Variables*, in Woodward, J. (ed.), 1970a.

REEVES, K. T. (1967), 'Constrained and Facilitated Behaviour: A Typology of Behaviour in Economic Organisations'. *British Journal of Industrial Relations*, 5 (2).

REEVES, K. T., TURNER, B. A. (1972), 'A Theory of Organisation and Behaviour in Batch Production Factories', *Administrative Science Quarterly*, March.

REEVES, K. T., WOODWARD, J. (1970), *The Study of Managerial Control*, in Woodward, J. (ed.), 1970a.

SELZNICK, P. (1949), *TVA and the Grass Roots*, Harper, New York.

SILVERMAN, D. (1968), 'Formal Organisations or Industrial Sociology: Towards a Social Action Analysis of Organisations', *Sociology* 2 (2), 221–38.

SILVERMAN, D. (1971), *The Theory of Organisations*, Heinemann, London.

SORGE, A., WARNER, M. (1978), 'Manufacturing Organisations and Work Roles in Great Britain and West Germany', Discussion Paper, International Institute of Management, December.

TIMPSON, J. D. (1967), *Organisations in Action*, McGraw Hill, New York.

VEBLEN, T. (1904), *The Theory of Business Enterprise*, Scribner.

WARMINGTON, A., LUPTON, T. GRIBBIN, C. (1977), *Organisational Behaviour and Performance*, Macmillan.

WEDDERBURN, D., CROMPTON, R. (1972), *Workers Attitudes and Technology*, Cambridge University Press.

WOODWARD, J. (1958), *Management and Technology*, HMSO.

WOODWARD, J. (1965), *Industrial Organization: Theory and Practice*, Oxford University Press.

WOODWARD, J. (ed.) (1970a), *Industrial Organization: Behaviour and Control*, Oxford University Press.

WOODWARD, J. (1970b), *Behaviour in Organisations*, Inaugural Lecture, Imperial College of Science and Technology, 3 March.

ZWERMAN, W. L. (1970), *New Perspectives in Organisation Theory*, Greenwood Pub. Co., Westport, Conn.

Part One

THE SURVEY

1   *Aims and Methods*

FORMULATING THE RESEARCH PROJECT

When the decision was taken to establish a Human Relations Research Unit at the South East Essex College of Technology in 1953, the first problem was to define an area of study and to find out what research facilities were available. The Joint Committee on Human Relations in Industry gave a preliminary grant to the College to finance one research worker for three months, the objective being to formulate a research project and to make a realistic assessment of the chances of getting the required co-operation from local industry. If all went well, firm proposals were to be submitted to the Committee at the end of this period together with an application for further financial support.

Preliminary discussions with some of the industrial representatives on the Governing Body of the College suggested that local firms were interested in problems of organization and would be prepared to provide the necessary research facilities for an investigation in this field. Studies of management organization would, it was felt, be useful to the College too. Like approximately a hundred other colleges in the United Kingdom, it prepared students for the examinations of all the principal professional management associations and provides courses for the Diploma in Management awarded jointly by the British Institute of Management and Ministry of Education.

Research into aspects of organization would be likely to produce information for feeding back into these courses. It might also help to evaluate them by showing how far theories implicit in the teaching were applied in practice locally, and whether such application was linked in any way with management behaviour or commercial success.

Formulating research of this kind did, however, present difficulties. Most of the work done in this country by sociologists interested in industrial problems prior to 1953 had been concerned more with working groups and management-worker relationships than with organizational problems. Co-operation between sociologists and industrialists had generally been slow to develop, and in the initial stages industrialists were more willing to open their doors to students of operator behaviour than to students of management behaviour. Top management were probably afraid that any examination of the delicately balanced and highly complex relationships between members of a management team would upset its equilibrium and have serious repercussions on the success of the business. Sociologists were equally unwilling to enter any doors that had been opened; they probably recognized that the methodological problems arising from sociological research are encountered in their most extreme form in the study of management behaviour.

These problems arise from the fact that the sociologist becomes part of any situation he studies and forms relationships with the people with whom he comes into contact. Thus he may affect attitudes and behaviour by his mere presence, or change a situation by becoming involved in it. It is almost impossible to analyse a social system while living it, because of the difficulty of safeguarding against personal bias. In the study of management groups these relationships could be particularly intimate, for the guinea-pigs would be fewer in number, more articulate, and from much the same background as the sociologists themselves. While such intimacy would make the collection of information relatively easy, it would increase the difficulty of evaluating and publishing it. Much of it would be of a personal and confidential nature, and its publication in a research report might cause embarrassment to individuals whose identity could not be concealed from readers familiar with the situations described. This concealment is easier to achieve in studies of larger groups of operators where striking characters stand out less clearly.

In this instance, however, the research workers were aware of these problems and regarded them as a challenge. In spite of the difficulties involved—in particular the possible conflict between the need to maintain scientific integrity by disclosing all the relevant facts and the reluctance to publish information that might prove harmful or embarrassing to certain individuals or firms— they felt that it was important to try and supplement the work which had already been done on operator behaviour with more detailed information about attitudes, behaviour, and relationships inside management groups.

Neither was the definition of the problem easy. The research workers felt that any research project based on a technical college should be narrowly conceived and directed towards the solution of immediate and practical problems. A technical college, because of its close relationship with industry, is ideally suited to research of a problem-centred kind, whereas its limited resources restrict the contribution it can make to theoretical development. Of course the danger of de-limiting the project so that its results would be trivial was foreseen; a project had to be devised which, although problem-centred, might make a contribution to the development of industrial sociology.

One problem of organization with wider implications, mentioned in the early discussions, was the dichotomy between executive and advisory responsibilities, and the resultant relationship between line supervision at different levels, and the various technical and administrative specialists being introduced in increasing numbers into industry. It was felt that this problem might be a useful one to study as practical results helpful to local industry might be obtained through the definition of the factors which determine the quality of line-staff relationships. Moreover, although the scope of such a study would be limited it was felt that any conclusions reached would extend our knowledge of the administrative process generally.

With this in mind, brief preliminary studies were made in eleven local firms, and it soon became clear that such a project was impracticable. Segmental analysis proved to be impossible in this area of study. In the first place firms differed considerably in the extent to which their organizational structure discriminated between executive and advisory responsibilities. Moreover, even where there was a clear-cut distinction, line-staff relationships could not be looked at in isolation, as they were inextricably woven into and conditioned by the overall pattern of personal relationships and by the social structure of the firm, both formal and informal.

Thus it was recognized in the final formulation of the project that industrial firms would have to be studied as complex social systems and line-staff relationships looked at as parts of a whole rather than in isolation. Moreover, the wide differences between firms revealed from the preliminary studies indicated that to get a generaι picture of the area as a whole it would be necessary to include in the research as many of the local firms as were prepared to co-operate. This raised the problem of the level at which the research was to be conducted. Broadening it in this way might mean that the analysis would be at too superficial a level to be useful; but to cover the whole management structure of all the firms in South Essex would undoubtedly be too formidable a task.

It was finally decided to develop a two-level project to concentrate first on making a broad survey of the whole area and then if time allowed make some more detailed studies of individual firms. This was the plan of research submitted to the Joint Committee. The second stage was not planned in detail. It was not known how long the survey would take or what problems would be encountered. In fact, it was hoped that the survey itself would show where and how more detailed work would most usefully be undertaken.

Financial help for four years was applied for, detailed plans for the survey were put forward, and it was suggested that an interim report should be submitted on the completion of the survey which would include proposals for the case studies. The research workers bore in mind the fact that during the survey they would have to build up the kind of relationship with the firms visited that would enable them to return at a later stage if necessary.

THE FIRMS STUDIED

The application having been granted, the next step was to delimit the area in which the work would be done and to locate the firms within it. The catchment area of a technical college is not clearly defined. For general courses it draws students from firms in its immediate vicinity, for special courses it goes further afield. It was decided to cover the wider area, moving along the north bank of the Thames from the metropolitan boundary to the oil wharves at Coryton and the hinterland back as far as Chelmsford.

This particular part of Essex had been almost wholly agricultural until the beginning of the twentieth century, isolated by its distinct boundaries, the marshes of the Lea to the west and the Thames Estuary to the south. The first factories were built in the lower Roding Valley about 1904 and since then the area has become steadily more industrialized. A large number of well-known firms now operate there; the latest developments being concurrent with the research: the establishment of industrial estates at Basildon, Hainault, and Harold Hill.

In order to reduce the variables in the situation as much as possible, the research workers decided to limit research to manufacturing firms, that is to firms classified into one of the fourteen categories listed under the heading of 'all manufacturing industry' in the statistics prepared by the Ministry of Labour and published quarterly in the Ministry of Labour *Gazette*. Mining and quarrying firms, building contractors, and laundries were excluded, as were transport undertakings and public utilities.

Identifying firms presented problems. Not least of these was that information could not be obtained from a single source as the research area did not coincide with any one local government, Ministry of Labour, or telephone area. On-the-spot checks had to be made, and the industrial estates already referred to had to be kept constantly under review so that newly established firms could be included. Eventually, a list of 203 firms was compiled and contact made with each. It is impossible to say how comprehensive this list was as the research workers may easily have missed some very small firms. It is unlikely, however, that any sizeable firms slipped through the net.

This preliminary survey showed that the comparatively late development of the area was reflected in the nature of its industry. Although every category included in the Ministry of Labour breakdown of manufacturing industry was represented on the list, it was the newer industries such as oil refining, telecommunications, photography, pharmaceuticals, and vehicles that predominated. South Essex firms employed in total approximately 3 per cent of the industrial labour force of England and Wales, but firms engaged in the manufacture of chemicals and vehicles employed as high a proportion as 7 per cent of the national total.

Factory buildings were modern and amenities good, and there was evidence of deliberate planning, factories being concentrated in zones rather than scattered widespread. This zoning of industry facilitated the research; in organizing the field work it was found possible to study factories in groups rather than as single units.

There seemed to be few family businesses, probably because the functions of ownership and management had already separated when the firms in the area became established. The few there were had moved out from East London, and their history suggested that the move had provided an occasion for radical changes in management structure.

The firms ranged in size from 11 to approximately 40,000; the complete distribution being given in Table I and Fig. 1.

Table I. *Size Distribution of Manufacturing Firms in South Essex*

Firms employing	Number of firms	% of total firms	Total number employed in group	% of total labour force
100 or less	93	46	3,255	3
101–250	48	24	8,321	7
251–500	25	12	8,852	8
501–1,000	18	9	13,559	11
1,001–2,000	8	4	11,991	10
2,001–4,000	7	3	17,513	14
4,001–8,000	2	1	10,383	9
8,000 and over	2	1	45,526	38
TOTALS	203	100	119,400	100

The proportion of firms employing 1,000 people or more is larger in South Essex than in England and Wales generally; 9 per cent as against 1·7 per cent. This high proportion of large firms reflects the late industrial development of the area, a characteristic of modern industry being the increased size of industrial units. It is possible of course that the figures show a greater disparity than is in fact the case, for, as indicated above, some small firms may have been missed. It is, however, fairly safe to assume that the number of small firms missed was not sufficient to have brought the percentage down to the national level.

Preliminary contacts suggested that few firms employing less than 100 people had an elaborate formal organization. Visits were paid to a 1 in 4 sample of these firms. In the majority there was no clearly defined level of management between the board and the operators. There were few organizational problems, and it appeared that little would be lost if the smaller firms were omitted.

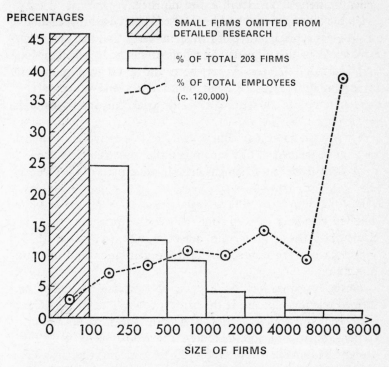

Fig. 1. Size distribution of manufacturing firms in South Essex

This left 110 firms on the list; 36 were branch factories with commercial headquarters outside the area. A letter was sent to each describing the research project and asking for co-operation. In the case of many of the branch factories, the research workers were referred to headquarters. After further correspondence and some discussion, 100 of the firms approached (91 per cent) agreed to co-operate. This magnificent response enabled the research results to be analysed and presented as a census of the firms in the area, rather than as a sample survey. As far as the research workers could judge, the ten firms unable or unwilling to co-operate did not differ fundamentally from the rest. They were not restricted to any one size group, industrial category, or industrial zone; six were self-contained firms, while four were branches of large organizations. It is probably safe to assume, therefore, that the information presented in this report is adequate as a basis for generalizations about South Essex industry.

On the other hand it must be stressed that these firms cannot be regarded as representative of British industry, and that generalizations about British industry as a whole cannot be based on the facts and figures given here. As has been said there are a number of important differences between South Essex and other parts of Britain in the size and nature of its industrial firms and its historical development.

This does not mean, of course, that the descriptive and analytical material presented in this report and the conclusions reached are necessarily irrelevant to similar firms in other parts of the Country.

THE INFORMATION OBTAINED

The survey was carried out between September 1954 and September 1955. From the outset it was recognized that it would have to be limited to formal organization and operating procedures.

Formal organization is the stable and explicit pattern of prescribed relationships inside the firm; it covers a defined system of jobs, each of which carries a definite measure of authority, responsibility, and accountability, the whole being consciously designed to enable those employed to work together in accomplishing their objectives. The number of firms involved would make it impossible at this stage of the research to find out very much about the second social process which goes on inside any institution and results in the establishment of informal organization. How formal organization worked in practice and whether people lived up to the specific definition of their offices were questions which would have to be left to the second phase of the research, as would the tracing of the patterns of informal relationships actually emerging from day-to-day operations.

The information obtained from each firm was therefore limited under the following headings:

1. History, background, and objectives.
2. Description of the manufacturing processes and methods.
3. Forms and routines through which the firm was organized and operated.
4. Facts and figures that could be used to make an assessment of the firm's commercial success.

The shortest period of time spent in any one firm was half a day, and the longest a week. The time taken to collect the required information depended not only on the size of the firm and the extent to which it was organization-conscious, but also on the detail of the records kept and the status of the person providing the information. Some kinds of information were easier to obtain than others. Under the first heading, for example, tracing the background history of a firm in terms of the expansion of its premises or personnel was a relatively straightforward matter; getting a precise definition of its objectives at each stage of its development was not.

All the firms studied had a common objective in that they were manufacturing goods and offering them for sale, but the nature of their markets, the type of customers they served, the methods they employed, and the targets they set themselves differed considerably. In some firms the managers were consciously aware of the firm's objectives and knew how these objectives had been modified from time to time by policy decisions; in others, difficulty was experienced in defining objectives, and their history showed that there had been occasions when means had been allowed to determine ends. For example, the changes in production methods that had taken place in some firms had resulted in changes in the quality of the products and in the type of customers aimed at, without those responsible for policy formulation being consciously aware of what had happened. Some firms too had a clearer idea of their social purposes and responsibilities than others.

When information about manufacturing processes and methods was being obtained, a number of technical variables were taken into account; these included the density of production, the flexibility of production facilities, the diversity of products, the time span of operations, and the way in which production programmes were initiated and controlled. A note was made of recent technological developments, particularly those involving automation. Automation, although a convenient term, is difficult to define because it has several different meanings in popular usage. The report *Automation* prepared by the Department of Scientific and Industrial Research[1] identifies three different streams of technical progress implied by the term: the expansion of mechanization by transfer devices; techniques of automatic control over manufacturing processes; and processing of technical and business information by electronic digital computer.

In respect of the third heading under which information was sought, a start was made by asking to see the organization chart. In about half the firms studied charts were available. Some were very elaborate. In one firm the general manager had a chart more than 20 ft long on his office wall; in another, detailed departmental charts were bound together in a book the size and weight of a family Bible. In a third firm, a manager produced two charts; one displayed on his office wall showed the existing organization, the other, kept in a drawer in his desk, showed how it would be if he could ignore the personal idiosyncrasies and weaknesses of his present managers.

Where no organization chart was available the research workers built one up for themselves through a process of question and answer. They found that the absence of a chart did not always imply a lack of organization consciousness. In some firms the answers to questions showed that the organizational structure, although not written down on paper, was definite and clearly understood. In others it was difficult to find out exactly who was responsible to whom and to trace the pattern of prescribed relationships.

Another difficulty encountered was that of defining offices and roles; different titles were used in different firms for the same office, while different offices sometimes had the same title. It was important, therefore, to define precisely the duties and responsibilities of each office studied.

Only in eight firms did the chief executive make, rather than approve, organizational decisions (the chief executive could be the chairman, managing director or general or works manager).

[1] *Automation*, Department of Scientific and Industrial Research (H.M.S.O., 1956).

In every case he represented the highest level of authority operating full-time on the spot.

One firm had an Organization Planning Committee, and four had Organization and Methods Departments responsible for making organizational decisions. In the remaining firms the responsibility was delegated by the chief executive to one of his subordinates; accountants, company secretaries, personnel managers and production controllers being some of the people involved. In some cases this delegation was formal, in others informal, the nominal responsibility remaining with the chief executive.

When an overall picture of organizational structure had been obtained, the research workers studied in more detail the history and responsibilities of the principal staff and specialist departments, including sales, research, development, personnel, inspection, maintenance, and purchasing; they examined the documentation associated with planning and control procedures and the methods used in costing and budgetary control.

A superficial analysis was made of cost structure. Although this amounted to little more than allocating a proportion of total turnover to wages, materials, and overheads, it produced some interesting comparisons. Information about costs was surprisingly easy to get, as in many cases it had already been assembled for presentation to joint consultative committees. As this information had often been presented pictorially, the research workers were given a number of illustrations of cakes cut into slices, piles of pennies, and pound notes placed end to end. In general they got the impression that the results of the efforts made to inform workers' representatives about the finances of the company were felt to have been disappointing.

Finally, a detailed analysis was made of labour structure; most of the information needed being obtained from personnel or wages departments. Lists were made of the different grades both of staff and of industrial workers, showing the numbers employed in each grade. These figures were then related to the organization chart. Certain labour ratios were also worked out, including those of managers and supervisors to total personnel; of clerical and administrative staff to hourly-paid employees, of maintenance to production workers, and of direct labour to total personnel. In making this analysis of the labour structure, problems of definition were again encountered; firms seem to differ widely, for example, in what they regard as indirect labour charges.

The research workers also obtained as much information as possible about the qualifications of managers and supervisory staff and each firm's development and training policy. Reliable information about management qualifications was not always readily available. Attitudes to professional qualifications were prejudiced, and in some firms the possession of academic or professional qualifications was regarded as a handicap; managers were said to succeed in spite of rather than because of their qualifications. In others, the recruitment each year of several first or second class honours graduate was not only an established practice, but regarded as an important one. To obtain the services of large numbers of such graduates was considered a desirable objective, and in some firms of this kind, staff who were able to pass a professional examination were rewarded financially. These extremes of attitude tended to bias the information obtained, the difficulties being increased by the fact that staff records were often insufficiently detailed or up to date to provide the correct factual information. The qualifications of the person providing the information also coloured the picture given.

ASSESSMENT OF BUSINESS SUCCESS

Finally the research workers tried to find out not only how the firms studied were organized and operated, but whether any particular form of organization was associated with management efficiency and commercial success. The assessment both of the efficiency of particular administrative expedients and of commercial success presents problems; the circular argument that an arrangement works because it exists is difficult to avoid. All that was done therefore was to assemble from each firm any available information having a direct or indirect bearing on its achievements. The first thing taken into consideration was the state of the industry in which the firm operated, for although many of the firms included in the research were in the newer and expanding industries, there were exceptions. Moreover, some industries were more competitive than others and firms in some luxury trades competed more with firms in other luxury trades than with firms in their own industries.

Next, the position of each firm inside its own industry was considered; what percentage of the total volume of the industry did its production represent; had this percentage increased or decreased in recent years, and had the firm been successful in acquiring new markets.

Over a five-year period annual reports and financial accounts were examined for profits made and the amount of capital invested in expansion programmes. The history and rate of development in terms of personnel and plant were taken into consideration as was the future of the decisions being taken about production policy. Where appropriate, questions were asked about works accounting; how far were works accounts reconcilable with financial accounts; was a unit of measure of capacity and production employed; and what success had been achieved in the progressive reduction of unit costs.

Other factors taken into account included the fluctuation of the firm's shares on the Stock Exchange, its reputation as an employer, both in the industry and in the locality, the level of salaries paid to senior management, the rate of staff wastage, and relationships between the firm and outside organizations. The attitude of local authority and employment exchange officials to the firm, the speed with which requests were dealt with and the number of committees on which it was represented gave an interesting indication of its local standing. What the trade union officials thought about a firm from a negotiating point of view also had some significance.

Having collected as much relevant information as they could, the research workers immediately realized that it was inadequate as a basis for ranking the hundred firms in their order of merit. Success, like anything which varies continuously from a minimum to a maximum value, may be classified in two ways: first, according to a division into sections; and secondly, by deciding upon some parameter which is both representative of what is being classified and capable of numerical expression. As the information obtained was inadequate for the second method of classification, some way of dividing firms into sections had to be devised. Because of the limited number, it was felt that there was little point in attempting to classify firms into more than three groups, the obvious categories being 'average', 'above average' and 'below average' in success. The research workers therefore reviewed the information they had collected about each firm weighting some items—progressive reduction of unit costs and expanding volume of trade inside the industry, for example, more heavily than others—and allocated each firm to one of the three categories. It was realized, of course, that in making this assessment, particularly in relation to the more marginal factors, subjective judgments were involved but it was felt that for a simple classification into three categories and as a basis for comparison the methods used were adequate.

The field work of the survey took approximately twelve months, and when it was completed all the information was assembled and analysed, a dossier being built up for each firm. This contained a descriptive account of its history and objectives, the research workers' subjective impressions of various aspects of its organization and policy, the assessment of success already referred to, and a schedule of information prepared on the lines indicated in Appendix I.

2 *Analysis of Organization*

TYPES OF ORGANIZATION

The assembly and analysis of the information collected during the survey showed that the hundred firms included were organized and run in widely different ways. It seemed that about half had made some conscious attempt to plan organization and to apply the precepts and principles of the systematic body of knowledge of organizational structure and processes contained in management theory.

The classical school of thought on organization distinguishes between three types of organization: line organization, functional organization, and line-staff organization.[1] In line organization, authority flows directly from the chief executive to various immediate subordinates, and from them to other workers. The pure form of line organization is found only where everyone does the same kind of job and where divisions exist only as a basis of control and direction. There is, however, a modified form of line organization, sometimes referred to as 'departmental line organization' in which personnel are grouped on a simple task basis, their activities being co-ordinated by the chief executive himself. Four basic activities are associated in a manufacturing organization—financing the enterprise, developing the product, production itself, and marketing, the simplest form of specialization being the delegation by the chief executive of the responsibility for one or more of these activities to separate individuals or departments. Where there is departmental line organization, specialization rarely goes further than this.

[1] See for example Wm. R. Spriegel and Wm. H. Lansburgh, *Industrial Management* (Chapman and Hall Ltd., 5th ed. London, 1955).

The concept of functional organization was first developed by Taylor (1911),[2] to try to overcome the problem of finding men with the wide range of skills required of the modern production supervisor. It was based on the idea that the main division of the production organization should be determined by a systematic analysis of the work to be done. At workshop level, the operator, instead of coming into direct contact with one supervisor would receive his orders from a group of specialized supervisors, each of whom would be responsible for a particular function.

The main reason why this form of organization never became popular was the deep-rooted conviction of most industrial managers that no one could work under more than one superior at a time. Thus the third type of organization, line-staff organization, developed as a compromise. It provides a means of utilizing special skills while maintaining a hierarchy of line authority; it allows not for functional supervisors but for functionalized staff departments working through a line supervisor.

The research workers examined the organizational structure of each of the firms studied in their frame of reference dividing them into three main types; Table II gives the result.

Table II. *Types of Organization*

	No. of firms
(i) Predominantly line organization	35
(ii) Functional organization	2
(iii) Line-staff organization	59
Unclassifiable	4
TOTAL	100

In none of the thirty-five firms in the first category did specialization go beyond the four basic functions of manufacture, no specialists being employed inside the production departments themselves. In twenty the chief executive controlled production operations himself, together with any research and development work, delegating responsibility for finance and administration to the company secretary, and for marketing and distribution to the sales manager. Indeed, sales management appeared to be the most

[2] Frederick W. Taylor, *Shop Management* (Harper, New York).

highly developed specialist activity in South Essex industry. Eighty-one firms in all had specialist marketing departments. In eight firms in the first category, the chief executive retained the responsibility for marketing himself, delegating the production function to an immediate subordinate.

Although complete functional organization of the kind suggested by Taylor is rare in British industry, two examples of it were found; there was one firm in which departmental managers received direct executive instructions from five specialist divisional managers, and another in which foremen received instructions from eight departmental managers. In both cases specialists were collectively responsible for production operations.

In the fifty-nine line-staff organization firms, there was a wide variety of functionalized staff departments. Fig. 2 gives a list of the specialists employed in the production and personnel fields.

The status and prestige of the heads of staff departments varied from firm to firm and from one specialization to another. While in all cases there was a nominal distinction between executive and advisory responsibility, in twelve firms the specialists were so powerful that, in practice, line supervisors took instructions from them. The day-to-day operational relationship between any line manager and any specialist was determined by the relative status of the two people. The advisory nature of the specialist role was emphasized only when a mechanism was required through which conflict could be resolved.

At the other end of the scale were eight firms whose specialists were so restricted that there seemed little point in employing them; their advice was never taken, the services they rendered were trivial, and their control was meaningless.

In one large line-staff organization firm, a distinction was drawn inside every department between the line and staff personnel. The 'line' personnel of the sales department were responsible for such functions as market research, their job being to give advice to the staff and to help formulate sales policy. 'Line' personnel managers were responsible for day-to-day personnel administration, while the 'staff' personnel department was responsible for co-ordination, top level union negotiations, and the formulation of labour policy.

There were one or two firms which, although employing specialists, did not conform to the usual line-staff pattern. Their production departments were organized on a profit-centre basis, the specialists employed in them being directly responsible to the line supervisor in charge. In addition, there were several high-level

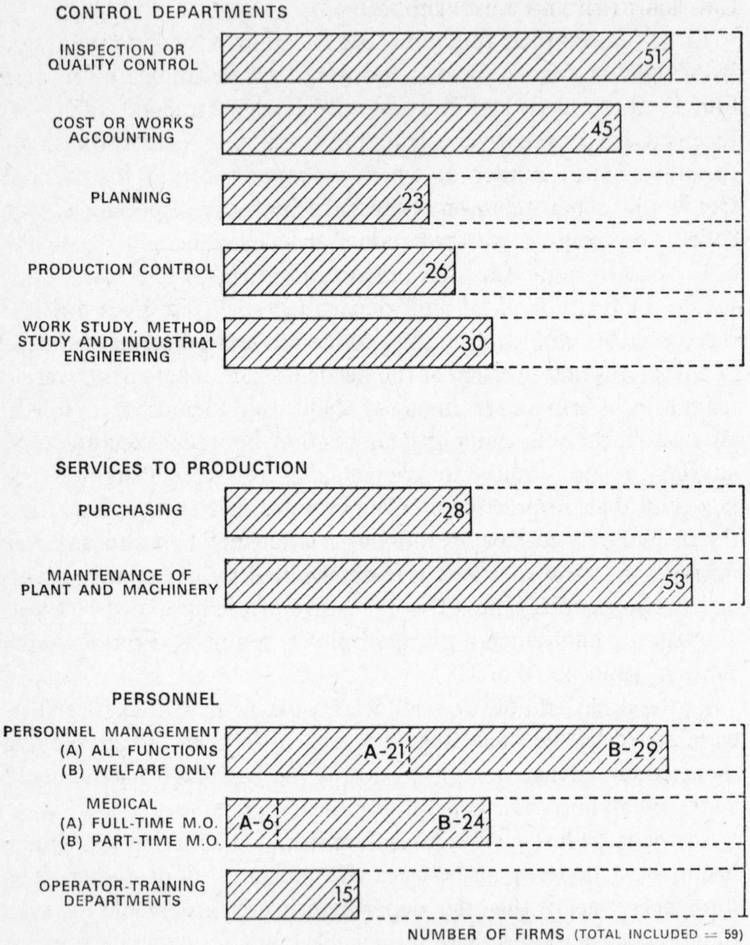

Fig. 2. Specialist departments associated with production

specialists who advised top management on the formulation of policy but had no executive responsibility for their specialisms; for example, the senior executive who advised top management on quality control had no control over the inspection personnel who were working in the various production departments of the factory.

These firms provided examples of divisionalized organization in which all the different kinds of work necessary to accomplish a specific end result were put into one organizational unit. There were signs that this kind of organization is growing in popularity.

GROWTH OF SPECIALIST DEPARTMENTS

Tracing the history of specialist departments provided the research workers with an interesting insight into the way in which organization grows. In many firms it was almost impossible to find out why a particular department had become established at a particular time. Only a minority of organizational changes seemed to have resulted from dissatisfaction with the existing organizational structure. In the firms studied such changes seemed to have come about as a consequence of either a change in top management or an increase in the organization consciousness of the chief executive. In most cases, this increased organization consciousness had been stimulated by an outside contact, bringing management consultants into the firm, attending a high-level management course, or establishing a close identification with a professional management association by becoming either an honorary officer or a committee member. The one organization planning committee and the four organization and methods departments had resulted from such stimuli, and they in turn had initiated other organizational changes.

But most of the organizational changes were not so deliberately planned. They had come about almost spontaneously; as the result of a crisis, to accommodate individuals, or in response to a management fashion. Several inspection departments could be traced back to a specific problem relating to the maintaining of quality standards. In fifteen firms personnel departments had been set up at the beginning of the second world war to handle the paper work arising from such legislation as the Essential Work Orders and the Schedule of Reserved Occupations.

In all the firms studied, organization had to some extent been modified to accommodate individuals. 'Empire builders' had distorted organizational patterns in their search for higher status. Bright young men for whom the existing organization had provided inadequate opportunities had been given newly created posts with potentially wider scope. In a number of firms sinecures had been found for misfits who had been unable to hold down their jobs but who, for one reason or another, could be neither discharged nor demoted. At least ten of the personnel departments —in particular those of the predominantly welfare type—seemed to have originated in this way. These new departments persisted long after the people in charge of them had died, retired, or moved on. In some cases they had succeeded in making their new departments indispensable, in others the vacancies created when they left their posts became weapons in the hands of factory politicians. More often, however, the posts were filled simply because they had become an accepted part of the structure and the reason for their inception had been forgotten. The manager, mentioned earlier, who kept a second organization chart locked in his office drawer, was aware of the way in which the organizational structure of his firm had been modified to accommodate individuals, and he was trying to safeguard against the perpetuation of the modifications.

Management fashion also had an important part in organizational changes. The urge to 'keep up with the Joneses' seems to be as powerful a force in industrial circles as in social life. There were chief executives who tended to follow suit if they heard that a neighbouring firm was about to establish a new specialist department.

Some interesting examples of the combined effect of personal ambition and management fashion came up. In one case a young store-keeper who had attended a materials control course had been able to convince his chief executive that his firm needed a materials control department of which he should be manager. Within six months, three neighbouring firms also had materials control departments. Industrial engineers were other specialists who were becoming fashionable at the time of the research. Indeed, the research workers themselves probably benefited from this following of fashion. One of the reasons why so many firms agreed to co-operate may have been that they were situated in the same area and thus in close communication with each other. Once it was known that one local firm had agreed to co-operate in the research others were prepared to follow suit; as one manager said 'I heard you had been at X's up the road and at Y's down the road, so it's about time we were done.'

A wide variety of factors seemed to have played a part in the establishment of the thirty work study departments; some were as old as the firms themselves, some had grown out of rate-fixing departments, some had been established by management consultants—and fashion was undoubtedly important in this field too. In the majority of cases, however, work study departments had been set up to solve specific management problems. The problems were not necessarily related to the need to increase operator efficiency. One chief executive said that he had decided to have a work study department to 'wake up the production foremen'; another, because he would be able to offer higher wages through financial incentives and thus be able to attract labour in an area where there was full employment.

In ten of the firms with work study departments there were no financial incentives; the departments were concerned with the measurement of work rather than with its evaluation, and were important parts of wider control systems.

MANAGEMENT SYSTEMS

A new concept for classifying industrial organization was developed by Burns (1958)[3] and subsequently applied to the survey data. His empirical investigations suggested that firms follow two fundamentally different organizational procedures, one resulting in the establishment of a 'mechanistic' system and the other an 'organic' system. 'Mechanistic' systems are characterized by rigid breakdown into functional specialisms, precise definition of duties, responsibilities and power, and a well developed command hierarchy through which information filters up and decisions and instructions flow down. 'Organic' systems are more adaptable; jobs lose much of their formal definition, and communications up and down the hierarchy are more in the nature of consultation than of the passing up of information and the receiving of orders. In this type of situation the chief executive is not regarded as omniscient.

This concept of a mechanistic as opposed to an organic system of management was found useful in the analysis of the data

[3] Tom Burns, *Management in the Electronics Industry—a study of eight English Companies*. Social Science Research Centre, University of Edinburgh; see also Honor Croome, *The Human Problems of Innovation* (H.M.S.O., 1960).

obtained from the survey. Reference has already been made to the fact that some firms seemed more organization-conscious than others. In most cases, lack of organization consciousness—inability to produce an organization chart or to state precisely who was responsible to whom in the hierarchy—indicated an organic management system.

There were some exceptions to this general rule, most of them were the small line organization firms. Although there was little functional specialization and little definition of duties and responsibilities in these firms, the omniscience of the man at the top was obvious and unchallenged; hierarchical communication was not consultation. Even if unaware of their precise function, individuals knew where they stood and how to conduct themselves, management as an authority system was well understood and accepted.

But while, in the main, a lack of organization consciousness was associated with an organic management system, the reverse was not the case. The ability to produce and discuss an organization chart was not always an indication of a mechanistic management system. Even at this early stage in the research, discussion showed that in many firms organization was less rigid in practice than it appeared on paper. In some firms, role relationships prescribed by the chart seemed to be of secondary importance to personal relationships between individuals. In others, roles were interchangeable; line supervisors could be transferred or promoted to specialist jobs or vice versa. The possibility of this happening restrained those concerned from pursuing their individual tasks as something distinct from the overall task of the firm as a whole.

Another interesting difference was shown in the methods of inter-management communication; in some firms communication was almost entirely oral, either face to face or by telephone, in others it was written. Inter-departmental memorandum and production documentation were more elaborate and more extensively used in some firms than in others. There was a tendency towards written communication in mechanistic systems and towards verbal communication in organic systems.

Organic systems, both those consciously planned on organic lines and those planned on mechanistic lines but operated on organic principles, outnumbered mechanistic systems by approximately two to one. This distribution might have been expected in view of Burns's earlier findings. As a result of his researches he came to the conclusion that mechanistic systems are appropriate to stable conditions and organic systems to conditions of change. It will be recalled that South Essex is an area in which the newer and developing industries predominate, and it might therefore be expected that organic systems would also predominate.

DETAILED ORGANIZATIONAL DIFFERENCES

Firms differed not only in the general character of their organizational structure but also in such detailed respects as the length of the hierarchy, the sizes of the span of control at various levels, the labour breakdown, and the cost structure.

The command hierarchy could be anything from two to twelve distinct levels of management between the board and the operators. The complete distribution is given in Fig. 3.

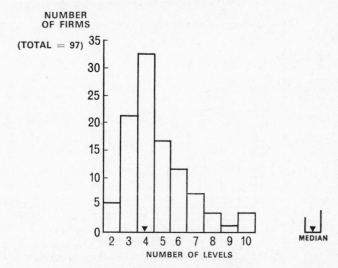

NUMBER
OF FIRMS
(TOTAL = 97)

NUMBER OF LEVELS

MEDIAN

Fig. 3. Levels of management

Just as the height of a firm's management pyramid can be measured by the number of levels in a command hierarchy, an indication of its breadth can be obtained from the size of the span of control at each level. The size of the span at the top and bottom of the hierarchy is given in Figs. 4 and 5. Fig. 4 shows the number of people directly responsible to the chief executive, and Fig. 5

the average number of operators responsible to first-line supervision, namely the first level of authority spending more than 50 per cent of the time on supervisory duties. Usually this was the foreman; in a few firms, however, there were non-working chargehands under the foreman.

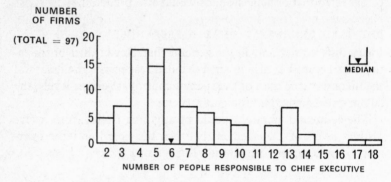

Fig. 4. Span of control of a chief executive

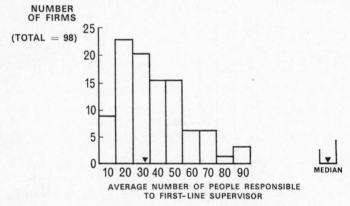

Fig. 5. Average span of control of a first-line supervisor

The varying lengths of the command hierarchy made it impossible to make direct comparisons between firms of the size of the span of control at the intermediate levels of management. In general, however, long command hierarchies seemed to be associated with small spans of control. Pyramids tended to be either long and narrowly based or short and broadly based. The number of levels in a command hierarchy did not appear to be a function of the total size of the management and supervisory group.

The number of levels in a firm's command hierarchy, together with its horizontal breakdown into departments, defines the network of roles comprising its social structure. An indication of the relative size of the vertical and horizontal sub-groups so formed can be obtained from an examination of its labour figures. The simplest vertical breakdown of personnel is into two groups, supervisory and non-supervisory. As Fig. 6 shows, these groups varied considerably in size. In all the firms studied non-supervisory personnel outnumbered supervisory and management personnel, but whereas in some firms the non-supervisory group was forty times as large as the supervisory, in others it was only five times as large.

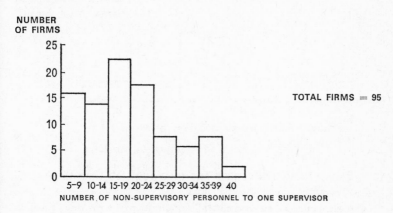

Fig. 6. Ratio of managers and supervisors to non-supervisory staff

Although most firms drew a formal distinction in their records between supervisory and non-supervisory personnel, and normally offered different conditions of employment, the research workers found that it was not always easy to distinguish between those who gave and those who took orders. Many clerical and administrative staff, although not formally recognized as supervisors, were nevertheless exercising authority. In some cases this authority was inherent in the job itself; inspectors, project engineers, progress chasers, and work study men all influenced and controlled others. In many firms the initiation of the paper work of production was tantamount to the giving of orders to production supervision.

In others, control was exercised through close association with a member of management. Clerical and administrative staff were scattered in units or small clusters throughout management organization and tended to reflect the attitudes and behaviour, and to share the authority of the manager or supervisor to whom they were attached. Many personal assistants and secretaries to senior managers exercised authority in excess of their formal roles. This 'middlemen' group—the non-supervisory staff who exercised authority—was larger and more firmly established in some firms than in others. The group was largest in firms with a mechanistic system, line-staff organization, high-powered specialists, and elaborate planning and control procedures. In three firms there

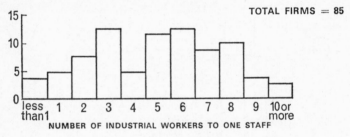

Fig. 7. Ratio of staff to industrial workers

were more production control and planning staff than there were managers and supervisors.

Non-supervisory personnel fell into two main groups; clerical and administrative on the one hand, and industrial workers on the other. Eighty-five firms provided figures for this breakdown. In eighty-two of them clerical and administrative staff were paid on a weekly or monthly basis, and industrial workers on an hourly basis. In the other three, both staff and industrial workers were paid on a weekly basis, industrial workers being given staff privileges after a period of probationary service. The relative size of the two groups varied from firm to firm, the range being between one industrial worker to three staff, and thirteen industrial workers to one staff; the complete distribution is given in Fig. 7.

The composition of the industrial labour force in terms of knowledge and skill differed from firm to firm. The oldest and most traditional differentiation between hourly-paid workers in British industry is based upon skill; skilled, semi-skilled, and unskilled categories being recognized in the wage structure of most industries, and in the class structure of society. Although it is impossible to define these categories with any degree of precision, the terms are commonly used and understood throughout industry. It is generally accepted that a skilled worker is a craftsman whose training has been spread over several years and is formally recognized outside an individual firm; a semi-skilled worker is one who, during a limited period of training, usually between two and twelve weeks, has acquired the manual dexterity or mechanical knowledge needed for his immediate job, and an unskilled worker is one whose job requires no formal training of any kind. In seven-eighths of the seventy-six firms from which

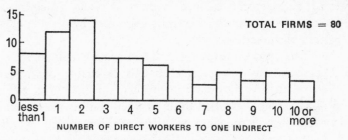

Fig. 8. Ratio of direct to indirect labour

sufficiently detailed information was obtained to make the calculation possible, semi-skilled workers were the largest single group, and unskilled workers were the smallest group. In the remainder, skilled workers were still in the majority.

Fig. 8 gives the breakdown between the direct and the indirect labour in eighty firms. Many of the firms employing a majority of skilled men had a high ratio of indirect to direct labour, the skilled men being employed mainly in maintenance and inspection departments.

Wages, salaries, and related expenditure accounted for anything between 3 per cent and 56 per cent of total turnover. Percentages were not evenly distributed between these two extremes but clustered around specific points: 5 per cent, 12 per cent, 30 per cent, and 50 per cent. One possible explanation of these clusters is that the figures obtained were approximations only; as indicated already, they had originally been prepared for presentation to joint consultative committees.

MANAGEMENT QUALIFICATIONS AND TRAINING

Graduates and professionally qualified staff were employed in fifty of the firms studied; twenty-two employed them in staff departments only, three in line departments only, and twenty-five in both line and staff departments. Thirty firms promoted their managers almost entirely from within, five recruited all managers and supervisors from outside, and the remaining sixty-five used both sources of recruitment according to circumstances. Systematic management training courses were held in fifteen firms, and executive development schemes involving regular training were in operation in a further three. Fifty firms had either held some short internal management training courses or sent managers and supervisors to similar short courses organized by outside educational establishments.

There were sixteen firms where the information obtained about qualifications was not precise enough to enable the research workers to calculate the exact proportion of qualified to unqualified staff. The ratio of qualified to unqualified staff in the remaining thirty-four firms employing gr luates is given in Fig. 9, which

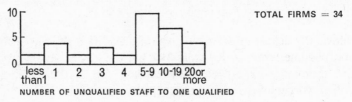

Fig. 9. Ratio of qualified to unqualified staff

shows that whereas in some the employment of graduates was on a fairly large scale, in others they were very much in a minority.

THE RELATIONSHIP BETWEEN ORGANIZATIONAL AND OTHER DIFFERENCES

Although the analysis of the information had shown that firms differed considerably in the way they were organized and operated, it was not easy to find the common threads underlying these differences.

Firms classified under the same Ministry of Labour category, for example, had little in common organizationally. Moreover, size did not appear to affect organization as much as might have been expected. The generally accepted opinion that specialization inside the management field is a direct result of growth was certainly not confirmed by the research findings. A line-staff type of organization was highly developed in eighteen firms employing less than 250 people. The administration of production in these firms was almost completely separated from the supervision of production operations. Seven had highly developed personnel departments covering the full range of personnel activity, while one had a full-time medical officer, supported by a nursing staff. Some of the larger firms, on the other hand, retained a line type of organization. For example, in one firm where as many as 5000 people were employed there was no personnel department; indeed, there was not even centralized recruitment; foremen were still engaging their own labour.

Neither did the length of the command hierarchy appear to be related to size, and as can be seen from Fig. 10—in which the information illustrated in Figures 4 and 5 is broken down on a basis of size—the number employed did not have as much effect on the size of the span of control of the first-line supervisor or chief executive as might have been expected. It is true that in none of the firms employing over 1000 people was the average size of the span of control of the first-line supervisor less than ten, and in no firm employing less than 250 was it more than sixty; but within these limits the range was wide.

Size seemed to have little effect either on the quality of a firm's industrial relations or on the extent to which it was organization-conscious. The larger firms were not always those in which relationships were less harmonious. It is equally true to say that the smaller firms were not in all cases those with the least clearly defined organizational structure. It seemed that in South Essex the informally organized but 'happy' small firm was more of a myth than a reality.

As neither size nor type of industry seemed to be the variable on which organizational differences depended, consideration was given to the possible explanation that these differences reflected the different personalities of the chief executives. It is commonly

assumed that both the form of organization and the degree of
success depend very much on the man at the top. Organizational
differences might also be attributable to the historical background
and tradition of the firms concerned. The research workers felt,
however, that while it was obviously true that such factors were

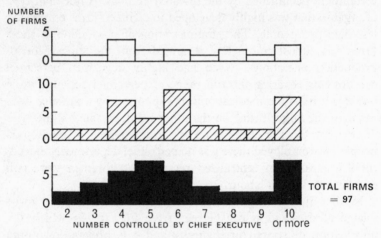

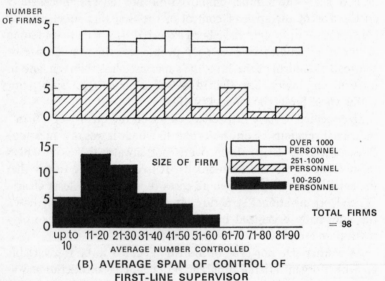

Fig. 10. Span of control analysed by size

variables in the situation and influenced it, they did not adequately explain it; the observed differences between firms either in organizational patterns or in the quality of human relations could not in all cases be related to personality or tradition.

ORGANIZATION AND SUCCESS

In the final stages of this first analysis of the survey data, consideration was given to whether the type of organization as analysed from the classical point of view was related in any way to record of achievement; was any particular form of organization associated with success? The conclusion reached was that the twenty firms assessed as 'above average' in success had little in common organizationally. Nine seemed to be organization-conscious, eleven were not. The successful firms included the two with a functional type of organization; this suggested that in some circumstances people can and do work effectively under more than one supervisor.

In five successful firms the chief executive controlled more than twelve immediate subordinates. This is interesting in view of the fact that one of the 'rules' of classical management theory is that in the interests of administrative efficiency the span of control at the highest echelon should be limited to five or six; this number being based on a calculation of the combination of reciprocal relationships likely to arise in the course of contact between one superior and an increasing number of subordinates.[4]

Advanced production control techniques were not in operation in all successful firms. In approximately one in four, commercial success still appeared to depend upon the skill in making clinical judgments by relatively junior line supervisors.

The twenty firms assessed as 'below average' in success differed equally widely. Here again nine were organization-conscious and eleven were not, and those with organic systems outnumbered those with mechanistic systems by approximately two to one. There were wide variations in the size of the span of control at the different levels of the hierarchy, and whereas in some unsuccessful firms command hierarchies were very long, in others they were very short.

[4] V. A. Graicunas, 'Relationship in Organization' in *Papers on the Science of Administration*, ed. Luther Gulick and L. Urwick (Institute of Public Administration, New York, 1939).

Up to this point in the analysis, therefore, the only conclusion to be drawn was that the systematization of the information obtained in the way described had produced entirely negative results. No relationship of any kind had been established between organizational and other characteristics, and to a research team based on a College that spent so much time and effort on the teaching of management subjects, the lack of any inter-relationship between business success and what is generally regarded as sound organizational structure was particularly disconcerting.

3 *Analysis of Technical Variables*

SYSTEMS OF PRODUCTION

There still remained for examination the data relating to the methods and processes of manufacture. One interesting characteristic of classical management theory, the concepts and formulas of which formed the basis of analysis in the previous chapter, is that it was developed in a technical setting but independently of technology. In general the formulas are closely linked with the personalities of those who worked and wrote in this field. It is true that several of the people concerned, including Taylor himself, were engineers with a technical background who had practised successfully in manufacturing industry. But they tended to generalize on the basis of their experience, and the expedients they found effective in practice were often given the status of fundamental truths or general laws by those attracted to their ideas. The result was that the assumption first put into words by Follett (1927)[1] that 'whatever the purpose towards which human endeavour is directed, the principles of that direction are nevertheless the same' became an accepted part of management theory. There has been a tendency to develop ideas about the administrative process independently of technical considerations, and the technical backgrounds of the people who practised successfully as managers tend to have been overlooked or forgotten in the evaluation of their work.

[1] Mary Parker Follett in *Papers on Dynamic Administration*, given at the annual conference of the American Bureau of Personnel Administration 1924–8. The majority of these reports are reproduced in a memorial volume entitled *Dynamic Administration* edited by Henry Metcalfe, and L. Urwick (Management Publication Trusts Ltd., West Willow and Harper Bros., New York).

Sociologists who turned their attention to problems of either administration or industrial behaviour, from Weber and Veblen onwards, took a different point of view in theory, assuming that the technological circumstances, either of a society in the wider sense or of a social system such as a factory was a major variable in the determination of its structure and behaviour. For example, the assumption that technical change has a profound effect on social relationships underlies the industrial relations studies undertaken by the Department of Social Science of the University of Liverpool.[2] Trist and his colleagues of the Tavistock Institute of Human Relations have done a good deal of interesting and exciting work on the basis of a similar assumption. The phrase 'a sociotechnical system' was coined and has been used extensively to explain the interplay of social and technical factors in the work situation.[3]

Dubin (1959)[4] went so far as to contend that technology is the most important single determinant of working behaviour. He also defined his use of the word technology by sub-dividing it into two major phases; first, the tools, instruments, machines, and technical formulas basic to the performance of the work, and secondly, the body of ideas which express the goals of the work, its functional importance, and the rationale of the methods employed. Indeed, a considerable part of the literature of industrial sociology in the last five years is concerned with the relationship between behaviour and technology at either the 'tool' or the 'control' level.

Having reached negative conclusions from the initial analysis of their material, the research workers turned almost automatically to their technological data. Was it possible to systematize this data in such a way as to show whether there was any relationship between organizational characteristics and technology? A difficulty immediately arose, for although the existence of a link between technology and behaviour is more or less taken for granted by

[2] W. H. Scott, J. A. Banks, A. H. Halsey, and T. Lupton, *Technical Change and Industrial Relations* (Liverpool University Press, 1956).

[3] One of the earliest articles published on this theme was that which appeared in *The Manager* in December 1955: 'Some Contrasting Socio-Technical Production Systems', by A. T. M. Wilson.

[4] Robert Dubin, 'Working Union-Management Relations', *The Sociology of Industrial Relations* (Prentice Hall, Englewood Cliffs, N.J.).

social scientists, the technical variables on which the differences in structure and behaviour depend, have not yet been isolated. Except in relation to specific case studies the concept of a socio-technical system remains largely an abstraction and is therefore of little value as a predictive tool in the study of industrial behaviour.

What was needed by the research workers at this point in the analysis was a natural history of industry, something in the nature of a botanist's 'Flora' that they could use to identify in tech-nological terms the firms they had studied. Without a precise instrument of this kind all that could be done was to group to-gether on a rough and ready basis all the firms in which manu-facturing processes and methods appeared to be similar. The first point of interest to emerge from this grouping was that Dubin's two phases of technology are closely related. It soon became obvious that firms with similar goals and associated manu-facturing policies had similar manufacturing processes—the range of tools, instruments, machines, and technical formulas was limited and controlled by manufacturing policy. For example, a firm restricting itself to the manufacture of bespoke suits was not able to use the same advanced techniques of production as a firm making mass-produced men's clothing.

Indeed, the first important breakdown of the firms studied was between those where production was of the 'one off' kind, to meet customers' individual requirements, and those where production was standardized. Firms making products on a 'one off' basis were further sub-divided according to the nature of these products. Some were simple from a technical point of view (like the bespoke suits referred to above); others were more complex—for example prototypes of electronic equipment. The size of the unit product was important too; large equipments such as radio transmitting stations had to be fabricated in stages, the manufacturing methods differing considerably from those used in the production of smaller prototypes.

Firms making standardized products could also be sub-divided; in some, production went on continuously, in others it was inter-rupted at more or less frequent intervals. Furthermore, whereas in some firms there was considerable diversity of products, in others there was relatively little flexibility in production facilities.

Another possible way of dividing firms was to differentiate

between those making integral products and those making
dimensional products measured by weight, capacity, or volume.
Firms making integral products are sometimes referred to
collectively as manufacturing industry, and firms making dimensional products as process industry. Dimensional products
are normally manufactured in chemical plants. Here again, in
analysing the data a distinction could be drawn between the
multi-purpose plant in which production was intermittent and
the single-purpose plant in which production was continuous,
stopping only in the event of a breakdown or for a complete
overhaul.

It soon became obvious to the research workers that there were
so many variations in manufacturing methods that every situation
which they examined was to some extent unique. Nevertheless, if
an attempt was to be made to assess the effect of technology upon
organization, some system would have to be devised for dividing
the firms studied into sections and for classifying firms with
technical characteristics in common within each section. It was
felt that the system of division normally used by production
engineers into the three categories of jobbing, batch, and mass
production was inadequate for this purpose, as each of these
headings covered a very broad field. On the other hand it had to be
borne in mind that the research data related to a hundred firms
only. Thus too many categories would make the numbers in each
too small to reveal trends or relationships.

In the final analysis, therefore, production systems were
grouped into the eleven categories illustrated in Fig. 11. It will
be seen that in eighty firms a single system of production predominated, while in a further twelve, two systems were combined
into one process of manufacture. These combinations were of two
main kinds; one, agricultural engineering, for instance, consisted
of the production of standard parts subsequently assembled into
diverse products. The other, found in such industries as pharmaceutical chemical manufacture, combined the manufacture of a
product in a plant with its subsequent preparation for sale by
packaging. Dimensional products, measured by weight or volume,
became integral products after further processing; a quantity of
acetylsalicylic acid, for example, became a number of aspirin
tablets.

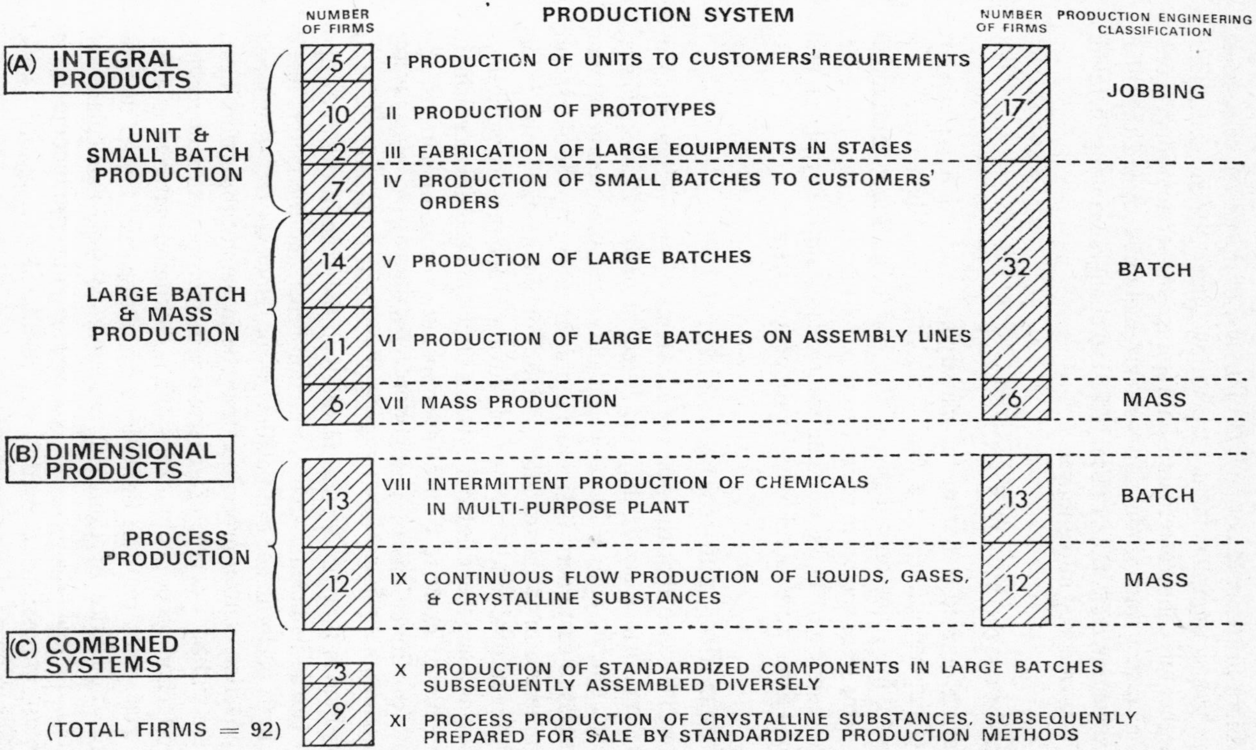

NUMBER OF FIRMS	PRODUCTION SYSTEM	NUMBER OF FIRMS	PRODUCTION ENGINEERING CLASSIFICATION
5	I PRODUCTION OF UNITS TO CUSTOMERS' REQUIREMENTS		JOBBING
10	II PRODUCTION OF PROTOTYPES	17	
2	III FABRICATION OF LARGE EQUIPMENTS IN STAGES		
7	IV PRODUCTION OF SMALL BATCHES TO CUSTOMERS' ORDERS	32	BATCH
14	V PRODUCTION OF LARGE BATCHES		
11	VI PRODUCTION OF LARGE BATCHES ON ASSEMBLY LINES		
6	VII MASS PRODUCTION	6	MASS
13	VIII INTERMITTENT PRODUCTION OF CHEMICALS IN MULTI-PURPOSE PLANT	13	BATCH
12	IX CONTINUOUS FLOW PRODUCTION OF LIQUIDS, GASES, & CRYSTALLINE SUBSTANCES	12	MASS
3	X PRODUCTION OF STANDARDIZED COMPONENTS IN LARGE BATCHES SUBSEQUENTLY ASSEMBLED DIVERSELY		
9	XI PROCESS PRODUCTION OF CRYSTALLINE SUBSTANCES, SUBSEQUENTLY PREPARED FOR SALE BY STANDARDIZED PRODUCTION METHODS		

(A) INTEGRAL PRODUCTS

UNIT & SMALL BATCH PRODUCTION

LARGE BATCH & MASS PRODUCTION

(B) DIMENSIONAL PRODUCTS

PROCESS PRODUCTION

(C) COMBINED SYSTEMS

(TOTAL FIRMS = 92)

Fig. 11. Production systems in South Essex industry

Eight firms could not be fitted into any of the eleven categories: one was a Remploy factory operating under special conditions, another was concerned mainly with storage and servicing operations. In a further four production was extremely mixed, and the other two were in transition, radical technical changes bringing them out of one category into another.

PRODUCTION SYSTEMS AND SIZE

Having devised a system for classifying production systems, it was important to ensure that something more than merely re-classifying firms on a basis of size had been done; production systems were therefore related to size. As Fig. 12 shows, however, there appeared to be no significant relationship; both large and small firms were found in each production category.

INCREASING TECHNICAL COMPLEXITY

It will be seen that the first nine systems of production given in Fig. 11 form a scale; they are listed in order of chronological development, and technical complexity; the production of unit articles to customers' individual requirements being the oldest and simplest form of manufacture, and the continuous-flow production of dimensional products, the most advanced and most complicated. Moving along the scale from Systems I to IX, it becomes increasingly possible to exercise control over manufacturing operations, the physical limitations of production becoming better known and understood. Targets can be set and reached more effectively in continuous-flow production plants than they can in the most up-to-date and efficient batch production firms, and the factors likely to limit performance can be allowed for. However well-developed production control procedures may be in batch production firms, there will be a degree of uncertainty in the prediction of results. Production proceeds by drives and a continuous attempt is made to push back physical limitations by setting ever higher targets. The difficulties of exercising effective control, particularly of prototype manufacture, are greatest in unit production. It is almost impossible to predict the results of development work either in terms of time or money.

In general it is also true to say that prediction and control are

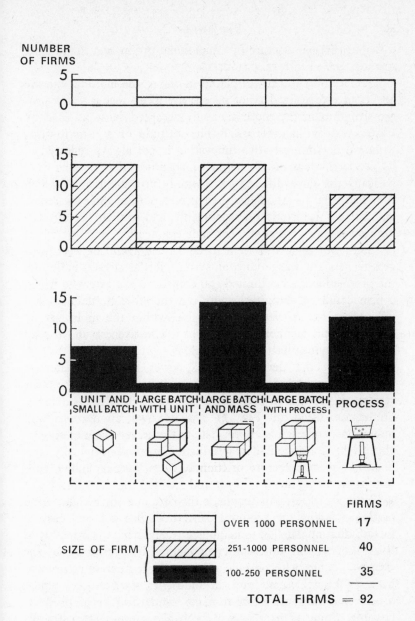

NUMBER
OF FIRMS

UNIT AND SMALL BATCH   LARGE BATCH WITH UNIT   LARGE BATCH AND MASS   LARGE BATCH WITH PROCESS   PROCESS

	FIRMS
OVER 1000 PERSONNEL	17
251-1000 PERSONNEL	40
100-250 PERSONNEL	35

SIZE OF FIRM

TOTAL FIRMS = 92

Fig. 12. Production systems analysed by number employed

easier in the manufacture of dimensional production than in the manufacture of integral products.

The fact that a firm was placed in one of the more technically advanced categories did not necessarily mean that it was a progressive firm in the more generally accepted sense as used by Carter and Williams (1958).[5] The attitude of a firm towards technical or administrative innovation is not always reflected in its production system. Firms in which production systems were basically the same differed considerably in the extent to which they had tried to rationalize their production, in their awareness and interest in technical developments, and in their use of techniques such as work study, methods engineering, and operations research. But there did seem to be a relationship between progressiveness and the production system, for, as already indicated, the production system limited and controlled the extent to which a firm could go. Progressiveness can therefore be defined as a willingness to do everything possible within the limits set by objectives and technology, to increase effectiveness and extend control over manufacturing operations.

Moreover, the development of newer and more effective methods of manufacture does not necessarily mean that the older systems of production become outmoded. Each of the systems of production listed in Fig. 11 has its own applications and limitations, and each is appropriate to the achievement of specific objectives. Continuous-flow production methods originally confined to the manufacture of liquids, gases, and crystalline substances are being increasingly introduced into the manufacture of solid shapes. Steel, paperboard, millboard, and some engineering parts are among the products concerned. But it is not easy to foresee their application to manufacture involving the assembly of large numbers of different components. Unit production, the simplest system, will continue as long as large items of equipment have to be fabricated and in industries where development proceeds at too rapid a rate to make standardization of products possible. Some firms also will probably continue to cater for individual idiosyncrasies.

Industrial administration theorists tend to be intolerant of

[5] P. Carter and B. Williams, *Industry and Technical Progress* (Oxford University Press).

individual idiosyncrasies. Urwick (1943)[6] says: 'to allow the individual idiosyncrasies of a wide range of customers to drive administration away from the principles on which it can manufacture most economically is suicidal—the kind of good intention with which the road to hell or bankruptcy is proverbially paved.' Standardization, specification, and simplification are the ideals on which modern manufacturing methods are based, and it is, of course, true that our increased standard of living depends upon standardized production. It is also true that increases in the standard of living are likely to result in greater demands for goods manufactured to customers' individual requirements; more people will want and be able to afford such things as bespoke suits or gold-plated limousines. Thus the number of firms catering for individual idiosyncrasies is more likely to increase than decrease; unit production will probably be with us for many years to come.

As has already been pointed out, some firms seemed less explicitly aware of their primary tasks and manufacturing objectives than others. The history of these firms suggests that means had sometimes been allowed to determine ends. An enthusiasm for a new technique of manufacture or for a more elaborate system of programming or control would lead to a modification in manufacturing policy without those responsible for its determination being consciously aware of what was happening. The effects of the innovation on quality standards or on the type of customers served had not always been thought out in advance.

One such firm employing approximately 500 people was concerned with batch production; it made large batches of standardized products, and small batches of customers' individual requirements. Management consultants had been brought in, their brief being the rather general one of increasing the firm's efficiency. The first thing the consultants had done was to introduce a better system of cost accounting, demonstrating to the management how unit costs could be progressively reduced by increases in batch size. They recommended that the firm should reduce the variety of its production and concentrate on a small number of standard lines. The firm did this and then found that their customers were not particularly interested in the standard lines. The retailers said they had accepted them only because the firm was prepared

[6] L. Urwick, *Elements of Administration* (Pitman, London).

to make smaller quantities of special products to customers' individual requirements. Sales dropped when those special facilities were withdrawn, and the firm lost ground to one of the larger industrial organizations operating in the same field.

The research workers visited this firm about a year later. A drop in sales had forced the firm—incidentally, one of the oldest in the area—to declare redundant workers who had been with them for many years and for whom no alternative employment was available locally. It then decided to revert to its earlier practice of catering for individual requirements on demand. The decision caused some heart-burning, for the management was now more sophisticated about the costs of such production. Nevertheless the firm survived and continued to fulfil a useful social function, thus demonstrating that there is still a place for a firm prepared to cater for individual idiosyncrasies in an industry where production methods are on the whole more advanced.

THE NATURE OF TECHNICAL CHANGE

Reference has already been made to the difficulties experienced by the research workers in classifying firms where radical technical changes were in progress, and to the fact that the area studied was one in which newer and developing industries predominated. The field work of the survey happened to coincide with the speeding up of the pace of technical change in South Essex industry. The research workers were therefore in a good position to study the nature of technical change and its effects on organizational structure.

Changes seemed to come about in two ways. Some were initiated by a policy decision to modify objectives in order to introduce a more advanced system of production. Others came about as a result of a technical or administrative development (sometimes originating inside the firm and sometimes outside) making it possible to achieve the original objective in a newer and more effective way. Among changes of the first kind were those that had followed decisions to standardize production. There were, too, the changes that had taken place in the pharmaceutical chemical industry as a result of the increased demand for prepared and packaged drugs intensified by the introduction of the National Health Service; and in the oil industry at the end of the second world war when, for both political and economic reasons, a high-level decision was taken to distil crude oil in this country.

The changes leading to the more effective pursuit of original objectives were of two main kinds: those resulting from a radical re-thinking of the manufacturing operations, the outcome being a more formal structuring of the decision-making process, and those that were entirely technical. Many but not all of the latter were associated with one of the three main streams of engineering progress covered by the term 'automation'. In one firm in which a computer was being installed to programme production, the two kinds of development had come together, the computer itself being the result of technical advance while its effective use depended on a complete re-thinking of the manufacturing operation and an analysis of all the contingencies that would have to be allowed for in its programming.

Techniques of work measurement and operations research were changes of the first kind. Moreover, the standardization of parts, which was an essential feature of the production system operating in the three firms classified in category X of Fig. 11, had necessitated a complete re-thinking of manufacturing operations. For many years those responsible for the determination of policy in these firms had taken for granted the fact that modern methods relying on standardization, simplification, and specification were inappropriate to the manufacture of unit products. An analysis of their production into component parts had shown, however, that the production of parts, as distinct from products, could be standardized. Thus in some respects these three firms were getting the best of two production worlds—reducing production costs and still continuing to satisfy individual customers.

In one firm a reorganization of this kind had failed to give the desired results, and a reversion to the older and less complex system of production was in progress. This firm made scientific instruments and had standardized part of its production operations, not only to reduce costs but also because in the immediate post-war period instrument makers were in short supply. This firm had also been taken over by a big industrial organization in which large batch and mass production techniques were highly developed. In moving towards standardized production, the firm had therefore had the wealth of accumulated experience of the parent company on which to draw. The changes appeared to be made without much resistance from those employed, and production costs were undoubtedly considerably reduced. But within a year or so a gradual deterioration in standards of performance at every level of the hierarchy was noticed—caused, it was felt, by the new methods. The reputation for high-class workmanship on which the firm depended for its success seemed to be in danger. It was therefore decided that some of the newer methods would have to be abandoned.

Changes initiated by a radical re-thinking of the manufacturing operations were not restricted in their application to any one production system, although the techniques to which they gave rise seemed particularly appropriate to·the production of small and medium-sized batches and to the type of line production that depends upon the assembly of large numbers of component parts. Neither were changes initiated by technical developments restricted in their application. There were areas of production in which particular kinds of technical change were most easily and most often applied. Automatic control seemed most suited to continuous-flow processes and to mass production. Nevertheless there were firms operating in the unit, and small batch production fields, where automatic devices had been introduced to control individual machines.

The examples of automation seen during this research ranged in scale from such large installations as transfer-lines for cylinder block manufacture, automatic plants for the distillation of crude oil, and electronic computers to small transfer machines (for example, one on which barley sugar sticks were made), electronic devices for machine tool control and non-destructive testing appliances of various kinds.

Moving from one firm to another, the research workers soon realized that it would be impossible to reach generalized conclusions about the effect of technical change on organization and relationships. In some cases technical changes fundamentally altered the system of production, the firms concerned moving from one of the categories listed in Fig. 11 to another. In others they had relatively little effect. Moreover, the scale of the change did not necessarily indicate the extent of its effect. For example, the cylinder block transfer-line accounted for only about one per cent of total production operations in the firm concerned, the basic system of production remaining as before: large batch production of the line type, based on the assembly of a number of different components. The barley sugar stick machine, on the other hand, although it represented a very much smaller capital investment, brought about a fundamental change in the production system, the technology becoming continuous-flow production instead of small batch production.

Where technical change resulted in a change in a production system, the tendency was to move towards a newer and more complex system; from unit and small batch to large batch and mass production, and from large batch and mass production to continuous-flow and process production. As far as could be foreseen, however, no production system listed in Fig. 11 was likely to disappear altogether from the area in the immediate future, nor was there any indication that completely new systems were likely to emerge. The distribution of firms between the categories given in Fig. 11 will undoubtedly change. Continuous-flow production not only of liquids, gases, and crystalline substances, but also of solid shapes will probably predominate in time. Indeed, it was interesting to find that even at the present time the large batch and mass production methods, normally regarded as typical of modern industry, were in operation in only one in three of the firms studied.

Continuous-flow production methods were being applied to an increasingly wide range of products; the canning and packaging of food, for example. The preparation of products for sale in the firms included in category XI of Fig. 11, the cutting, tabletting, wrapping, and bottling operations were rapidly being integrated in the actual manufacturing process. This was particularly noticeable in a brewery studied. The empty beer bottles were fed into the bottling machines by hand, but the sterilizing, filling, stoppering, labelling, counting, and crating of the bottles was done automatically. Developments in the manufacture of paperboard and millboard were changing the system of production to continuous-flow in these industries too.

ATTITUDES TO CHANGE

Moving from one factory to another and questioning people about the manufacturing processes and methods in operation in them, the research workers obtained an impression of the way that people reacted to change. The surprising thing was the almost complete lack of resistance. Not only the managers and supervisors, but also the industrial workers with whom the new technical developments were discussed appeared to take pride in the fact that their firms were technically up to date. Much trouble was taken to explain in simple and non-technical terms the way in which new plants and machinery operated, and in spite of the slight trade recession that coincided with part of the field work, people seemed optimistic about the future and managers seemed prepared to take risks either by expanding premises or by employing more people.

Indeed, the general impression was that the industrial population of South Essex had been conditioned not only to accept change but also to welcome and enjoy it. In one firm the operators told a research worker that if the workshop looked the same for more than three months at a time they would begin to think the firm was going downhill. In another, the research workers were given a pamphlet, prepared and circulated by the Shop Stewards' Committee, on how current technical developments might affect their industry. It was obvious that in preparing this pamphlet they had been advised by people who were technically well informed and, naturally, the pamphlet dealt at length with what the operators themselves were likely to get out of these new developments. Nevertheless it was moderate and non-alarmist. This moderation was particularly significant in that the publication of the pamphlet coincided with Press articles on automation in which the effects of automation had been exaggerated and over-dramatized.

It seemed to the research workers that this lack of resistance to change was due to a number of factors. Probably the most important was that change was not seen as a threat to employment. The comparatively recent development of the area and the predominance of the newer industries meant that for most people change was something that led to prosperity and expansion. Many had followed the new industries into South Essex in the 1930s, coming from East London, Southern Ireland, and what were then known as 'the depressed areas'; their subsequent prosperity had given them faith in the future of the firms for which they worked.

Indeed, attitudes to employment in the area were extremely

interesting and might repay further and more intensive study. On one hand people were aggressive and militant in their relationships with management, political and industrial behaviour were closely linked, and patronage of every kind was resisted. On the other, there was high productivity, low labour turnover and absence rates, and a close identification with the employer.

Change was rarely a threat to the pay-packet either; firms operating incentive systems of payment were in the minority. Between 80 and 90 per cent of the industrial workers in the area were paid on a time basis and their wages were not affected even temporarily by changed methods of working. Thus one of the major causes of insecurity associated with changes in production methods was eliminated.

Although not associated with incentive systems, work study techniques and control procedures were highly developed in many of the firms studied. In some circumstances these techniques can reduce resistance to change, as they tend to shield the shop floor worker from any direct impact. In some of the firms production was so broken down and circumscribed that one job became very much the same as another when it reached the shop floor, thus quite substantial changes could occur both in products and in production methods without the operators being fully aware of what was happening.

Finally, factory managements seemed to be particularly skilful in presenting change. For example in one firm where there were no incentive bonuses, the new machines were being operated alongside the old ones. It was obvious to all concerned that the new way was the better and easier way.

4 *Technology and Organization*

ORGANIZATIONAL TRENDS

The next step in the survey was to relate the information about the way firms were organized and operated to the technical framework. This was done, and for the first time in the analysis patterns became discernible: firms with similar production systems appeared to have similar organizational structures. There were, of course, differences between some of the firms placed in the same production category, but the differences inside each category were not, on the whole, as marked as those between categories. The figures relating to the various organizational characteristics measured tended to cluster around medians, the medians varying from one category to another.

Therefore the main conclusion reached through this research project was that the existence of the link between technology and social structure first postulated by Thorstein Veblen (1904)[1] can be demonstrated empirically. It is not suggested that the research proved technology to be the only important variable in determining organizational structure, or that such factors as the history and background of a firm and the personalities of the people who built it up and subsequently managed it were unimportant. For example, the research workers soon became aware, going from firm to firm, that individual managers differed considerably in their willingness and ability to delegate responsibility for decision-making to their subordinates. Nevertheless, in spite of individual differences, there was more delegation and decentralization in process industry than in large batch and mass production industry.

[1] Thorstein Veblen, *The Theory of Business Enterprise* (Scribner).

Technology, although not the only variable affecting organization, was one that could be isolated for study without too much difficulty. The patterns which emerged in the analysis of the data indicated that there are prescribed and functional relationships between structure and technical demands. Trends in organization appeared to be associated with an increasing ability to predict results and to control the physical limitations of production. These trends were of two kinds, for whereas some organizational characteristics were directly and progressively related to the scale of technical advance formed by the first nine systems of production listed in Fig. 11 others formed a different pattern; the production systems at each end of the scale resembled each other, while the greatest divergences were between the extremes and the middle ranges.

THE DIRECT RELATIONSHIP

Among the organizational characteristics showing a direct relationship with technical advance were: the length of the line of command; the span of control of the chief executive; the percentage of total turnover allocated to the payment of wages and salaries, and the ratios of managers to total personnel, of clerical and administrative staff to manual workers, of direct to indirect labour, and of graduate to non-graduate supervision in production departments.

Fig. 13 shows how the number of levels of management in direct production departments increased with technical advance, the longest lines being found in process industry. This diagram indicates clearly the way in which inside each production group statistics relating to organization tended to cluster around the median. Included here are only the firms in which a single system of production predominated. It was found that in firms where two systems of production were combined there was a tendency to organize each system independently. In eight of the nine firms combining process production with mass production there were more levels of management on the process side of manufacture than in the departments where the products were prepared for sale, and a higher proportion of managers to operators. In the three firms where the production of components was associated with diverse assembly there were more levels on the components side than on the assembly side, and also a much higher ratio of operators to supervisors.

Technical factors also seemed to explain the wide variations in the span of control of chief executives, the people responsible to

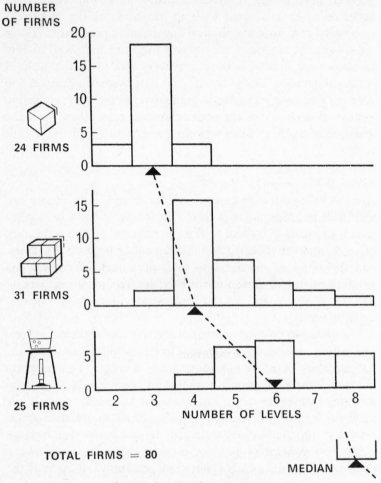

TOTAL FIRMS = 80

Fig. 13. Levels of management

the policy-forming body for the conduct of their firm's business. In unit production firms the number of people directly responsible to the chief executive ranged from two to nine, the median being four; in large batch and mass production firms the range was from four to thirteen, the median being seven, and in process production firms the range was from five to nineteen, the median being ten.

The information obtained indicated that not only the span of control of a chief executive but also the role and functions were modified by technical factors. 'Management by committee' was more common in process industry than in the less complex systems. Twenty of the twenty-five process production firms had management committees or executive boards, whereas the figures for large batch and mass production were ten out of thirty-one, and for small batch and unit production three out of twenty-four. This meant that in many process industries the chief executive functioned more as the chairman of a decision-making body than as an authoritarian decision maker.

As already pointed out, the variations in the number of levels of management made it difficult to compare the size of the spans of control at the intermediate levels in detail. The figures that were obtained, however, suggested that these too varied with the degree of technical complexity. In direct contrast to the span of control of the chief executive, which grew larger with technical advance, spans of control at middle management levels grew smaller. The small spans of control and the long lines of command characteristic of process industry meant that in this type of industry management structure could be represented by a long and narrowly based pyramid. In unit production the pyramid was short and broadly based.

As Fig. 14 shows, the proportion of total turnover allocated to the payment of wages, salaries, and related expenditure was another characteristic varying with the type of production, the proportion becoming smaller with technical advance.

It can be seen from Fig. 14 that the biggest difference in labour costs was between firms making integral products and firms making dimensional products. In firms making integral products, the decrease in labour costs associated with increasing technical complexity was relatively small. Labour costs in unit production firms tended to be largely development costs, whereas in large batch production they tended to be production costs. Moreover inside each production category the range was wide, the percentage distribution of costs being affected by a number of variables, the most important of which was the price of the raw materials used.

The firms in the process production categories not only had very much lower labour costs, but were also more homogeneous as far as their cost structure was concerned. Moreover, there was a more direct relationship with technical complexity. Labour costs were

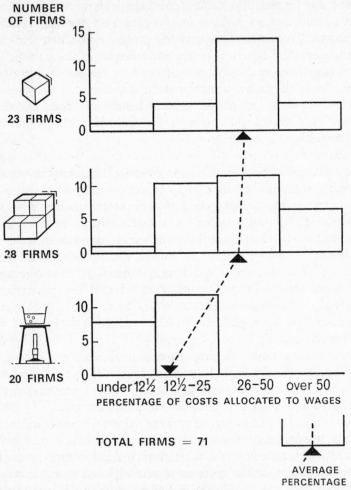

Fig. 14. Labour costs

lower in single-purpose continuous-flow plants than in multi-purpose plants producing batches of dimensional products.

It was interesting to find that the ten firms in which labour costs were less than $12\frac{1}{2}$ per cent of total turnover spent the greatest amount per head on employee welfare and services. There was also a tendency for firms in which labour costs were low to spend more money on the employment of specialists in the personnel management and human relations fields. Of the ten low labour cost firms, seven had high-status personnel departments covering all the accepted functions of personnel management, and a further two had welfare departments with more limited status and functions. Four of these nine firms employed fewer than 250 people. The obvious explanation was that firms in which labour costs were low and which were not so concerned with labour economies could afford the more highly paid specialists that function in the personnel management field. Industrial relations certainly seemed to be better in process industry than in large batch and mass production, but it is not safe to assume that the good relationships were due to the large number of specialist staff employed. As will be seen later, there were a number of contributory factors: less tension and pressure, smaller working groups, and smaller spans of control, for instance. In fact the firms that could afford these specialists may have needed them least.

There was also a link between a firm's technology and the relative size of its management group, the ratio of managers and supervisors to non-supervisory personnel increasing with technical advance. The sixteen firms shown in Fig. 6 as having one supervisor to between five and nine non-supervisory personnel were all process production firms. On average in this type of industry the ratio was 1 : 8, whereas in large batch and mass production it was 1 : 16, and in unit and small batch production 1 : 23.

In Table III (Fig. 15) the numbers are given for three firms in each main production group, these firms having been selected as representative of small, medium, and large firms respectively.

The figures are interesting; they show how labour structure is affected by technology, and they give an indication of the additional demand for managerial and supervisory skills likely to arise from technical change. Provision will have to be made in South Essex for the training of more technical and managerial personnel to meet the demands likely to arise from the technical changes described in the last chapter.

The research workers came to the conclusion that the size of the management group gave a better indication of the 'bigness' of a firm than the total number of employees. Some of the firms studied, although employing relatively few people, had all the other characteristics of large companies; including a well-developed management structure, considerable financial resources,

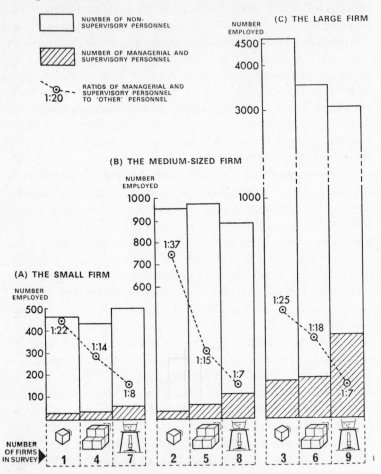

Fig. 15. Ratio of managers and supervisory staff to total personnel in selected firms (analysed by size)

long-term planning, generous employee services, and a highly-paid executive staff. This was particularly true of process production firms. It was found, for example that Firm 7 of Table III employed 55 managers out of a total labour force of 498; in all the above respects it resembled Firm 5, which had 60 managers to a total labour force of 975. The status and prestige of the two firms was also similar; they were represented on the same local committees and equally influential in local politics.

Table III. *Ratios of Managers and Supervisory Staff to Total Personnel in Selected Firms (analysed by technology).*

Production system	Total number employed	Number of managerial and supervisory personnel	Number of non-supervisory personnel	Ratio
Unit and small batch				
Firm 1	455	20	435	1 : 22
„ 2	948	25	923	1 : 37
„ 3	4,550	175	4,325	1 : 25
Large batch and mass				
Firm 4	432	30	422	1 : 14
„ 5	975	60	915	1 : 15
„ 6	3,519	180	3,329	1 : 18
Process				
Firm 7	498	55	443	1 : 8
„ 8	888	110	778	1 : 7
„ 9	3,010	375	2,635	1 : 7

Not only were there relatively more managers and supervisors in process industry but they were also better qualified; the degree of technical complexity being related to the number of graduates employed on production management. As Fig. 16 shows, twenty process firms employed graduates on line management, whereas only two unit production firms and one mass production firm did so.

Moreover, twelve of the fifteen firms operating regular and systematic management training courses were process firms; so were twenty of the thirty firms whose policy was to fill managerial posts almost exclusively by promotion from within. Most of the process production firms studied seemed to take in a group of graduate trainees each year and then promote from this group.

It will be seen from Fig. 16 that there were seven unit and small batch production firms and four mass and large batch

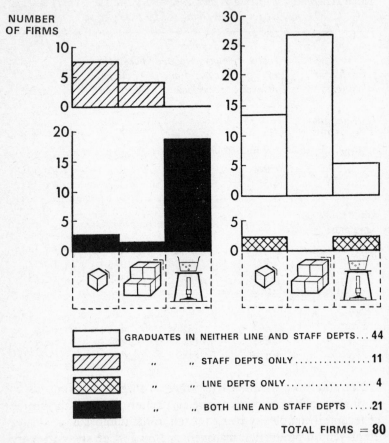

Fig. 16. Employment of graduates

production firms in which all the graduates employed were in staff departments. The majority were concerned with research and development or inspection functions, and their firms were those whose products themselves, rather than the methods of manufacturing, were technically complex.

In Fig. 17 the information given in Fig. 7 is broken down on a basis of production system. The clerical and administrative group, like the management and supervisory group, grows larger with technical advance. In the unit and small batch system of production, however, the range is wider than in the other systems.

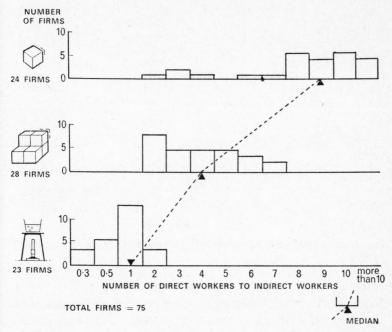

Fig. 17. Ratio of direct to indirect labour in different systems of production

This is because the different types of unit production varied considerably; the firms making technically complex products, both prototypes or large equipments, had a higher ratio of clerical and administrative staff to hourly-paid than those making simple products to customers' individual requirements, either as unit articles or in small batches.

Fig. 18 breaks down the information already given in Fig. 8 on a similar basis and shows that the ratio of indirect workers to direct workers gets larger with technical advance. It is process industry that employs a majority of indirect workers, many of whom are responsible for the maintenance of plant and machinery.

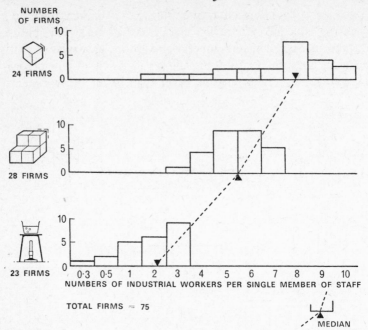

Fig. 18. Ratio of staff to industrial workers analysed by production system

SIMILARITIES AT THE EXTREMES

Turning now to the figures that rose to a peak in the middle of the technical scale, the first discernible trend of this kind related to the size of the span of control of the first-line supervisors in production departments. Fig. 19 shows the average number of hourly-paid workers controlled by first-line supervisors in the different systems of production, the highest averages being in the large batch and mass production firms. Fig. 20 gives the averages for individual firms and shows clearly the similarity between the extremes of the technical scale.

The small spans of control in unit production and process production were an indication of the breakdown of the labour force into small primary working groups. As a result, the relationship between the group and its immediate superior was more intimate and informal in these types of production than in the large batch and mass production firms studied; this was probably a contributory factor to better industrial relations.

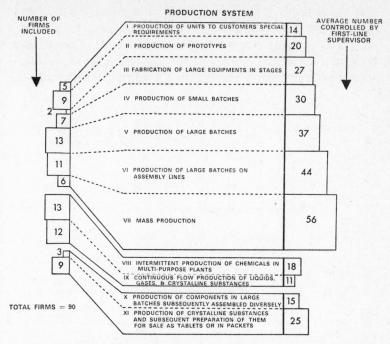

Fig. 19. Average number controlled by first-line supervisors in the different systems of production

Another resemblance between unit production and process production was that it employed a large number of skilled workers in comparison with large batch and mass production; there were nineteen firms in which skilled workers outnumbered semi-skilled workers, nine of them being unit production firms and ten process production firms. In all the large batch and mass production firms, the skilled workers were the smallest group. The skilled workers employed in unit production firms were concerned directly with production, the more mechanical parts of their job being delegated to semi-skilled workers, while unskilled workers serviced the craftsmen and fetched and carried for them. Occupational status was linked not only with numerical superiority and high pay, but also with a close identification with the immediate production objective. All the elements of skill, conceptual and perceptual, as well as the manual and motor, were brought together in the work of the craftsmen.

62 *The Survey*

In the large batch and mass production firms studied, the semi-skilled workers not only outnumbered the craftsmen but were also the people actually responsible for production, the skilled men being in the main the indirect labour responsible for the mainten-ance of tools and plant. The unskilled workers did very much the

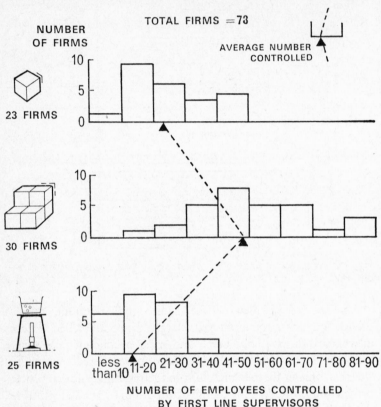

Fig. 20. Size of the span of control of first-line supervisors in three main types of production

same kind of job as they did in unit production, except that they were concerned more with the servicing of sections or departments than individuals. Standardized production and all that it implied had taken the perceptual and conceptual elements of skill out of the main production task, although much of the work still required a fair degree of motor skill and manual dexterity. In most of the large batch and mass production firms studied, the patterns of behaviour were no longer determined by the skilled men. Moreover, in the firms which ran incentive schemes, their earnings were hardly higher than those of the semi-skilled production workers.

It was interesting to notice how the role and functions of the draughtsmen differed from one production system to another. In unit and small batch production the draughtsman was a bridge between the development function and the production function; a main channel both of communication and control. In large batch and mass production he no longer filled this dominant role; he was merely one of a number of intermediaries who had some part to play in bridging the gap between the design of a product and its manufacture.

In process production, although the organization of work was basically the same as in large batch and mass production, the skilled men were the indirect labour force responsible for the servicing and maintenance of plant. The maintenance function was of great importance, the maintenance department being the largest single department in most firms. Thus the skilled men were able to influence the situation more than their counterparts in mass production, and were in a more dominant position.

The main problem in this type of industry appeared to be establishing the occupational status of the plant operators; these men, although often highly skilled, were not formally recognized as skilled outside their own firm. The traditional differentiation between the skilled and the semi-skilled worker does not allow for a situation in which the manual and motor elements of skill have been taken out of the main production task, while the conceptual and perceptual elements remain.

The skill of a plant operator is of the perceptual and conceptual kind in that over a period of time he has to learn to absorb a great deal of information and to act on it continuously. But, this skill not being recognized formally, the plant operator has to be recruited as a semi-skilled worker at a comparatively low rate of pay. Several firms felt that this created difficulties for them, as in the competitive labour situation of the area it was very difficult to find and keep men of sufficiently high calibre at this low figure. A job in which the emphasis is laid more on the intellectual elements of skill, and which calls for articulation in both speech and writing, can attract only those with the minimum educational qualifications.

Firms at the top and bottom of the technical scale resembled each other in a number of ways, not so easy to illustrate by reference to figures. First, there was a tendency for organic management systems to predominate in the production categories at the extremes of the technical scale, while mechanistic systems predominated in the middle ranges. Clear-cut definition of duties and responsibilities was characteristic of firms in the middle ranges, while flexible organization with a high degree of delegation both of authority and of the responsibility for decision-making, and with permissive and participating management, was characteristic of firms at the extremes. There was less 'organization consciousness' at the extremes; it was the firms in the middle ranges which found it easier to produce organization charts.

The second trend was for the line-staff type of organization to be more highly developed in the middle ranges of the scale. The two firms in which there was functional organization and fifteen of the firms in which line organization predominated were process production firms. The other line organization firms were in the unit production categories.

In unit production firms, where relatively few specialists were employed inside production departments, the line supervisors themselves had to be technically competent. Their technical competence was, in most cases, of the kind acquired by long practical experience, and was based on 'know-how' rather than professional training. It was interesting to find that in this type of production, supervisors and managers were on average about ten years older than their counterparts elsewhere.

In each of the three firms in which unit production had recently been superseded by standardized production of parts and subsequent diverse assembly, the number of specialists employed had increased by about 25 per cent as a result of the reorganization.

Firms in the large batch production categories employed the largest number of specialists. In many cases the managerial and supervisory group broke down into two distinct sub-groups, general managers comprising one and specialists the other; these sub-groups had differing and sometimes conflicting objectives and ideologies. In these firms too there was the most rigid application of line-staff organization. On paper, at least, there was a clear-cut distinction between executive and advisory responsibility. On the organization charts some positions were linked with continuous lines and others with dotted lines, indicating line and staff roles respectively.

In process industry, it was extremely difficult to distinguish between executive and advisory responsibility. Not only was organization more flexible but in many cases it was also changing. The tendency seemed to be for firms to move away from the line-staff type of organization towards either functional or predominantly line organization. In some firms the line of command seemed to be disintegrating, executive responsibility being conferred on specialist staff. Eight of the twelve firms in which the status and prestige of the specialists were so high that it was impossible, in practice, to distinguish between advice, service, and control on the one hand, and executive responsibility on the other, were process production firms. In the other process production firms, specialist skills and knowledge were being increasingly incorporated in the line. In these firms, as in the unit production firms studied, stress was laid on the importance of the line managers being technically competent. Here, of course, the technical competence required was of a different kind; it was intellectual rather than intuitive and based on qualifications and knowledge rather than on long experience and 'know-how'. In comparison with the managers in unit production, those employed in process production were young. In one process production firm a hundred of the hundred and twenty managers and supervisors were under thirty-five.

It was interesting to find that two oil refineries, approximately equal in size and situated in the same area, were moving away from line-staff organization in opposite directions. In one, specialist skills were being incorporated into the line, line management being technically competent and of high status. In the other the line managers had limited status and were not professionally qualified, their functions being no more than the routine supervision of production operations. They worked alongside highly trained specialist staff who, although nominally advisory, did in effect make executive decisions.

Even in those process production firms with an organizational pattern of the line-staff type there was not the same dichotomy between general managers and specialists as in large batch and mass production firms. There were no clear-cut distinctions between the objectives and ideologies of the two kinds of management. The main reason for this seemed to be that in most of these firms line managers and specialists were interchangeable. Firms tended to recognize 'specialisms' rather than specialists: the laboratory chemist of today could become the line manager of tomorrow. In some cases this interchangeability extended as far as the personnel management staff. A number of the personnel managers and officers in the process production firms included in the survey were scientists and engineers with general management experience, who expected to return to general management after a period in the personnel department.

Another distinction that was most clear-cut in the middle of the technical scale was that between production administration and the supervision of production operations. It was here too that production control procedures were most elaborate and sanctions most rigorously applied. At the bottom of the technical scale the difficulties of controlling production and predicting results appeared to be so great that few firms were prepared to attempt the task. On the other hand, the exercise of control in process production firms was such a relatively simple matter that conflict or stress was rarely associated with it; in many cases the mechanism for exercising control was built into the manufacturing processes themselves.

It would not be true to say that all the firms in the middle ranges of the scale had introduced equally elaborate production control procedures. Some of them still seemed to rely almost entirely on the clinical judgements of their line supervision. This meant that there was greater variation in the way in which production operations were planned and controlled between firms in the middle ranges of the scale than between firms at the extremes.

A similar pattern emerged in relation to communication methods. As might have been expected, the production control procedures in operation in the middle ranges of the scale gave rise to a considerable amount of paper work. Even allowing for this, however, it was interesting to find that in firms at the extremes of the scale communications between managers and departments tended to be verbal, while in the middle ranges they tended to be written. The amount of paper work—inter-departmental memoranda, operating instructions, and policy directives—increased as technology advanced, reaching a peak in assembly-line production firms. As technology advanced beyond this point, however, the amount of paper work began to decrease, and in process production, communications were almost entirely verbal again.

The research workers got the impression that this tendency to communicate in writing in the middle ranges of the scale was linked with the pressures and stresses arising from batch production. The reduction in the area of discretion of line supervision, and the conflicts that arose between them and the specialist personnel encouraged them to safeguard themselves by communicating in writing. They felt it necessary to be able to produce copies of the memoranda they had sent to other managers so that they could clear themselves in the event of a dispute. Life in firms in the middle ranges of the technical scale was therefore less pleasant and easy-going than in firms at the extremes. The research workers themselves soon became aware of this, for they found that it was easier and less arduous to obtain information in unit production and process production firms than in large batch and mass production firms.

5 Technology, Organization, and Success

TECHNOLOGY AND SUCCESS

One of the objectives of this survey was to find out how far the principles and ideas which formed the basis of the teaching of management subjects were accepted and applied in practice, and whether such acceptance and application ensured business success. In approximately half of the firms studied, these principles and ideas were reflected in the form of organization established—but there seemed to be no direct link between them and business success. As far as organization was concerned, successful firms seemed to have little in common. Indeed, in analysing the research data the only variable found to be demonstrably related to variations in organization was the system of production in operation.

At this point in the analysis, the research workers thought it might be useful to take a second look at the organizational characteristics of firms graded as above and below average in success in each production category.

Of the twenty firms in the above average category, five were unit production firms, a further five were large batch and mass production firms, and six were process production firms. The remainder operated combined systems; in one, the combination was of mass production with unit production, and in three, of process production with mass production. Of the seventeen firms classified as below average, five were unit production firms; six were mass production firms; four were process production firms, and two had combined production systems. In each production category there were both successful and unsuccessful firms; the figures suggesting that chances of success might be slightly higher in process production than in other types of manufacture.

The re-examination of the organizational figures revealed one other interesting fact; the five successful unit production firms had organizational characteristics in common, so had the five large batch and mass production firms, and the six process production firms. It was found that the figures relating to the organizational characteristics of the successful firms in each production category tended to cluster round the medians for that category as a whole, while the figures of the firms classified as 'below average' in success, were found at the extremes of the range. An illustration of the pattern is given in Table IV (Fig. 21), which is concerned with the average size of the span of control of first-line supervisors in the 'above average' and the 'below average' firms.

Table IV. *Average Span of Control of First-Line Supervisors Analysed by Business Success*

Production system	Less than 10	11 to 20	21 to 30	31 to 40	41 to 50	51 to 60	61 to 70	71 to 80	81 to 90	Un-classi-fied	Median	Total
Unit and small batch:												
All firms	1	6	8	4	3	1	–	–	–	1	23	24
'Above average' in success	–	–	4	1	–	–	–	–	–	–		5
'Below average' in success	1	1	–	–	2	1	–	–	–	–		5
Large batch and mass:												
All firms	–	1	2	5	9	4	5	1	3	1	49	31
'Above average' in success	–	–	–	–	3	2	–	–	–	–		5
'Below average' in success	–	1	1	1	–	–	–	1	2	–		6
Process:												
All firms	6	12	5	2	–	–	–	–	–	–	13	25
'Above average' in success	1	5	–	–	–	–	–	–	–	–		6
'Below average' in success	1	–	1	2	–	–	–	–	–	–		4

The figures relating to the span of control of the chief executive the number of levels in the line of command, labour costs, and the various labour ratios showed a similar trend. The fact that organizational characteristics, technology, and success were linked together in this way suggested that not only was the system of

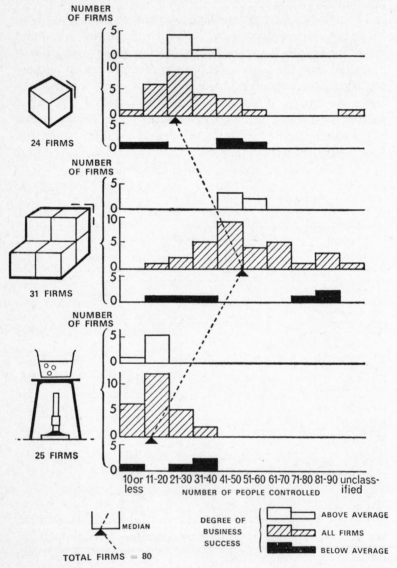

Fig. 21. Average span of control of first-line supervisor analysed by business success

production an important variable in the determination of organizational structure, but also that one particular form of organization was most appropriate to each system of production. In unit production, for example, not only did short and relatively broadly based pyramids predominate, but they also appeared to ensure success. Process production, on the other hand, would seem to require the taller and more narrowly based pyramid.

It was also interesting to find that, in terms of Burns's analysis,[1] successful firms inside the large batch production range tended to have mechanistic management systems. On the other hand, successful firms outside this range tended to have organic systems.

There were administrative expedients that were linked with success in one system of production and failure in another. For example, the duties and responsibilities of managerial and supervisory staff were clearly and precisely defined on paper in most of the successful large batch production firms studied and in none of the unsuccessful firms. In process production, however, this kind of definition was more often associated with failure. It was found too that as technology became more advanced, the chief executive seemed able to control an increasing number of direct subordinates successfully. All the successful firms in which the span of control of the chief executive was ten or more were process production firms.

In general, the administrative expedients associated with success in large-batch production firms were in line with the principles and ideas on which the teaching of management subjects is based. In all the successful large batch production firms there was not only a clear definition of duties and responsibilities of the kind already referred to, but also an adherence to the principles of unity of command; a separation (at least on paper) of advisory from executive responsibilities, and a chief executive who controlled no more than the recommended five or six direct subordinates.

The tendency to regard large batch production as the typical system of modern industry may be the explanation of this link between success and conformity with management theory. The people responsible for developing management theory no doubt

[1] Burns, op. cit., p. 23.

had large batch production in mind as they speculated about management. In general, the experience on which their generalizations were based had been obtained in large batch production industry.

In the final analysis the conclusions reached earlier had to be modified. While at first sight there seemed to be no link between organization and success, and no one best way of organizing a factory, it subsequently became apparent that there was a particular form of organization most appropriate to each technical situation. Within a limited range of technology this was also the form of organization most closely in line with the principles and ideas of management theory. Outside the limited range, however, the rules appear to be different; the most suitable form of organization being out of line with these principles and ideas.

ASSESSING THE EFFECTS OF TECHNICAL CHANGE

The demonstration of a link between technology, organization and success has practical significance for the industrial manager; it can lead not only to the development of techniques helpful in the appraisal of organizational structure but also make it possible to plan organizational change simultaneously with technical change. The industrial manager need not wait to see the effects of technical change before modifying organizational structure. The varied technical changes that were taking place in South Essex at the time the field work of this research was being done have already been described. Further investigation showed that any technical changes which did not radically affect the nature of the production system only resulted in minor modifications to organization. On the other hand, the kind of technical change involving change in the production system was followed by a fundamental organizational change. This was as true of the change resulting from developments that made possible the more efficient realization of original objectives as it was of the changes resulting from modifications of objectives.

For example, automatic devices for the control of individual machines introduced into unit and small batch production had relatively little effect on anything other than the nature of the work done by the machine operators themselves. The introduction of the transfer-line for the manufacture of cylinder blocks led to modifications in the size and composition of primary working groups and affected supervisor-subordinate relationships on the job, but because so small a percentage of total production operations was affected, the overall organizational picture remained as before. On the other hand, in those firms where technical change had transformed what had been either large batch production or a combination of process production with large batch production into continuous-flow production, fundamental organizational changes had come about.

The work done by Scott and his colleagues (1956) on technical change and social structure in a large steel works,[2] showed that significant organizational changes resulted from the introduction of the continuous strip-mill. This is in line with the results of this survey, for the introduction of the new strip-mill was a technical change of the kind that involved a fundamental change in the production system of the firm. Traditionally the manufacture of steel was a batch production process, but recent technical developments had turned it into a continuous-flow process.

In South Essex most of the organizational changes that had followed changes in production systems were neither dramatic nor planned for in advance. Organizational problems seemed to have arisen as a result of technical changes, and the finding of solutions to these problems had led to modifications in the organization. For example, in firms where large batch production had been superseded by continuous-flow production, the command hierarchy had lengthened, the span of control of the chief executive had widened, and the ratio of managers and supervisors to total personnel had increased. In the firm which had reverted to unit production,[3] abandoning the standardized production of parts, the reversion had been followed by organizational change of a dramatic kind, the command hierarchy being reduced overnight from eight levels of authority to four.

The fact that organizational change brought about by technical change resulted in modifications to structure in line with the results of the survey, suggests that facts and figures of the kind given in this report could help the industrial manager to foresee the

[2] W. H. Scott, J. A. Banks, A. H. Halsey and T. Lupton, *Technical Change and Industrial Relations* (Liverpool University Press, Liverpool).
[3] See p. 45.

organizational results of any technical change he contemplated. Thus, no problems need arise from technical change to which at least partial solutions cannot be found from the accumulated experience of manufacturing industry. This implies, of course, that such experience must be adequately documented and systematized information made available. There is a pressing need for more factual description of manufacturing situations. Information of this kind would also be helpful if amalgamations or take-overs were contemplated, enabling the parent company to understand the organizational problems of any subsidiaries that were concerned with production processes different from its own.

TECHNOLOGY AND SOCIAL STRUCTURE

The fact that it was possible to demonstrate that there is a link between technology and organization has significance not only for the industrial manager but also for the social scientist. The concept of the socio-technical system was of course already familiar to and accepted by social scientists, but progress in social science, unlike progress in social philosophy, proceeds by way of demonstration as much as by way of ideas. Thus the demonstration of the link could be a step forward in the pursuit of knowledge relating to the formulation of social structure and to the administrative process generally. For the social scientist the most interesting question raised by the survey is this: how far does technology influence the formulation of social structure inside an industrial setting?

Formal organization is not of course the whole of social structure. The social scientist sees an industrial or commercial enterprise as a social system within a social system; a small but complete society of individuals bound together into a functioning team operating against a wide social background. Social structure is the framework on which the system operates. The variables in the system include occupational structure, the enterprise consisting of members of different occupational groups which are linked with various social groups in the community; formal organization, i.e the stable and explicit pattern of prescribed relationships designed to enable those employed to work together in the achievement of objectives, and informal organization, i.e. the pattern of relationships which actually emerges from day-to-day operations.

Formal organization can arise imperceptibly and gradually from informal organization and spontaneous relationships, or it can be consciously planned without reference to informal organization. As already indicated, the basic idea underlying the development of scientific management is that formal organization in industry should be consciously planned. Indeed, the general trend in modern society is towards this kind of planning, with the result that firms who consciously plan their formal organizational structure tend to regard themselves as more progressive and up-to-date than firms that do not.

The link between technology and the occupational structure element in social structure is obvious, and research has shown that informal organization too is influenced by technology. But because conscious planning of formal organization has been based on principles and ideas that have become increasingly divorced from technical development, it has generally been assumed by social scientists that formal organization is the part of social structure least affected by technical considerations.

The information obtained from this survey demonstrates quite clearly, however, that in the firms in South Essex formal organization too is affected considerably by technical factors. The reason for this may be that conscious planning is not as commonplace as might be supposed; nor the only distinction between formal and informal organization as clear-cut. Approximately only half the firms studied showed any organization-consciousness, and in many of these its effects were limited to a few aspects of formal organization. The formalization of spontaneous relationships still seems to play an important part.

There appears to be some conflict here between the findings of this research and those of other researches carried out by social scientists in the industrial field.[4] Generally speaking, social scientists seem to find more conscious planning of formal organization in the firms they study than was found here. A possible explanation of the discrepancy might be found in the way the firms were chosen for this present study. The research covered a geographical area in an intensive way and probably brought in smaller and less well-known firms of the kind that normally escape the social science net. It seems reasonable to suppose that, in general, firms likely to be approached by social scientists and

[4] See, for example, W. H. Scott, *et alia*, op. cit., p. 73.

to accept them would be the more progressive, and therefore more organization-conscious firms.

The survey findings did confirm, however, that conscious planning of organization rarely seems to be based on technical considerations. In many firms those responsible for making organizational decisions had only a limited knowledge of the manufacturing processes, the majority of organization specialists being non-technical people.

In the final stages of the survey the research workers tried to find out not only whether organizational changes accompanying technical changes had been planned in advance but also whether the managers of successful firms were conscious of the requirements of their production systems, or had tried to satisfy these requirements in making organizational decisions. This appeared to be the case in only three firms. On the whole managers had a limited awareness of the requirements of their production systems. Many, when discussing particular administrative expedients, made some such comment as 'it would not work here'; they all seemed to regard their own situation as unique. People with industrial experience will no doubt be familiar with this kind of comment. Management consultants, for example, would probably regard them as evidence of rationalization or prejudice against new ideas. The research workers recognized that there was an element of prejudice in them; nevertheless, in much of what was said, there was an implicit recognition of the situational demands of the production system. But this recognition seldom became explicit; it was found, for example, that although all the successful unit production firms had short-command hierarchies, there was little evidence to suggest that the lines had been kept short as a result of deliberate decisions. The managers concerned did not even seem to be aware that the command hierarchies in their firms were short in comparison with those of other firms in the area.

Against the background of facts and figures linking technology, formal organization, and success, it must be remembered that the firms studied fell into two approximately equal groups: those in which formal organization had arisen imperceptibly and gradually from informal organization, and those in which it had been consciously planned. It was interesting to find that among the successful firms in the first group, unit and small batch production and continuous-flow production predominated, while the majority of successful firms in the second group were in the large batch production category. This suggests that conscious planning produces better results in some kinds of industry than in others.

There may be a simple explanation of this. Conscious planning is based on the principles and ideas of classical management theory. These principles and ideas were the result of the speculative thinking of individual managers, the majority of whom obtained their industrial experience in large batch production. Basically, therefore, conscious planning may be no more than the formalization of the informal pattern of relationships found to be most appropriate in the management of large batch production.

This would support the assumption that formal organization depends more on technical considerations than is generally realized, and that any tendency to divorce it further ought to be resisted.

One of the dangers of conscious planning is that it can lead to a belief that the building of a formal organizational structure for an industrial enterprise is an end in itself rather than a means to an end. This is probably because much of the thinking about organization and the teaching of management subjects has to be done outside a real situation, and it is rarely possible to consider organization in relation to the objectives it serves. If we take Barnard's work (1955),[5] for example, in describing the functions of the executive as he saw them, he was writing against a specific background of knowledge and experience. Few readers of his book are likely to be familiar with the background. They therefore have to assess the work in a vacuum or relate it to their own experience. This does not make the work less valuable, but its value is as a basis for speculative thought about management rather than as a guide to action.

The approach to the study of organization suggested here, that is, the approach through empirical sociology, must also be regarded at this stage as a basis for speculative thinking rather than as a guide to action. It does, however, provide a framework for further study.

The survey findings suggested that the link between technology and organization persists in spite of, rather than because of,

[5] Chester I. Barnard, *The Functions of the Executive* (Harvard University Press).

conscious behaviour or deliberate policy, and in defiance of the tendency in management education to emphasize the independence of the administrative process from technical considerations. The examination of the situational demands arising from different kinds of manufacture might therefore lead to a deeper understanding of the administrative process.

If we could find answers to such questions as why unit articles can be produced successfully only where the lines of control are short, why mass production demands the definition of duties and responsibilities, and why the chief executive in a process production firm can successfully control more subordinates than his counterparts in other types of production, we would have come a long way towards the discovery of cause and effect relationship between systems of production and the forms of organization they demand. These cause and effect relationships might in turn provide us with a basis of reasoning in the field of management.

If it could be demonstrated not only that technology is limited and controlled by objectives, but also that technology itself limits and controls both organization and certain aspects of behaviour, Follett's assertion that the principles and direction of human endeavour are the same no matter what its purpose is,[6] would have to be regarded as true only at a very general and superficial level of analysis. The understanding of certain elementary principles of human behaviour is obviously helpful in any situation in which people have to form relationships. But although at one level of analysis all firms may appear to have similar organizational problems, at a deeper level constants may become variables, and the purpose towards which human endeavour is directed could ultimately prove to be one of the important determinants of the principles of that direction.

Finally, what implications would this new approach have for the selection and training of managers? It would immediately raise a doubt as to whether decisions relating to organizational structure can be made effectively except by people with a knowledge and appreciation of the requirements of its technology. This would mean that the possibility of developing general managerial competence, except in association with technical knowledge or skill, would be questionable.

[6] Follett, op. cit., p. 35.

At present much of the management education and training undertaken inside industry and the teaching institutions is based on the assumption that management skills can be isolated from any technical background: that there is, in fact, a management vocation. There is a fairly widespread belief that at a certain level of responsibility managers and administrators are interchangeable between one industry and another and even between industry and other institutions. It is true, of course, that some people can and do move around successfully in this way, but the fact that they tend to be the exceptionally able people with a wide range of knowledge and skill may obscure any difficulties inherent in the interchange. Talent of this kind may not be available in sufficient quantities to make possible the planning of all executive development along these lines.

Formal organization theory is impersonal in so far as it defines a number of positions or roles and the relationships between them without reference to the personalities of those occupying them. Each person employed by a firm occupies a definite position in this organization and the role and status thus conferred upon him determine to a considerable extent the actions he initiates and the results and responses he can expect.

Technology, because it influences the roles defined by formal organization, must therefore influence industrial behaviour, for how a person reacts depends as much on the demands of his role and the circumstances in which he finds himself, as on his personality. There can be occasions when the behaviour forced on him by his role is in conflict with his personality. If so, role considerations may lead him to alter or modify his personality, or to leave his employment and seek a more congenial job elsewhere.

It will be remembered that at one stage in the analysis of the survey data the research workers considered whether the differences between firms both in organization and achievement could be attributed to differences in the ability of their senior managers, and rejected this as a complete explanation. In considering the personality differences between managers, it did appear, however, that senior executives in the firms in each production category had characteristics in common. This might imply that one of the ways in which situational demands impose themselves is by bringing individuals to the top of the management ladder whose personal qualities best fit the technical background in which they have to operate.

In general, the senior executives of firms in the batch production categories, where efforts were continuously being made to push back the physical limitations of production, seemed to have more drive and push and to be more ambitious than their counterparts in unit production or process production. Whether this was the result of natural selection or conditioning it is, of course, impossible to find out through studies of this nature.

The research results suggested too that some technical environments impose greater strains than others on individuals at all levels of the hierarchy. Reference has already been made to the differences in communication behaviour. Both inter-managerial relationships and employee-employer relationships seemed to be better at the extremes of the scale than they were in the middle; pressure was greater in the middle and it seemed more important to build mechanisms into the organizational structure which would resolve the conflicts likely to occur.

Thus it seems that an analysis of situational demands could lead not only to the development of better techniques for appraising organizational structure and for conscious planning, but also to an increased understanding of the personal qualities and skills required in different industrial situations, and to improve methods of training directed towards giving those concerned a better understanding of the strains and stresses associated with the roles they are likely to occupy.

Part Two

THE CASE STUDIES

6 *The Case Study Approach*

TERMS OF REFERENCE

It will be remembered that in the proposal originally submitted to the Joint Committee on Human Relations in industry of the Department of Scientific and Industrial Research/Medical Research Council, allowance was made for undertaking case studies should it be thought worth while to follow up the survey results. The main idea emerging from the survey—that the technical demands of the production system shaped the organization of a firm to a greater extent than has so far been recognized, limiting and controlling the behaviour of the people employed— did seem to the research workers to warrant further investigation.

It must be stressed, of course, that what had emerged so far was a hypothesis rather than a firm conclusion. Logically, therefore, the next step would have been to try and validate this hypothesis through the collection of facts and figures about organizational structure on a country-wide and representative basis. Had this been possible, we would by now have been well on the way towards finding out whether empirical sociology can prove a valid theory of management, theory being interpreted as the basis of an applied science rather than as the basis of speculative thought.

But this was obviously impracticable; no one research team operating on a limited scale could possibly collect the information required. Indeed, the mind boggles at the amount of work involved. The collection and systematization of the survey data had been difficult enough and this was a mere fragment of the information that would be required before any definite conclusions could be reached. Moreover, even if adequate research resources were available, the collaboration between social scientists and industrial managers has not yet reached the stage at which access can be obtained to all the required information.

Having accepted that the hypothesis could not be tested on a broader scale, the question arose as to whether anything else could usefully be done. It would have been unfortunate from an expediency point of view if use could not have continued to be made of the research facilities available in the area, for a great deal of interest and goodwill had been engendered by the survey. In some of the firms contacted, managers had begun to interest themselves in the implications of this link between organization and technology, and were anxious for the investigations to be taken further.

Moreover, even if the hypothesis could not be validated, it seemed important to try and find out more about it The ideas put forward in the last chapter, for example, are all dependent on the link between technology and organization revealed by the survey being causal rather than casual; this was merely an assumption. It was felt that if the firms could be revisited and further information obtained this assumption could be made with more confidence. It ought also be possible to obtain a better understanding of this link and of the social processes involved in the interaction of technology and organization; only through investigations of a more detailed kind than those undertaken so far would it be possible to trace the relationship between the methods of manufacture operating in a firm and their associated organizational pattern, or to obtain answers to any of the questions raised at the end of the last chapter.

Having decided to deepen the research, the research team then had to consider how deep to go. Was it better to go back and get a little more information from all the firms included in the survey, or to concentrate on a few? In order to avoid superficiality in the investigations a strong case could be made for dealing in considerable detail with a very small number of firms. On the other hand, a wide range of production techniques had been covered, and it seemed important to include in any further investigations examples of all the different production systems listed in Fig. 11. The advantages and disadvantages of making extensive and intensive investigations seemed so evenly balanced that the final decision was to work at two levels; to go back to twenty of the firms included in the survey and collect more data, and in addition make a small number of very detailed studies.

THE LESS DETAILED CASE STUDIES

In choosing firms for the more extensive studies, the research workers restricted themselves to the fifty-eight firms included in the survey employing more than 250 people. It was impossible to select firms at random, one difficulty being the adequate coverage of the different systems of production. Thus, the firm chosen cannot be regarded as being in any way representative either of the group as a whole or even of their production category. Six were unit or small batch production firms, six were large batch or mass production firms, five were process production firms, and in the remaining three process production was combined with the preparation of a product for sale by standardized production methods.

The interest shown in the research by the firms restudied was also a factor influencing their selection. This may help to explain why there was a preponderance of successful firms. As many as nine of the twenty firms had been classified as above average category in success in the earlier research; eight had been classified as average and only three as below average. Most sociological research in industry has been carried out in firms with reputations as good employers where it could be assumed that managements felt relatively secure. The classification of a firm as above average did not necessarily imply that it was a good employer in the more commonly accepted sense of the term, but it can be assumed that the feeling of security that appears to be necessary to the acceptance of social science research will be found more often in successful than in unsuccessful firms.

One or more of the research team spent approximately a month in each firm selected for study, concentrating on various aspects of organization. First of all they found out more about the way in which the organization structure had evolved. The history of the firm and the principal changes in organization were studied, special consideration being given to the question of how far the prejudices and preferences of the individuals responsible for organizational decisions had influenced development at various stages.

Secondly, a longer-term and more detailed study was made of existing organization with particular reference to the nature and number of decisions taken at the different levels of the hierarchy, the co-operation required and the regular contacts established between the various members of the management team, and the way in which control information was produced and corrective action taken. Doubt had been thrown by the survey on the concept of formal and informal organization as separate parts of a whole and in these deeper studies it was hoped to see how the pattern of relationships actually emerging from day-to-day operations differed from the prescribed pattern. It was also hoped to obtain more information about the way in which organization had been modified either explicitly or implicitly to accommodate individuals and about the effect on individual personality of the strains and stresses arising from formal organization.

Finally, the technology of production was to be examined in more detail. The information obtained during the background survey had serious gaps, because its significance to the research had not been adequately recognized earlier. In each firm a detailed analysis was made of the situational demands arising from technology, and consideration given to the organizational and operational expedients likely to be effective in meeting these demands. On the basis of this analysis an assessment was made of the appropriateness of the existing structure of a firm in meeting the situational demands arising from its technology.

The methods used were observation and interview, the interviewing programme being worked out in collaboration with the chief executive of each firm. Between thirty and fifty people were interviewed, the number depending on the size of the firm and the complexity of its formal organization.

In all, about 800 people were interviewed at this stage of the research. The majority were senior executives, that is, people directly responsible to the chief executive, and the departmental heads responsible to senior executives. In several cases junior supervisors were also interviewed about various aspects of organization and in a small number of firms information about operating procedures was obtained from the industrial workers involved.

The interviewing was of the open-ended kind; no set questionnaire was used. Nevertheless, each interview followed a similar pattern. The schedule of information prepared for the firm from the material obtained during the background survey and given in Appendix I was used as a basis, and each person interviewed was asked to provide additional information on any aspects of organization about which he was particularly knowledgeable. Before doing this, he was asked to tell the interviewer something about himself; he was questioned about his employment history and technical training, the content of his job, his attitude to it, his attitude to his employers, and his promotion prospects. This background information was useful in putting into perspective what was said about the organizational problems of the firm. It also provided some interesting material about management incentives and about the way in which managers were selected and trained in different technical situations.

The research workers were allowed to move about freely in the factories studied; much of the interviewing was done in the offices of the people concerned. The interviews varied considerably in length; in some cases the time taken was less than an hour, in others the research workers spent several days with individual managers. They found that in the case of these longer interviews, normal departmental business was carried on in their presence. This was extremely useful, enabling them to check, through first-hand observations, the answers to questions. Many of the organizational procedures described were seen in operation and a greater understanding was obtained of the way in which the problems referred to in discussion could and did arise. Informal discussions at the lunch table, attendance at management meetings, and participation in some of the firm's organized social activities added to the picture. When analysing and systematizing their data, the research workers found that the broad impressions they had obtained in this less formal way supplemented and confirmed the information obtained from the interviews; contradictions were few.

THE INTENSIVE STUDIES

For the more detailed studies the research workers decided to concentrate on firms in which manufacturing methods were either changing or mixed, because if organization and technology are linked in the way suggested, it is in such firms that the most difficult organizational problems are likely to arise. Where technical developments involve a change in a production system, formal organization will have to be modified to meet a new set of situational demands. It was felt that it would be useful and interesting to study this process in operation. Where production systems are mixed there is a possibility of two incompatible sets of situational demands arising from the technology and a way would then have to be found of reconciling them in organizational structure.

Three firms were particularly appropriate; they were all in the 2,001–4,000 size group. In one, manufacturing methods were changing, and in the other two, they were both mixed and changing. On the basis of the survey results two had been graded as 'above average' in success, and one as 'average'. It seemed therefore that all three had successfully overcome the organizational problems associated with technical change. They were all willing to participate in the intensive investigations. These firms are referred to as A, B, and C throughout this report.

In firm A, electrical and electronic components were produced in large batches and subsequently assembled diversely. This firm was one of the oldest in the area and for the first fifty years of its life had been concerned entirely with jobbing production. Earlier in this century the keen competition in the radio-communication equipment industry had made it necessary for the firm to concentrate its resources on research and development, and by so doing had built up a reputation for high quality that was the key to its survival and success. Throughout its earlier development the firm had considered the techniques of standardized production inappropriate to its type of manufacture.

Soon after the second world war this firm had been acquired by a large and important industrial group with wide interests outside the specialized field of radio-communication equipment. The group covered a number of different systems of production mainly in the engineering field, but it is true to say that its interests were largely concentrated in the large batch and mass production ranges, and 'production efficiency' featured more prominently in its policy than 'the best'. While the new owners did not deliberately put into effect any reorganization, Firm A felt the effect of the change in ownership partly through the infiltration of new blood and partly through association with a different kind of tradition and culture. So the change in ownership led indirectly to changes in methods. By analysing the various products and breaking them down into their component parts, it was found that some of the products and many of the parts could be standardized, and where necessary, diversity retained in the assembly operations.

There was nothing revolutionary in this new approach to manufacturing; its main features were an increasing separation of production administration from the actual supervision of production operations, an increase in specialization, and a tightening of controls. Workshop supervision was required to operate to more detailed specifications; the Methods Department now told them how each piece of equipment had to be manufactured; the Production Control Department indicated when each phase of manufacture should begin and end, and the Rate Fixing Department controlled the wages paid and told them what their labour costs should be. This is all familiar enough in large batch and mass production. In this particular firm, however, the interest lay in the fact that the change was stimulated by a desire to find out whether manufacturing operations could be made more efficient by introducing some of the techniques of standardized production into what was essentially jobbing production, without a reduction in quality. The firm appeared to provide an example of a situation in which technical and administrative development had made possible the achievement of original objectives in a different way.

Firm B, one of the nine firms covered by the survey in which process production was combined with the preparation of the products for sale through large batch and mass production methods, was operating in the fine and pharmaceutical chemicals field. Developments during and after the last war, in particular, the introduction of the National Health Service, led to changes in the pharmaceutical chemicals industry. Original objectives were modified by changed demands. Less dispensing is now done by retail chemists and more proprietary drugs and medicines are sent out by manufacturers ready for use. Preparing the products for sale has involved the development of production lines for bottling, packaging, tabletting, and ampouling the drugs and medicines. Thus, a different system of production has been introduced alongside the plants in which the drugs are made. Personnel has greatly increased, the larger proportion of those employed now working on the new production lines. Another result of the change is that pharmacists have to be employed in the manufacturing as well as in the retailing side of the industry where the dispensing of drugs is now largely being done.

Firm C was an oil refinery; it too was one of the older firms in the area, although from 1916 to 1945 its main function had been installation work—the importing, storing, and distributing of products refined abroad—rather than manufacture. Small and semi-automatic distillation plants had been built on the site from time to time during this period to refine further some of the imported oils, the main products being lubricating oils, bitumen, and paraffin wax. These plants were still in operation at the time of the research, production being mostly of the kind classified in Fig. 11, category VIII, as intermittent production of chemicals. Some of the plants were single-purpose, others multi-purpose.

At the end of the second world war, for both strategic and economic reasons, a government decision was taken to distil crude oil in this country. This resulted in a tremendous expansion of the oil industry, and at firm C a plant was specially built for this purpose, the new plant operating for twenty-four hours a day, seven days a week. Much of it was automatically controlled, the production being of the kind classified in category IX of Fig. 11 as continuous-flow production. Thus inside firm C both methods of making dimensional products were in operation.

Change in firm A had resulted almost entirely from the introduction of new methods to achieve original objectives, whereas in firm B technical change had resulted from a change in objectives. In firm C there was a combination of both processes; a change in objective combined with the technical developments in the automatic control field had made it possible to build the larger continuous-flow plants.

Approximately six months was spent in each of these three firms. The methods used were those of social anthropology—direct and prolonged observation until patterns of interaction were discernible. A large number of interviews were also carried out. In firm A, all staff from the first-line supervisor upwards were interviewed; in firms B and C, all the senior and middle management staff were interviewed; in firms B and C, all the senior and middle management staff together with a one in two random sample of the first-line supervisors. The number interviewed at each level is shown in Table V.

Table V. *Interviews in Firms A, B, and C*

	Number interviewed		
Grade of staff	Firm A	Firm B	Firm C
Chief executive and senior executives	5	9	14
Heads of departments (other than above)	8	26	15
Intermediate management levels	28	50	40
First-line supervisors (charge hands and foremen spending more than 50 per cent of their time on supervisory duties)	69	66	57
TOTALS	110	151	126

In the case of firms A and B both the manufacturing and commercial activities were carried out on the same site. Until the outbreak of the second world war, firm A had a headquarters in London, where much of its selling and administrative work was done. This had been evacuated to the factory site at the beginning of the war and remained there. But it has never been completely absorbed into the social system of the factory and has retained several characteristics of a headquarter's organization, with the associated relationship problems.

Firm B was self-contained from the outset; expansion after the war had been contained within the original site. But at the time of the research plans were in hand for the building of a second production unit in another area. This added interest to the research, for discussions were taking place about how the existing organization would have to be modified to meet the new situation. This meant that everyone interviewed was particularly organization-conscious at the time of the research.

Firm C, one of four production units in different parts of the country, had commercial headquarters in London; to complete this case study it was necessary therefore to visit these. A number of management meetings were attended and fifteen senior executives were interviewed. These are not included in the figure given in Table V.

The content of the interviews was much the same as in the earlier studies. It was possible to go more deeply into each question, however, and to check one person's reaction to an administrative expedient or problem with another's. Some of the managers and supervisors interviewed co-operated with the research workers by keeping diaries covering the period of research, maintaining contact and reporting on any incidents in which they were involved. This time a set questionnaire was used to obtain personal and background information. The interviewing was still open-ended in character, those interviewed being asked to talk freely around the questions and give as much information as they could about the aspects and problems of organization with which they were most concerned. The questionnaire was used because it was thought that it might be interesting and useful to compare the backgrounds and previous experience of the managers and supervisors in the three firms.

As these studies were to be more detailed than those previously undertaken and the research workers were going to operate inside each firm for a longer period, the initial arrangements were made even more carefully. In each firm an office was put at the disposal of the research workers. They then set out to obtain the complete approval and understanding of the purposes and methods of the investigations from the people who were going to take part. In the main the firm's regular communication channels—in particular, departmental memoranda and formal management meetings—were used. These were supplemented with informal discussions.

In all three firms co-operation was very good; the research workers felt that the response showed that the aims and methods of the research were fully understood and accepted. Stress was laid upon the fact that individual participation in the research was entirely voluntary, and only one, a manager selected for interview, refused to take part. This high degree of participation did not mean, of course, that no feelings of insecurity were aroused.

Studies at depth almost inevitably give rise to a certain amount of anxiety, as relationships between senior managers are often highly complex and most firms have some skeletons in their cupboards which the top management is reluctant to reveal to outsiders. More uneasiness seemed to be aroused in firm B than in either firm A or firm C. This had an effect on the investigations: the research workers found that they could not probe as deeply here as in the other two firms. Of the three studies, the one carried out in firm C was probably the most intensive. There were a number of reasons; the first was that inter-personal relations were exceptionally good, relatively little anxiety was therefore aroused by the research, and people were willing to talk very freely. The second was that the people interviewed began to develop an interest in social science research and debated at considerable length with the research workers such questions as whether it was possible to be 'scientific' in studying human behaviour. The third was that the lack of pressure, characteristic of process industry, helped the research workers. As long as they kept out of the way if an operating crisis occurred, people were willing to give them as much of their time as was needed.

In each case a senior executive of the firm acted as a liaison with the research workers; in firm A this was the assistant works manager, in firm B, the personnel manager, and in firm C, the training manager. Without this liaison far more time would have been spent in making contacts and finding the way around, and the research workers were extremely grateful for the help they received. It was realized, however, that here was another possible source of bias, for identification of the research workers with a particular department might have influenced the quantity and quality of the information given.

These differences in approach and intensity made the research data more difficult to handle. Indeed, from the point of view of research method, one of the most interesting aspects of the studies described here, both extensive and intensive, was the impossibility of repeating in one firm exactly what had been done in another. It became only too obvious that in the field of empirical sociology, research methods have to be modified to some extent to fit the circumstances of each situation studied.

ANALYSIS OF RESULTS

The major part of the field work was completed by the beginning of 1958. As each study was completed, the main points that had arisen were discussed with the chief executive; detailed reports of individual firms were not prepared at this stage unless specially asked for.

In preparing the report of the follow-up studies, difficulties were experienced of the kind foreseen at the beginning. The problems were how to disclose all the relevant facts without publishing information that was harmful or embarrassing to individuals or firms, and how to conceal the identity of individuals from readers familiar with the situations described. It was realized that in view of the changes taking place in South Essex industry a lapse of time would ease the situation considerably. It was therefore decided to publish a short account of the background survey, together with the main findings of the follow-up studies almost immediately, and to proceed more slowly with the more detailed account of the research.

Before doing anything further, however, a series of meetings were held at the College with representatives of the participating firms to discuss the findings, the conclusions reached, and the publication policy. All the firms involved in the follow-up studies, and about a third of those involved in the background survey only, sent representatives to these meetings. A brief account of the discussions that took place and the main points raised are given in Part III together with the implications of the research findings and an outline of the follow-up work that was done subsequently.

Although clearance for publication had been obtained, it was found impossible to make use of all the information available even in the more detailed account of the research because of its sheer bulk. Each firm studied warranted a report of its own. All that could be done within the space of a single volume was to pick out a number of aspects of organization and compare firms in these respects. The technological framework used in the background survey remained the basis of comparison. One of the drawbacks of handling the material in this way was that although the social systems of the firms studied had been looked at as integrated wholes, they could not be presented as such. This means that it is impossible for the reader to get a complete picture of the organizational structure of individual firms from the chapters that follow.

The three main aspects of organization selected for examination were: the type of organization with particular reference to the breakdown between line roles and staff roles; the relationships between the three main functions of manufacturing—research and development, production, and marketing; and the organization of production, including the way in which results were predicted and controlled.

7 The Anatomy of Organization

MANAGEMENT FUNCTIONS

The background survey had shown that the majority of the firms studied employed specialist managers and that just over half had a line-staff type of organization. Interesting organizational trends had emerged. As production technology advanced, moving towards continuous-flow and process systems, the distinction between line roles and staff roles became less clear-cut, and specialist skills (although of greater importance) became increasingly incorporated into the line and linked with executive responsibility. Moreover, in the middle of the technical scale, i.e. the large batch and mass production field, where the distinction between line and staff roles still persisted there was a tendency to move towards divisionalized organization, the overall and comprehensive line-staff pattern being replaced by a series of line-staff patterns covering particular products or geographical areas. In the more detailed studies these trends were examined more closely, and the associated problems of organization were discussed with those responsible for organization planning.

A difficulty experienced in these discussions sprang from the fact that there is no universally accepted vocabulary of management, the same words are used in a number of different ways. The greatest confusion in terminology encountered related to the use of the word 'function'. Sociologists studying organization tend to use this word in a special sense, almost as a synonym of *raison d'être*. Follett (1927)[1] in her writings on management, gave it a mathematical meaning, implying any aspect of management so

[1] Follett, op. cit., p. 35.

connected with another that a change in the one produced a corresponding change in the other.

It was used in two other ways by the people interviewed. In some contexts it simply meant a task or activity, being used to describe what managers and departments did. In others it was used to imply specialization of the kind advocated by Taylor (1911).[2] When he recommended that the management process should be broken down into elements, each element to be the responsibility of a specialist supervisor, he used the word 'function' to describe these elements and the phrase 'functional organization' to indicate the kind of structure which would arise from such a breakdown.

The indiscriminate use of the word 'function' tends to obscure the fact that organizational structure can differentiate between two completely different kinds of functions; there are task functions of which the most important are the basic activities already referred to, financing the enterprise, developing the product, manufacturing, and marketing it; and there are element functions such as personnel, planning, control, inspection, and maintenance which are intrinsic parts of the management process. The two kinds of functions differ from each other in a number of ways and the differences have important implications for organization.

Task functions are directed towards specific and definable end results, and to ensure the efficient achievement of overall objectives these results must be co-ordinated. The co-ordination required is not necessarily of a day-to-day operational kind, however, for in some types of industry, task functions can, within limits, be carried on almost independently of each other, and are frequently separated in time and place. This was apparent from the fact that nine of the firms studied in the second phase of the research did not cover the full range of management activities; of these, two were concerned with manufacture only. In two, financial policy was determined and executed by separate holding companies. A further three had no marketing functions; one was working entirely on a contract basis, while in the case of the other two the manufactured goods were disposed of by separate and independently controlled marketing companies. In seven firms, there were no research activities; two of these were linked with larger

[2] Taylor, op. cit., p. 18.

industrial organizations and used the parent firms' laboratories.
A further two drew on the research associations covering their
industries. The other three had no formal contact with research or
development. Their managers picked up new ideas as and when
they could, but there was no systematic procedure leading to
planned changes either in the product or the production methods.

Moreover, four of the sixteen firms with research departments
had sited them away from the main factory; the research laboratories operated independently and the research staff had no
day-to-day operational contact with the other management
personnel.

In some of the larger firms studied, these basic activities broke
down into a number of subsidiary task functions. The breakdown
inside the production function was mostly related to the type of
product or process, although there were exceptions; in one firm,
for example, the type of material handled provided the basis for
differentiation. Here again, it was found in some types of industry
that these subsidiary task functions could be separated from each
other in time or place. Examples of this were found in firms
where some of the production work was sub-contracted.

Element functions are seldom directed towards specific and
definable results. It is rarely possible to separate them in time and
place, and even when not differentiated in the way suggested by
Taylor, they will still be present as intrinsic parts of the management process. Taking the personnel function, for example, while
it is true that in a few organizations such as employment agencies,
it is a task function, in the manufacturing field, those responsible
for the personnel function are not normally held directly accountable for any primary task. Companies are not brought into
existence solely for the purpose of hiring and handling personnel,
and the personnel function cannot be carried out independently
of other activities. Moreover, a personnel management element
is contained in all task functions even though it need not be
differentiated as a specialism. It would obviously be impossible
to carry out research, to produce, to sell or even to handle the
funds required to run a business effectively without hiring and
handling personnel.

Another example of an element function is production control:
the measuring of actual against anticipated results in terms of

quantity and cost. Inspection is also an element function; it is concerned with maintaining quality standards.

The failure of many managers to distinguish between task functions and element functions when planning and discussing organization seemed to have led to another misconception: the confusion of functional organization with line-staff organization. Many of the people interviewed used these phrases indiscriminately.

When Taylor first suggested that the process of management should be broken down into elements and these elements differentiated as specialisms, he almost automatically assumed that the group of specialists so formed would have joint accountability for end results. It was this concept of joint accountability which failed to gain acceptance and as a result the functional type of organization never became widespread. The line-staff concept taken over from functional organization was a compromise; it provided for the development and utilization of special skills in the way Taylor suggested, but at the same time a hierarchy of line authority was maintained, line managers formally retaining the complete responsibility for end results.

Thus, line-staff organization is based not on a differentiation between specialist skills but on an assignment of roles. For conceptual purposes, the distinction between line and staff is rigid and theoretical; 'line' defining the positions in the organization which have responsibility and authority in that those occupying them are directly accountable for end results, and 'staff' the positions which provide support and service to the line; those occupying staff positions are not accountable for end results either individually or collectively.

The research workers found, however, that the phrase 'functional organization' was generally used to denote not the specific form of organization suggested by Taylor, but the kind of structure which emerges when all the work done in a firm is grouped into departments or divisions, the basis of the grouping being special knowledge or skills. In common usage the phrase 'functional management' meant little more than specialized management, and in several firms the staff part of line-staff organization was referred to as functional organization. There was a tendency to confuse differentiation on a basis of role with differentiation on a basis of knowledge and skill; to identify line responsibility with general management and staff responsibility with specialist management. As a result many of the people concerned with organization planning did not realize that a specialist manager can have a line role; that however specialized he may be from a knowledge and skill point of view, he remains a line manager if he is responsible for specific end results.

LINE SPECIALIZATION

It has already been pointed out that the earliest and most wide-spread form of specialization in South Essex industry appeared to be line specialization, the organizational structure differentiating between the basic task functions only. In five of the firms studied in more detail, specialization went no further than the full range of these functions. These five firms had few organizational problems and in none of them was there any evidence of conscious planning. Only in one case was an organization chart produced; the outline of this organization chart is given in Fig. 22.

This chart illustrates the simplicity of formal organization in these five firms. The role of the chief executive was clear-cut, all his immediate subordinates being specialist line managers. His job was to co-ordinate the efforts of the specialists and to ensure that the end results for which they were accountable contributed to the successful achievement of overall objectives. The co-ordination was almost entirely a matter of direct and personal contact between individuals, and in each case the management system had the organic characteristics of easy communication and a high degree of involvement and participation.

Three other firms in which only part of the range of basic activities was covered also had an organizational structure of this kind, there being line specialization only.

All the firms with an organizational structure similar to that illustrated in Fig. 22 were either 'average' or 'above average' in success; therefore, from a business point of view, a very simple form of organization can be effective. Three of these firms were

---

[3] A wide variety of titles were used in the firms studied; in all the diagrams in this chapter, titles have been standardized, the same title being used in each diagram to indicate the same function.

small, employing less than 500 people, but four were in the 500–1,000 range, and one employed over 1,000; thus it is not only in the very small firms that a simple form of organization is effective. These firms were all, however, at an extreme of the technical scale; they were either small unit production firms or large process production firms of the single-purpose plant type. There were no

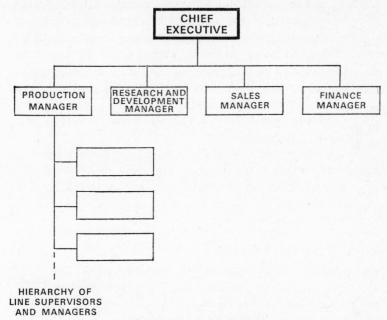

Fig. 22. Line specialization

successful large batch or mass production firms with this simple form of organization.

In two other firms the organizational pattern was similar to that illustrated in Fig. 22, the only difference being that on the production side there was differentiation between products. One had two production departments, and the other three; the managers of these departments being directly responsible to the chief executive. In both firms production was of the jobbing and small batch type, the products being prototypes of scientific instruments and electronic equipment. These firms like those already described had relatively few organizational problems. Role relationships were simple and clear-cut, and the chief executive co-ordinated the activities of the line managers. The line managers were in control of all the elements in the process of managing their departments; they were not serviced or supported by any staff managers.

All the line managers, including the production managers, were specialists themselves, the production managers being highly qualified and responsible for technically complex articles. An outline of the organization chart of one of these firms is given in Fig. 23.

In all, therefore, there were ten firms with a predominantly line type of organizational structure, management activities being differentiated on a basis of knowledge and skill, and some specialists being employed. There were no staff positions as such, as all the specialists were line managers; i.e. they were given responsibility and authority because they were accountable for specific and definable end results.

On the whole, the relationship between general managers and specialists seemed better in these ten firms than in the other firms studied. This suggests that the general manager's suspicion of the expert is not as important a cause of conflict in industry as the differentiation between line and staff roles.

LINE-STAFF ORGANIZATION

In the other thirteen firms studied, including all the large batch and mass production firms, specialization went further. Differentiation existed not only between task functions but also between element functions. Two were the firms already referred to in an earlier chapter as having a functional type of organization.[4] These will be described in more detail later. In view of the confusion in terminology, however, it is important to stress here that their organization was functional in the Taylorian sense, joint accountability being implied. The specialist staff employed in these firms were held jointly responsible for end results.

The remaining eleven had a line-staff type of organization; there was a clear-cut distinction in formal organization between line roles and staff roles. Line managers were held accountable for end results while staff managers were formally responsible for giving advice and guidance to line managers. In four firms, the organizational structure was described as functional by some of the

4 See Table II, p. 18.

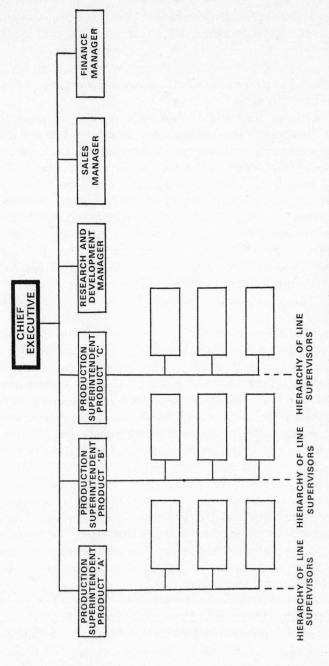

Fig. 23. Product-centred organization

managers and supervisors interviewed. Here, however, the word 'functional' was being used in the less specific sense and implied no more than a high degree of departmentalization based on differentiation between task and element functions. Formally, at least, there was no question of staff managers having any responsibility for end results.

These eleven firms all had their own way of interpreting the line-staff concept. The number and nature of the specialist departments varied from one to the other, and so did the preciseness with which duties and responsibilities were defined. The relative prestige of line and staff managers varied too. A business firm is not only a social and an economic system, but also a political one, and factory politics played a large part in determining the prestige and status of staff managers. Although at a formal level joint accountability was not recognized, the power and prestige of the staff managers in some of the firms were so high that at the informal level of organization it was almost impossible to distinguish in practice between advice and executive instructions.

In spite of the individual differences between firms, three main types of line-staff organization emerged; these are illustrated in Figs. 24, 25 and 26 respectively. The first was departmentalized organization. There were five firms with an organizational structure of the kind illustrated in Fig. 24. In these five firms the only managers generally recognized as line managers were those with direct responsibility for the production operations. There was confusion of the kind already described; organization failed to distinguish both between staff responsibilities and specialist management and between task functions and element functions. In the firm to which Fig. 24 refers, the role of specialists such as the research manager, the financial controller, and the sales manager was not felt to be any different from that of the personnel manager, the production controller, the materials controller, and the purchasing manager. All specialist managers were indiscriminately assigned to staff roles.

The second type of line-staff organization illustrated in Fig. 25 was found in three firms. Here organization did differentiate between task functions and element functions: the functions co-ordinated at the top of the hierarchy were task functions.

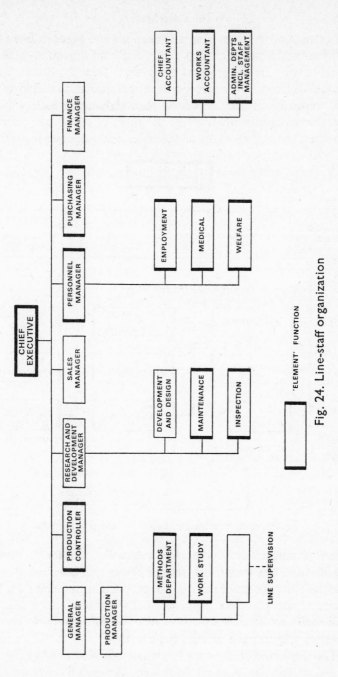

'ELEMENT' FUNCTION

Fig. 24. Line-staff organization

Differentiation between element functions and between line roles and staff roles came one step down, line-staff organization being found only inside the production function. Thus there was quite a marked difference in status between the specialists employed in staff departments and associated with production management, and the specialists heading up the finance, sales, and research activities, the higher status of the latter being derived from their

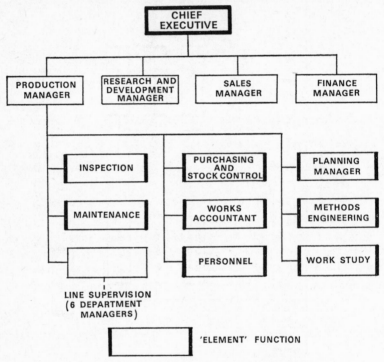

Fig. 25. Line-staff organization inside production

direct responsibility to the chief executive. As far as formal organization was concerned, those holding staff positions had no responsibility for anything outside production management. For example, the personnel manager in the firm to which Fig. 25 specifically relates was not responsible for the personnel function in either the research or sales departments.

The third kind of line-staff organization is illustrated in Fig. 26. It has characteristics in common with the organization depicted in Fig. 25 as well as with that in Fig. 23. It is based primarily on a differentiation between task functions, with a differentiation between element functions superimposed. A line-staff type of organizational structure is built up inside each task function.

This kind of organization was referred to by those interviewed as 'divisionalized organization'. Several people considered it the only workable alternative to the departmentalized or 'functional' kind of organization depicted in Fig. 24. It involved the creation of a series of relatively small autonomous units at the periphery of the organization. As far as production management was concerned, the basis of differentiation was not the nature of the work done, but the product being manufactured. Each of the product divisions was almost entirely self-contained, and covered all the activities necessary for the effective operation of the division.

The firm, whose organization is illustrated in Fig. 26, is the one already referred to, in which a large number of organization charts had been bound together in a weighty volume. It has not been possible to reproduce these charts in full. The chart in Fig. 26 was therefore drawn by the research workers and is a simplified version of the firm's charts; it merely indicates the principles on which the organizational structure was based.

It will be seen that in this firm a small group of specialists of senior status had been appointed to advise the chief executive and board on the formulation of policy relating to their own specialisms. The other two firms with divisionalized organization did not have this group of specialist advisers at the top of the hierarchy.

The eleven line-staff organization firms included one of the firms studied intensively—Firm A, in which the production of standardized parts had been a recent innovation—and one process production firm. The others were either large batch and mass production firms or firms in which this type of production was combined with process production.

These firms had a characteristic in common: more conscious planning of organization had been done than in the line organization firms. In nine of them responsibility for organization planning had been assigned specifically to one individual or department. Because of this it was possible to discuss organization in a more abstract and theoretical way than in the other firms

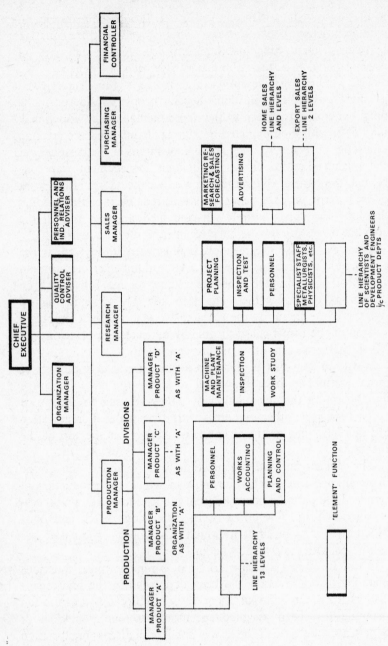

Fig. 26. Product-centred line-staff organization

studied. The research workers asked the people responsible for organization planning what they considered to be their most difficult problems, how organizational decisions had been made in the past, and whether any changes were contemplated.

ORGANIZATIONAL PROBLEMS OF LINE-STAFF FIRMS

(a) *The trend towards divisionalization*

The first point of interest emerging from these discussions was the confirmation of the impression obtained during the background survey: it seems that management fashion now favours divisionalization. Several people said that they thought departmentalized organization was out of date and that it was important to break up large functional empires and relieve senior specialists of their enormous administrative load. In three firms changes towards divisionalized organization were currently being planned. In two of these the changes were a consequence of technical changes, diversification, and a widening of the range of products manufactured which had created organizational problems, bringing home to top management the fact that there is a limit to the number of different products which can be effectively handled through an organizational structure of the departmentalized kind. In the third firm the people responsible for organization planning had gradually become aware of the fundamental differences between task functions and element functions. They had realized too that specialists could be and often were accountable for specific end results. This led them to consider whether it would be better for those responsible for end results (both specialist and general managers) to be given control over all the activities involved. Logically, it was felt, control should be complete, and any breakdown in line and staff roles should be contained within the framework of each task or product division.

Those responsible for this decision, like their counterparts in the two other firms moving in the same direction, were not certain about how far they would be able to go. They were aware that this fundamental change in organization would create problems as with any other change, and take a long time to implement.

The difficulties of making an organizational change of this kind were referred to by those responsible for organization planning in the firm illustrated in Fig. 26. Here the change-over from departmentalized organization to divisionalized organization had taken place about nine months before the more detailed studies were made. Those who had put the change into effect still remembered vividly the problems they had encountered in planning and putting the new organizational structure into operation. The breaking down of the existing organizational structure had resulted in the splitting up of social groups established over a long period of time. The relationships emerging from day-to-day operation had contained personal as well as role elements, and while roles had been changed overnight by organizational decisions, personal adjustment to the new roles had been a slow process.

In this particular case the difficulties were increased by the fact that the change resulted in the disintegration of functional empires, several senior executives being deprived of authority. In general those in line positions had been given more power and those in staff positions less. For example, under the old system, the manager responsible for product quality had also been the executive head of a large inspection department. The staff of this department were no longer under his direct control; they had been made responsible to the line supervisors of the departments in which they were located. He himself had retained his prestige position, for as Fig. 26 shows he was still responsible to the chief executive in an advisory capacity. His role had changed, but not his status.

It was the new high-level advisory roles which caused the greatest difficulty. They were neither understood nor fully accepted, line managers felt uncertain and insecure in their dealings with the people concerned. The roles had changed, but the people in them were the same, and it was very difficult for those who had previously worked in staff departments to sever personal ties and direct their allegiance elsewhere.

Even in this firm divisionalization had not gone the whole way; the purchasing department had remained intact. Indeed, the organization chart given in Fig. 26 suggests that purchasing was regarded as a task function. Those responsible for organization planning thought that it would have been better to divisionalize purchasing, and that the managers of the newly created product divisions should have been made responsible for their own buying. As might have been expected, this view was shared by the production managers interviewed. They resented the fact that purchasing was the only element in the process of managing their divisions over which they had no direct control. The reason for the anomaly was that the reorganization had coincided with a drive to cut down material stocks—inventory reduction was another phase managers were concerned with during the later stages of this research—and it had been feared that independent buying would lead to stock-piling, and buying of small quantities at high prices. The fear had also been expressed that the relationship of the firm with its outside suppliers would become extremely complicated if they were approached by more than one person. Thus, although the chief executive had been wholeheartedly behind the organizational changes, he had decided that the balance of advantage lay against the divisionalization of the purchasing department.

The need to present a united front to the outside world had created problems in the personnel sphere too. The divisionaliza-tion of the personnel management function had made it necessary for several members of the firm to maintain a contact with the same Ministry of Labour Employment Exchange and the same Trade Union officials. In practice, therefore, the adviser to the chief executive in the personnel and industrial relations field continued to exercise enough functional control over the personnel departments in the product divisions to co-ordinate the activities involving contact with outside organizations.

(b) *The confusion between task functions and element functions*

The second point of interest emerging from the discussions with the people responsible for organization planning in the depart-mentally-organized firms suggested that the failure to distinguish between task functions and element functions, characteristic of such organization, was not entirely due to the confusion in termin-ology already referred to.

One contributing factor was the tendency to take for granted that production is the central and dominating phase of all manu-facturing activities, and to look upon all organization as production-centred. Some of the people interviewed considered production management to be synonymous with line management and thought that it was only the production managers who could be held responsible for specific end results. This led them to take the view that all specialists, both those responsible for such element functions as personnel management, inspection, plant and machine maintenance, and methods engineering, and those responsible for the task functions of finance, research, and marketing, were employed to service and support the production managers.

A possible explanation of this attitude is that the generalizations on which organization planning is based have been mainly derived from the personal experience of those working in the field of standardized production. In this type cf industry, production itself seems to be the critical activity around which all organization is planned. As the following chapter will show, however, there are stages in a firm's development and manufacturing situations where the production function is subsidiary either to marketing or research. Included in these investigations were firms manufacturing unit articles, where production was a corollary to research and development, and process production firms where marketing was the dominating activity.

It seemed, too, that it is not always easy to interpret the classical principles of management, and confusion could arise as a result. Reference was made to Urwick's principle of specialization, which says that duties and responsibilities must be grouped together in such a way as to ensure an efficient and economic performance of the work to be done. People felt that it was not always easy to decide what this way was. Many of those who referred to this principle said that they had interpreted it in terms of the efficient and economic use of specialist personnel; they had tried to bring together in their organizational structure the activities and responsibilities requiring the same kinds of skill and competence. Problems arose, however, because such activities and responsibilities were not always related to each other in their relevance to end results.

This was especially true of finance. There are two quite separate financial functions essential to the efficient operation of a business: one is a task, the other is an element in the process of management. The task function has to do with the raising of funds for initiating or expanding the business, the keeping of accounts, and the determination of financial policy. The element function is management accounting; this is the part of production administration concerned with prediction and control. The prediction aspect of this function is the determining of 'ideal' standard costs and the control aspect is the keeping to a minimum of what Andrews (1948)[5] has called 'indirect costs'. The contributions to end results made by those two functions are not of the same nature, but in many of the firms studied they had been brought together, as they required the same specialist skills.

During the interviews a number of references were made to the bad relationships between accountants and other managers. The research workers came to the conclusion that one cause of their hostility was that the bringing together of the two financial functions tended to obscure the fact that the management accounting function is primarily a servicing and supportive one. People concerned with works accounting tended to assume responsibility for end results that was not properly theirs; they saw their role as a controlling and sanctioning one rather than as a servicing and supportive one. Line managers resented this attitude and retaliated by becoming aggressive and obstructive.

In firms where the two financial functions were separated in organization, relationships between the accountants and the other managers seemed better. This was particularly noticeable in the firms where there was divisionalized organization; in these firms each product division had its own accounting staff which provided the line managers with the information they needed to control their own departments. This meant that it was the servicing element in the role of the accounting staff which was the most important. The task function of finance was completely divorced from management accounting.

Many people seemed to have difficulty not only in interpreting some of the principles of management but in reconciling one with another. The reconciliation of the principle of specialization with the principle of unity of command was felt by some of the organization planners interviewed to be almost impossible. This is illustrated in the following quotation from one of the interviews:

> It is certainly difficult to be economical in your use of specialists and at the same time ensure that no one works either officially or unofficially under more than one boss. In my view, the only way of drawing up an organization chart is to weigh up the pros and cons of sticking to one of these principles or another. I favour

[5] P. Andrews, *Manufacturing Business* (Macmillan and Co., London).

product divisions; everybody knows exactly where they are in such a system but you certainly could not say that it is the best system if you are thinking in terms of economic use of specialists.

(c) *Personnel Management*

Finally, all the people responsible for planning organization referred to the difficulties of fitting the personnel function into the organizational structure. From what was said, it appeared that it was in relation to personnel management that the problems and dilemmas associated with the line-staff concept occurred in their most extreme form. As indicated already, personnel management is one of the element functions intrinsic to all task functions; problems of responsibility and co-ordination were therefore inevitable. The fact that the arguments between personnel specialists and line managers were usually about people made these problems more difficult to solve. Loss of face was an important consideration for all the parties concerned. Moreover, there seemed to be a greater danger of repercussions than there was in the case of the other element functions where conflict was more often centred around inanimate objects or abstractions.

It was felt that, generally speaking, there was a lot to be said for making the personnel department directly responsible to the chief executive. There were specialist personnel departments in all but one of the line-staff firms; three were the firms which had changed over to a divisionalized form of organization with the result that what had been large specialist personnel departments had been split up and each product division now had its own small group of personnel management staff. One of these was the firm already described which had a high-level personnel specialist responsible for advising the board; he was supported by a small staff whose main concern was personnel research and the co-ordination of information. The divisional personnel staff relied on this central department for advice and ammunition.

In four of the remaining seven firms, the man in charge of the personnel department was directly responsible to the chief executive. Only in one was he formally entitled 'personnel manager'; in another he was called 'personnel and industrial relations superintendent', and in the other two 'personnel director'. In general, the title 'personnel manager' seemed to be restricted to personnel specialists who were slightly lower in status.

Two of these four personnel executives were the people responsible for organization planning in their firms; this responsibility certainly seemed to increase the prestige of their departments. The other two, although directly responsible to the chief executive, were noticeably lower in status than other senior executives. In one, the lower status was indicated by an organization chart that showed the names of the senior executives on a sloping line, the personnel executive being at the bottom. In the other, the personnel executive had fewer status symbols, and was the only person directly responsible to the chief executive not included in the firm's 'top-hat pension scheme'.

The senior personnel executive in the other three firms was responsible to the senior production executive. In two of these the personnel department covered production personnel only, both the research and sales managers being completely responsible for recruitment and for dealing with the personnel problems arising in their departments.

An interesting incident occurred while the research workers were studying one of these firms. A trade union started a recruitment drive among the clerical workers in the sales department and subsequently claimed the right to negotiate on their behalf. The sales manager turned to the personnel manager for advice and the personnel manager became involved in the discussions that took place with the trade union officials. These took up a lot of his time, and the production manager to whom he was responsible began to protest. The ultimate outcome was the re-definition of the personnel manager's duties and responsibilities, and when the research ended he was about to be made directly responsible to the chief executive.

In the third firm the personnel manager was responsible to the production manager and provided a service for the whole factory. The research workers were told that he had been put under the production manager because the bulk of the labour force was employed in production departments; he had to be made responsible to someone, and the production manager seemed the most appropriate person. The close association with the production departments made the personnel manager's relations with other

departments more difficult. In the sales and research departments
he confined himself to the more technical aspects of the personnel
function: recruitment, staff grading schemes, record maintenance,
and welfare services. It was unusual for either the sales manager
or the research manager to come to him for advice, and he rarely
became involved either in the disciplinary problems that arose in
their departments or in the formulation of their personnel policy.
Some of the managers interviewed felt that it would be more
satisfactory if the personnel manager were made responsible to
the chief executive.

Both in this firm and in the two referred to above (where the
personnel specialist, although responsible to the chief executive,
was lower in status than the other senior executives) the principle
of unity of command had had an important influence on the
structure, the overriding consideration being that the personnel
manager should have only one boss. It soon became obvious,
however, that the pattern of informal relationships emerging from
day-to-day operations in these firms was not very different from
what it would have been if the personnel manager had been made
formally responsible to more than one. He regarded other senior
executives as his superiors and their requests as executive instructions. As so frequently happens, informal organization had
created the very situation which formal organization had been
devised to avoid. It seems that where the status system is out of
line with formal organization it is the former rather than the latter
which determines the pattern of relationships.

The general feeling that it was desirable to make the personnel
specialist responsible to the chief executive seemed to contradict
the trend towards divisionalization, which implies that the
responsibility for the executive part of the personnel function
belongs to the line manager. Some of the people with whom this
was discussed recognized that they were being inconsistent when
they said that, on the one hand, the breakdown between line and
staff roles should be contained within the framework of each
product division, and on the other, that the personnel manager
should be made responsible to the chief executive. Even the
strongest advocates of divisionalization were rather hesitant about
extending it to personnel management, and in firms where there
was a divisionalized form of organization it was felt that the

personnel staff in the product divisions needed the backing of a strong central department. (As might have been expected, it was the personnel specialists themselves who held these views most strongly.)

Several arguments were put forward in favour of having a powerful personnel department directly responsible to the chief executive. One was that as a very important part of the personnel specialist's responsibility was to brief the board on policy formulation, he had to be near to the top of the hierarchy and able to talk to board members on almost equal terms. Another was that the personnel manager needed power and prestige in order to make the other managers treat him with sufficient respect. In all staff roles there is an element of control; the personnel manager has to ensure that the labour policy laid down by the board is implemented throughout the organization. It was felt that he could only do this effectively if he had direct access to the chief executive and could call upon him to apply sanctions. A third argument was that for top management the only way of indicating either to the people employed or to the world at large that it regards good industrial relations as important was by putting the specialist responsible for personnel management high on the management ladder. There was one firm in which the personnel manager, although responsible for production personnel only, reported directly to the chief executive. This chief executive told the research workers he realized that, from an organization point of view, the personnel manager ought to report to the production manager, but as this was a difficult area as far as labour relations were concerned, it was essential to let everybody know that personnel management was regarded as an important function.

The extent to which the personnel specialist was involved in policy formulation was reflected in his status. This was equally true of other specialists. There were exceptions to the general rule, however; a few specialists seemed to have more say in the formulation of policy than their formal status warranted. All these people had a characteristic in common: they had in some way managed to opt out of factory politics. They had built up an independent reputation for themselves—often through involvement in the affairs of an outside management association. As far as their own firms were concerned, their role was more that of the visiting consultant than of the usual staff specialist.

There seemed to be little relationship between the status of the personnel specialist and the part he played in the solution of day-to-day shop floor problems. The personnel departments studied fell into two groups: those with high-status personnel executives concerned mainly with the development of policies and procedures; and those with low-status personnel managers who were responsible to line managers and who functioned as trouble-shooters on the shop floor. In their own way both groups were doing a useful job, but it seemed that these jobs were rarely combined. The research suggested that good personnel management policy did not guarantee (at least in the short run) good relations on the shop floor.

In spite of the reluctance to accept divisionalized personnel management, this is the most satisfactory arrangement in theory. The kind of organization which provides both a high-level personnel specialist advising the board on personnel policy, and lower-level specialists closely associated with line managers and involved in shop floor disputes, seems to get the best of both worlds.

FUNCTIONAL ORGANIZATION

The two firms with the functional type of production organization illustrated in Fig. 27 were process firms. This unusual organizational structure had been revealed by the background survey and the more detailed investigation provided an opportunity to study the behaviour and relationships associated with it. Both were successful firms, and it seemed that, on the whole, the people concerned did not find it difficult to adapt themselves to the organization.

In the firm to which Fig. 27 refers there were thirty supervisors, responsible either for departments or sections of the plant, who reported to and received executive instructions from five senior executives. All had had experience of working under a single superior, either in their present firm or outside. Twenty-eight said they thought the functional type of organization was better, their main source of satisfaction being the contacts they had with all the members of the top management group. The five senior executives were referred to as 'the Big Five', and the supervisors said that the close association between 'the Big Five'

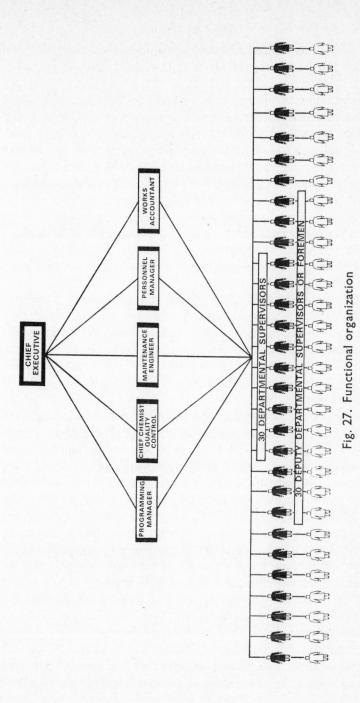

Fig. 27. Functional organization

and themselves meant that they knew about everything that was going on in the firm and about any developments contemplated. The other two took the opposite point of view; they were very disgruntled and said that a functional type of organization was a constant source of frustration and irritation. Both felt that they would be a lot happier if they were responsible to one person only. They talked a lot about 'the principle of unity of command' and about management organization generally. Both had taken the British Institute of Management and Ministry of Education Joint Diploma in Management studies, and were more organization-conscious than their colleagues, none of whom had been given any formal management training. They had definite views about what was right and wrong in organization, and much of their discontent arose from comparing their own situation with what they thought was the ideal one.

In the second firm more people were critical; but even here two-thirds of those interviewed said that on the whole they thought the organization worked well. First-hand observations led the research workers to the same conclusion. No evidence was found in either firm of incompatible or conflicting instructions being given, or of attempts being made to play one boss off against another.

It was interesting to find that in the two functionally organized firms both role and personal relationships between senior executives appeared to be good. In each case the people concerned formed a cohesive social group and spent quite a lot of their leisure time together. It was, of course, impossible to tell whether the close association was forced upon them by the circumstances in which they worked, or whether there was a natural affinity which drew them together and which in itself made an important contribution to the successful working of the organization. The fact that this was much the same in both firms suggests that the close association might have been brought about by circumstances.

The departmental supervisors were much more isolated and independent in these two firms than in those with a more orthodox type of organization; their only close association was with their immediate subordinates. They probably had more to do with the chief executive than those at a similar level in most of the other firms studied, but the relationship was not an intimate one. This independence and isolation seemed to have both advantages and disadvantages. The supervisors were able to control their own affairs; they could, for example, arrange their own holidays or take time off if they made the necessary cover arrangements with their subordinates. The salary structure was known and understood throughout the firm; increments came along almost automatically, and they were not dependent upon any single individual for increased pay or promotion. This independence seemed to result in harmonious if not intimate relationships with superiors.

The disadvantage seemed to be that they were deprived of the emotional security that can result from a close relationship with an immediate superior. There was no one to whom they could turn for help and advice on personal matters.

Organization of this kind requires supervisory staff who can stand on their own feet and work in isolation. It was probably significant that in both firms the supervisors were well qualified technically; in one they were all graduates. Thus, they tended to form closely knit groups, and lack of a close relationship with superiors was compensated for by a close relationship with colleagues. They turned to each other for help and advice, and there was less inter-departmental friction than in the other firms studied.

It was clear that in these two firms joint accountability was not only the basis of organization, but was associated both with business success and good inter-personal relationships. Moreover, these were not the only two firms in which joint accountability was a workable concept. At a higher level there were two firms with joint managing directors. At an informal level of organization, too, there were staff managers in line-staff organization with so much power that in practice their advice had the weight of executive orders. The two extreme cases were the firms with departmentalized organization in which a move towards divisionalization was not under discussion. Although the organization charts drew a distinction between line roles and staff roles, the status of the staff managers, and the way in which they were used, implied that they were jointly responsible with the line managers for end results. This showed itself in the way inter-departmental memoranda were routed and addressed, and in the composition of the different management and policy committees. One of these firms was a process production firm and the other a mass production firm. It seems that in some circumstances people can work quite happily under more than one boss.

THE FUNCTIONS OF ORGANIZATION

These discussions of organizational problems threw some interesting light on the attitudes of the people responsible for organization planning. Only a minority of those interviewed were strongly committed to one form of organization, insisting that one form, usually that of the firm in which they were working, was better than another. The majority felt that there was no one best way of organizing a firm. Their personal experience had convinced them that one system worked as well as another and they regarded the various forms of organization described in management literature as possible alternatives.

The follow-up studies also confirmed that in many firms the conscious process of organization-building proceeds independently of technical change and development, and that the link between technology and organization was not the product of conscious behaviour or deliberate policy. Examples were found where changes in organization had followed changes in technology. Reference has already been made to the two firms in which diversification and a widening of the range of products had preceded a change towards divisionalization. Even here, however, the changes had not been planned simultaneously. Changes in organization had come after technical change had led to a collapse of the existing organizational structure.

In general, therefore, there was no conflict between the impressions obtained from the broad and general survey and the more detailed analysis of organizational structure arising from the second phase of the research.

The more detailed analysis raised two further points, however. The first was that the research workers realized as they studied firms more deeply that not only the type of organization but also the functions of organization were linked with technology. Normally, organization is regarded as having a two-fold function; it has to produce a design or mechanism for the co-ordination of work and to identify the source of authority, establishing a network of relationships to enable people to work together for a particular purpose; thus it serves both technical and social ends. But even this, it seems, cannot be taken for granted. In the technically advanced firm the co-ordination of work does not depend upon organizational structure or on co-operation between people. In process industry, the design or mechanism for the co-ordinating of work is intrinsic in the plant itself, and in some of the mass production firms studied the control system fulfilled a similar function. In both these systems production emerged almost automatically once the production process had been set in motion.

This means that in the technically advanced firm organization serves primarily social ends, its function being to define roles and relationships within a social system. This means that the organization planner can concentrate on establishing the network of relationships which is best for people. Moreover, because co-ordination is independent of organization, the form of organization is not likely to have a critical effect on the success of the business.

In the less advanced systems of production, where organization serves both technical and social ends, there is likely to be a much closer link between business success and the form of organization, and the two functions of organization can come into conflict. The network of relationships best for production is not necessarily the best for people.

The recognition of the differences in the functions of organization between one firm and another make the differences in types of organization easier to understand. For example, it has been suggested that functional organization of the Taylorian type, characterized by a fusion of line and staff roles and by joint accountability, can be successful. But this type of organization was found only in technically advanced firms. Here, joint accountability implied a collective responsibility for the production machine, not collective responsibility for end results. There was no evidence to suggest that the principle of 'one man, one boss' was invalid in firms whose organization provided a mechanism for co-ordination.

Therefore a first step in building an organizational structure appropriate to the situational demands arising from technology, is to find what purposes the organization has to serve.

The second point emerging from the case studies was that the classical school of thought on organization appears to be inadequate not only because it fails to provide a direct and simple basis for relating organizational structure and business success, but also because its concepts and abstractions do not facilitate the work of those who plan organizational structure. In a real life situation, reference to these concepts and abstractions can add to the confusion and obscure the picture.

8 Development, Production, and Marketing

The last chapter drew a distinction between task functions and element functions. Following up this analysis, the next aspect of organization examined was the relationship between the task functions and the people responsible for carrying them out. Particular emphasis was laid on the relationship between the three main manufacturing tasks: development, production, and marketing.

It was not possible to include all the firms studied, for (as already indicated) there were eight firms in which the full range of these activities was not covered. In two cases the information obtained locally was supplemented by visits to sales departments at company headquarters. This chapter refers to fifteen of the twenty-three firms.

Another problem arising from the study of the relationship between functions was this: it is not easy always to discern where one phase of manufacture ends and another begins. Reference has already been made to the confusion between task and element functions, and so the lack of definition of areas of responsibility. There were two firms with the departmentalized form of line-staff organization, illustrated in Fig. 26, in which the two element functions of planning and control had not only been brought together in a single department, but the forecasting element of the marketing function had also been linked with them. The result was that there was practically no direct contact between the production and the marketing departments, the liaison between the two functions being effected entirely within a single department. In both firms the status of this bridge department was high; in one case the senior executive responsible was second in command to the chief executive, and the sales and production managers were responsible to him. This meant that even at departmental head level, communications between marketing and production went through an intermediary. There was a third firm in which the stores formed the bridge between production and sales.

But in spite of the difficulties of analysis and the anomalies in organizational structure, the link between organization and technology was clearly discernible, for not only the nature of the development, production and marketing functions, but also their sequence depended to a great extent on technical factors.

One of the differences between task and element functions discussed in the last chapter was the independence of the former in comparison to the latter. In certain circumstances, research, production, and marketing can be separated from each other in time and place, and a company can be brought into existence to develop a product only, to produce, or to sell. The analysis of the relationship between task functions showed that the extent to which they could be separated was closely related to the system of production. It was in the technically advanced systems of production that functions could be separated most easily. This is evident from the fact that the firms which had to be omitted from this chapter, because the full range of activities was not covered, included half the process production firms, but none of the unit and small batch production firms.

The relative importance of the various functions was also related to the system of production. In each production group there seemed to be one function that was central and critical in that it had the greatest effect on success and survival. The emphasis placed on the different functions was not of course entirely dependent on technology; economic factors and the stage of development were also important. In some of the firms studied, the emphasis shifted between marketing and production over the relatively short period of the research. Nevertheless, in the long run, technology remained the dominant factor in the determination of the critical factor.

The more detailed studies made at this stage of the research produced some interesting information about status systems. A characteristic that all the firms *above average* in success had in common was that their status systems gave adequate recognition to the importance of the critical function. In reply to direct questioning, the managers and supervisors interviewed were reluctant to admit that one department was more important than another in contributing to success, or that one department had higher status than another. A phrase used repeatedly in these discussions was 'the chain is as strong as its weakest link', implying that all departments were equally important. Nevertheless, much of what was said contained an implicit acceptance of a status system which discriminated between departments. As we have seen, there were firms where formal organization itself discriminated in this way, one example being the firm where the different departments shown on the organization chart were placed on a sloping line.

Barnard (1948)[1] points out that status systems are closely related to systems of organization, communication, specialization, and authority. They are determined by both technical and social factors. In many of the firms studied, the department with the highest status appeared to be that in which the chief executive had previously worked, and the *élite* was the group with which he had been closely associated.

The fact that the status system was linked with technology on the one hand, and with the background of the chief executive on the other, meant that there was a tendency for firms whose chief executive had been closely associated with the critical function earlier in his career to be the more successful ones.

For the purposes of this analysis, the fifteen firms studied were divided among the three main production categories. The characteristics of unit and small batch production, large batch and mass production, and process production respectively, are described below, and summarized in Fig. 28.

UNIT AND SMALL BATCH PRODUCTION

The unit and small batch production group consisted of four engineering firms operating mainly in the electronic and tele-communications equipment and scientific instrument fields, and

---

[1] Barnard, op. cit., p. 77.

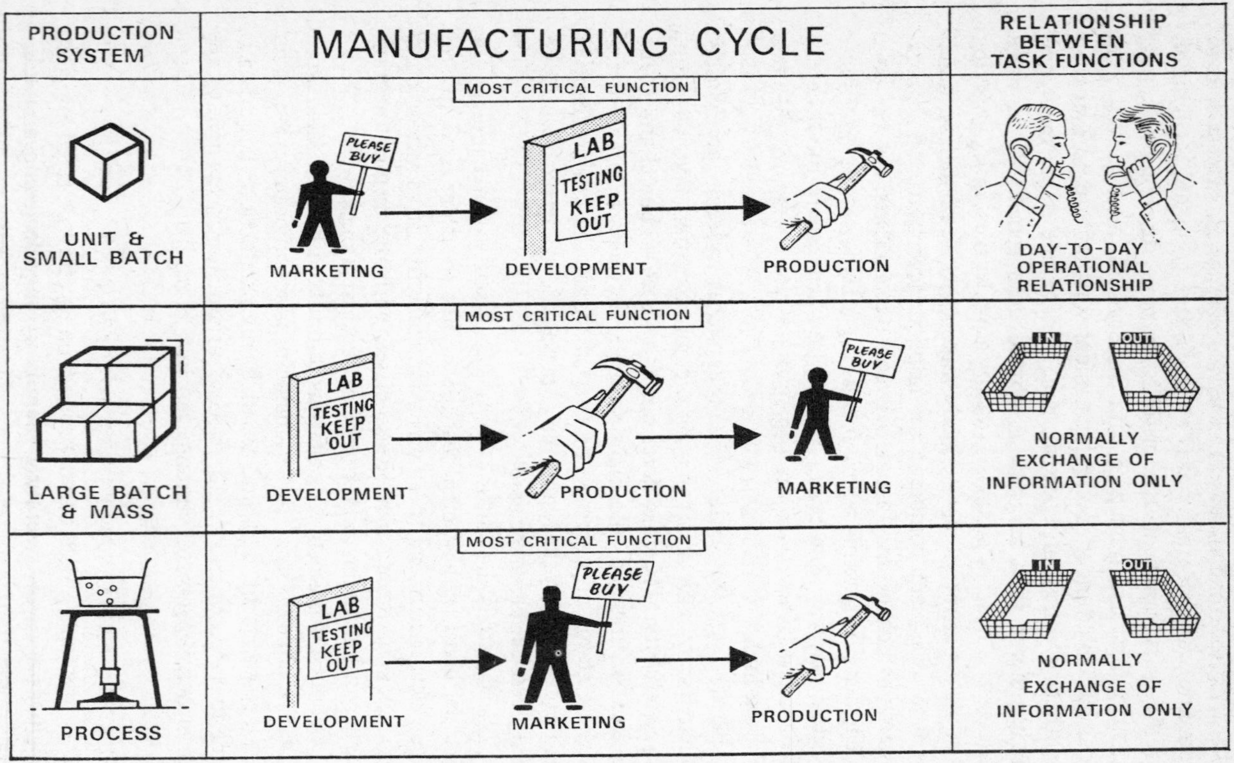

Fig. 28. Characteristics of production systems

two consumer goods firms, one making clothing and the other furniture.

The first characteristic these six firms had in common was that their production schedules were based on firm orders only. In theory, they had no future beyond the period covered by their order books, so that all their financial planning was short-term. It was interesting to find that this limited future did not seem to create insecurity amongst the people employed. All six firms had plenty of orders; on the engineering side the rapid technical advance in these particular fields was good for business, and on the consumer goods side, the high standard of living (particularly in the immediate locality) was creating a demand for individually made products. Thus, those employed felt optimistic about the future. Moreover, one of the most important assets of a unit production firm is the skill and experience of the labour force, and a falling off of work does not therefore result in a threat of redundancy. The people employed in these firms seemed to feel that they were likely to be retained even during slack periods.

But even though it did not create insecurity, the effects of short-term planning were evident in attitudes and behaviour. The managers and supervisors interviewed tended to be completely absorbed in current activities. It has already been pointed out that in this part of the country firms took a pride in being considered technically progressive. In unit production firms, the people interviewed illustrated the technical progressiveness of the firm by referring to work in hand. In the other systems of production greater emphasis was laid on plans for the future and on the large amount of capital being invested in new developments.

The fact that product schedules were based on firm orders only meant that marketing was the first phase of the manufacturing cycle. In many cases it was an idea rather than a product which had to be sold to the customer. The job of the salesman was to convince the customer that the article he required could be produced by the firm. In building up the image of the firm, greater stress was laid on technical expertise and on the quality and efficiency of the products, than on low cost and quick customer service. In all these firms the research workers were told by at least one of the managers interviewed that the firm produced 'not the cheapest but the best'.

The relationship between the firm and its customers was a close and continuing one; contact had to be maintained until each order was complete. One of the most important aspects of the marketing function was to provide a channel of communication between the customer and the development engineers and the production managers working on his order. To do this adequately, the salesman needed to have technical knowledge, not only of the products themselves and of the way they were made, but also of the production facilities available.

This called for a special kind of salesman. Technical qualifications were important, and a large proportion of the sales staff interviewed in unit production firms were graduates in science or engineering. The research showed that there is ambivalence in attitudes towards selling. Many of the salesmen interviewed, including those who admitted that they enjoyed selling, seemed to feel that there was a social stigma attached to it. This raises the interesting question of whether the sales effort throughout the country generally is weakened by social attitudes to selling. Illustrations of this ambivalence could be found in all production categories. In unit production, however, it was general and widespread. Many of the people responsible for selling objected to being referred to as 'salesmen' at all; in four of the six firms studied, the department responsible for obtaining orders was called not the 'sales' or 'marketing' department but the 'commercial' department, and those employed in these departments described themselves as 'technologists'. Few of them had spent their entire career in selling, and when speculating about their future they said there was no reason why they could not be transferred at a similar and higher level to a research or a production department.

Associated with this mobility of staff between departments were two assumptions; first, that a salesman in unit production did not require any special selling skill and, secondly, that sales management was not a specialized function of management. The following remarks were typical:

> To do the job properly, it is important to be good at getting on with people, but in this kind of industry there is no place for highly developed techniques of selling.

> In this firm we have to provide a service to our customers and

advise them about what is technically possible. We do not have to persuade them to buy something they do not want, or try to whet their appetites.

As far as the social structure of the unit production firms was concerned, one result of this attitude towards the sales function was that those responsible for selling were more closely integrated with the staff of other departments than their counterparts in other production categories. They did not get themselves involved in the activities of professional management associations and had little contact with sales personnel outside their own firms.

In the four engineering firms studied, the close integration of sales personnel with the other managers and supervisors was encouraged by the fact that organization was of the product division kind. The marketing function was organized on a product basis. There was a high degree of decentralization, the departments responsible for each product or group of products being almost entirely autonomous. In two firms the different product departments dealt with their own accounts; in the others, however, the accounting was done centrally.

There was a similar product breakdown in the development organization, and to a more limited extent in the production organization also. So there was a tendency for concern with the same product to break down the barriers between functional departments and to cut across departmental loyalties.

Development was the second phase of the manufacturing cycle; research and development were the central and critical activities of unit production, and the development engineers the *élite*. Nearly all the managers and supervisors with the necessary technical qualifications said that they would prefer to work in the development department if they had the choice. In three of the four engineering firms the chief executive had been a development engineer himself; the general impression was that it was only the people who had spent some time on development work who were likely to get to the top of the management ladder.

Research and development personnel spent far more time in the production workshops than their counterparts in the other production categories. Development was closely linked with production engineering; and when production ran into difficulties the development engineers quickly became involved.

A consequence of this was that the drawing offices also had high status, being the main channel of communication between development and production. When the intensive study of factory A was made, it was found that resistance to the change-over from unit production to the standardized production of parts was most marked among the drawing office personnel; the introduction of rationalized production techniques and of such departments as methods engineering and work study changed the function of the draughtsman and undermined his status. The new departments replaced the drawing office as the link between the development and the production departments—with the result that the drawing office became merely a service department. The draughtsmen were disgruntled and frustrated; one way in which this showed itself was that they were joining the appropriate trade union in large numbers. The research workers came to the conclusion that a detailed study of the way in which the increasing rationalization of production is affecting the role of the draughtsman would be extremely interesting and useful in that it might show how the problems arising could be overcome.

Development activity is notoriously difficult to control because of the uncertainty of its outcome. In the majority of the large batch and mass production firms studied, an attempt had been made to control development work, either by setting target dates for the completion of plant and product designs or by budgeting for research and development costs. It was felt that these attempts were not very successful, because if targets were not met or actual costs exceeded budgeted costs, the argument that it was impossible to work well with a gun at your back often provided an effective let-out for the people concerned. In some firms studied, the difficulties of controlling research complicated the relationships with other departments; managers in departments which could be controlled more easily tended to resent the research and development personnel. Several said in interview: 'research people get away with a lot more than anybody else'. This resentment of development personnel by production management was almost entirely confined to the large batch and mass production firms. In unit production, although envy of the high status of development engineers was implied in much of what was said, they were not resented. This was because everyone benefited from the fact that development activity is difficult to control; the dominance of the development functions make pointless the application of rigorous control elsewhere.

As the chief executive of one unit production firm pointed out, 'most of the time and money spent here goes in developing the product, so any attempt to tighten up on the production side would achieve very little and stir up a lot of bad feeling'.

The lack of pressure in unit production firms which had been noticed during the background survey thus seems to be almost entirely due to the dominance of the research and development function. The ethos of the unit production firm is the ethos of research. In unit production, production itself is chronologically the final activity. In three firms the relationship between development and production was complicated by the existence of development workshops under the control of development personnel. Some products were completed and dispatched to customers direct from the development workshops. There seemed to be no clear-cut line of demarcation between the development and the production workshops. In theory, prototypes of a complicated construction that were developed and fabricated simultaneously were the responsibility of the development workshops. In practice, however, there were a large number of other factors influencing the way in which a job was routed. These included the personal interests of the development engineers, the pressure of work in the development and production workshops respectively, and the nature of the product. Because the more complicated work was done in the development workshops, the fitters employed there had the reputation of being better craftsmen than those employed in the production workshops. The latter were often resentful of this.

In one firm a payment-by-results system operated in the production workshops, while those employed in the development workshops were paid on a time basis. In this firm it was not only the more complicated job, but also the jobs on which it was difficult or impossible to put a price, which were sent to the development workshops. The amount of production work that had to be dealt with in this way suggested that a financial incentive is not the most appropriate system of payment for unit and small batch production.

The firm making men's and women's suits to individual orders and the firm making furniture had many characteristics in common with the four engineering firms, although their products were so different. Here too it was difficult to draw a line between development and production functions. The cutting out of a suit, for example, was in part a design and in part a production activity. The most interesting difference between the tailoring firm and the other unit production firms was that the managers and supervisors were working under greater pressure. Each product took a relatively short time to make and target times were set for each stage of manufacture, as keeping to delivery dates was extremely important in building up the firm's reputation. Even so, the pressure was nothing like as great as in a second clothing firm studied, where products were standardized and the production system rationalized.

In most cases the production managers and supervisors in the unit production firms were not as well qualified from a technological point of view as their colleagues in development and sales departments. The proportion of graduate staff was very small. In one firm (the one referred to above where the men in the production workshops were paid on an incentive basis) an attempt was being made to introduce more complicated programming and control techniques, and associated with this there was a move to bring more highly qualified people into production management. These changes were associated with the appointment of a new general manager who had come from the production side himself.

It has already been pointed out that in unit production the main task functions were dependent upon each other and not easily separated in time or place. Close and continuous co-operation was required between the managers and supervisors responsible for development and marketing respectively; the activities of the various departments had to be integrated at a day-to-day operational level. The integration depended almost entirely on interpersonal contacts. Direct and speedy channels of communication between one department and another were essential at every level of the hierarchy. Bridge communications were important, for a crisis occurring at any stage in the manufacturing sequence could quickly involve all departments. The research workers saw this happening on a number of occasions during the course of the field work in the unit production firms. In one firm, for example, a crisis occurred as a result of a failure in the supply of a raw material required for a small component. This led to a modification in the design of the product. Development engineers became involved and in the long run it was also found necessary to refer back to the customer through the commercial department to get the contract modified.

The close integration of functions, the frequent personal contacts, and the lack of pressure associated with the dominance of the development function contributed to the development of good inter-departmental relationships. A feature of all the unit production firms studied was the closely knit homogeneity of the management group. Managers seemed to be as much aware of the overall objectives of the firm as they were of their own sectional interests. It will be seen later that unit production was the only type of industry in which this was the case.

As far as the functions of organization were concerned, there was no doubt that in unit production they were both technical and social. The basic task of organization was to create a mechanism for the co-ordination of work. It seems, however, that there is no conflict between technical and social functions. In unit production the network of relationships required to bring co-ordination about is also conducive to the development of satisfactory social relationships. What is best for production seems also to be best for people.

LARGE BATCH AND MASS PRODUCTION

The five large batch and mass production firms in which the full range of activities was covered were all operating inside the same industry, namely, engineering, four of them being 'federated firms'. Different branches of engineering were represented, however, and the type and range of product was wide. They varied from heavy mechanical engineering to light electrical engineering. Moreover, as far as organization was concerned, they formed a much less homogeneous group than the unit production firms and had different production organization. They had some characteristics in common, though; for example, planning was longer-term than in unit production, and the relationship between development, production, and sales was similar.

The production schedules were not directly dependent on firm orders. Programmes were determined and long-term plans made on the basis of a sales forecast. In three firms, whose products were stable and firmly established with little variety, production was entirely for stock. In the other two there was a mixture of production for stock and production to orders. In one firm where production was for stock, it was initiated by the stores department, the actual authority to manufacture coming from the stores. In all five firms capital costs recurred or products were re-designed at fixed periods. Thus, the life of the firm was in terms of future planning extended beyond the period covered by the order books.

The fact that in theory the future was longer-term did not make these employed feel more secure. It was interesting to note that the unit production firms where theoretically life was short, offered more secure employment conditions than the large batch and mass production firms. At the time of the research, the close relationship between the state of trade and the amount of labour required in large batch production was obvious. Some of the firms studied had been affected by the Suez crisis, and there was a lot of talk about redundancy and the problems associated with it. There was an atmosphere of insecurity which seemed to affect the lower echelons in particular. Their attitudes resembled those of lower grades of supervision in the retail distributive trades who are always made anxious by a worsening of the trading position.

Alongside this fear of redundancy there was optimism about the future of these firms and about their long-term prospects. This optimism was particularly noticeable at middle and upper management levels. Managers were much more interested in the future than their counterparts in unit production. A considerable amount of capital was being expended on development in four of the five firms, and there was a widespread feeling that the recession was temporary, and unlikely to affect pay and prospects. It would appear that one characteristic of this type of industry is a difference in outlook between the lower and upper levels of management, the lower levels being concerned with short-term planning and the problems created for them by fluctuating sales, and the upper levels with long-term planning and future prospects.

The sequence of operations was the same in all five firms, the first phase of manufacture being product development, the second production, and the third marketing. The functions were more independent of each other and more self-contained than in unit production. The research and development departments and programmes were elaborate and extensive in all five firms. Policy decisions taken as a result of product research, however, were long-term and far-reaching; in most cases considerable expenditure was involved. Decisions to modify existing products or to produce new ones in quantity were therefore taken only at the highest level of management. There was a hiatus between product research and production and between production and marketing—particularly in firms where production was mainly for stock.

The independence of functions meant that end results did not depend on the establishment of a close operational relationship between the people responsible for development, production, and sales respectively. This tended to encourage sectional interests and exaggerate departmental loyalties. A frequently encountered organizational problem was that of maintaining an adequate channel of communication between departments which were functionally independent. Although a close working relationship was not required between functions in this type of industry, there had to be exchanges of information between the people responsible. It was important for research managers to be informed about the manufacturing facilities available for new products and the customer's opinion of the firm's products. They had therefore to keep in touch with both production and sales managers. Similarly there were matters of common concern to sales and production personnel. The establishment of adequate communication channels between functions was a more difficult problem than in unit production firms, where information was exchanged freely and frankly as part of a day-to-day operational relationship.

The relationship between development and production was complicated in some cases by the lack of any clear-cut definition of responsibilities and by the tendency, already referred to, to interpret the principle of specialization as being the grouping together of duties requiring similar skills.

The main responsibility of all the research and development departments was the developing or modification of products, and as far as this responsibility was concerned, the relationship between research and production tended to be similar in all firms. In some, however, the development departments had additional responsibilities. In two firms, product development was linked with production engineering, and in a third, the senior executive responsible for research was also responsible for product inspection and testing. These additional responsibilities brought the development and production functions closer together. In another firm, although the bulk of the production was standardized, a few products were made to customers' special orders and the development and production staff had to work closely together on these.

Opinions were divided about whether development personnel should become involved in production routine. The people responsible for planning organization in firms whose development departments were responsible for production engineering or inspection argued that 'involvement in production problems kept the feet of the development staff on the ground'. It was also felt that an association between production and development personnel speeded up the pace of development, making it easier to control.

In the firms with development staff responsible for product development only it was argued equally strongly that the involvement of research people in production problems distracted them from their primary objectives, and slowed the pace. One firm had sited its development laboratories away from the main factory.

The research workers found it impossible, within the limited scope of these studies, to reach any conclusions about where the balance of advantage lay. Generally speaking, it seems that where there is a close association between product and process with single-purpose machinery, there was a lot to be gained from the association of development and production. It was obvious, however, that the attitudes and behaviour of those responsible for development work were influenced by the extent of their involvement in production routine. In firms with a link between the two functions, the development staff knew more about production problems, and the production staff knew more about their firm's research and development programmes. The two groups of staff also saw more of each other, both in the factory and outside.

On the other hand, it seemed that the distraction of the development staff from their primary objective was not the only disadvantage of involvement. The linking of production engineering with product development inevitably seemed to lead to a confusion of roles. The two functions can be incompatible. The basis of the relationship between product development and production is the need to exchange information, but production engineering is an intrinsic element in the process of production management. Anyone concerned with or responsible for both functions is therefore bound to be involved in an extremely complex pattern of role relationships. He is forced to rely on good personal relationships to make his position tenable. Moreover, it can be argued that it is a mistake to take the responsibility for product engineering away from the senior executive responsible for the production function and give it to the senior executive responsible for research.

Confusion of roles was also a problem for the firm that made a few special products to customers' individual requirements. The close co-operation necessary between development and production brought the development engineers on to the shop floor from time to time. Here they became involved in manufacturing problems other than those with which they were immediately concerned. The determination of priorities was a particularly difficult problem for it was sometimes necessary to break into production schedules to get components made for the special order. In these circumstances friction between development and production personnel was almost inevitable.

During the period of the research a dispute started when a foreman accused a development engineer of interfering in something which was not his business and refused to alter the schedules as requested. Senior executives on both sides became involved one by one. The general manager who had finally to arbitrate was also responsible for organization planning. He discussed the incident with one of the research team, condemning all the people concerned for their irrational and irresponsible behaviour. He did not seem to be aware that he was partly to blame himself or that he had allowed an organizational structure to develop which brought research and development people on to the shop floor, without adequately defining areas of responsibility.

In another firm studied, with both standardized and special order production, there was a development workshop in which the special products were assembled, the components being drawn from the stores of the main factory. Normal production routines were not interfered with here and quarrels of the kind described above could not arise.

The difficulties associated with the confusion of roles were probably exaggerated by hostility between research and production personnel. This was a noticeable feature of all the large batch and unit production firms studied. Whereas in unit production everybody benefited from the fact that research activity was difficult to control, pressure being reduced throughout, in large batch and mass production the only result was an uneven application of pressure. In unit production, people responsible for research and development were an *élite*. Their contribution to success and survival was recognized by other managers, who accepted the fact that they were more highly qualified as a right and proper state of affairs; they were therefore in a comparatively happy position. In large batch and mass production firms, the work of the research and development staff could be critical for the firm over a long period but it was not easy for the other managers and supervisors to accept this. The managers and supervisors interviewed in the large batch and mass production firms obviously realized that in the short run the success of the firm depended on the efficiency of the production organization, especially on the progressive reduction of unit costs. They tended to resent the fact that higher qualifications were required for research, and contact with research personnel seemed to arouse feelings of inferiority.

Not only were the production staff resentful of the research staff but the two groups tended to look at things differently. Research staff dissociated themselves from short-term objectives; they were less status-conscious among themselves, less involved in factory politics, and less closely identified with the profit-making ideology which tended to be a dominant feature of the production system of values.

The fact that in some firms research and production staff saw more of each other and knew more about each other's work than was the case elsewhere, did not mean that relationships were better. Indeed, the reverse seemed to be true, for the firm in which the research and production staff spoke most highly of each other was the one whose research laboratories were situated several miles from the main factory. In this firm, physical separation had not prevented the establishment of adequate communication channels. A lot of information was exchanged, the research staff visited the factory, and the production staff the laboratories; to some extent the research-production relationship was based on a guest-host feeling. There was also a good relationship between the research and sales departments; this was the only firm studied where the research department collaborated with the sales department in the interpretation of technical data and results.

It seemed that in the firms where research staff spent some time in the workshops, deliberate attempts were made to keep information from them. One production manager admitted this in an interview: 'These research people are always on our backs, and we have to be very careful what we let them know.'

These case studies suggested that, providing adequate channels of communication can be established, there is a lot to be said for keeping research staff away from production staff, and not allowing them to become involved in production routine. There is a complicating factor, however: while in normal circumstances the co-ordination between research and production is merely a matter of exchanging information, there are occasions when the two functions have to be brought together in an operational relationship—for example, when a new product is being brought into large-scale production.

The firms studied handled this problem in different ways. In three cases a mechanism for affecting the necessary co-operation had been built into the formal organizational structure. One firm had set up a product development department to form a bridge between research and production. This was a busy department, as modifications to existing products were frequently made, and routine procedures had been devised to cover most contingencies. This department will be described in more detail in the next chapter. The rationalization of production processes had gone so far in this firm that by the time the work arrived on the shop floor to be handled by the first-line supervisors, it was almost impossible to distinguish new production from old.

In two firms, changes were more radical, although occurring

less often. In one of these firms the mechanism was a product development committee which met regularly and was responsible for planning changes. In the other a product team consisting of the production and research staff most closely concerned was organized when a new product was being introduced. It met regularly under the chairmanship of the general manager for a limited period until problems arising from the new production had been solved.

In the remaining two firms, top management seemed to take it for granted that the necessary co-operation would come about automatically, and that managers and supervisors normally suspicious of each other and on the defensive would work together on an operational level when asked to do so. It was not surprising to find that change and innovation were resisted more strongly and created more problems in these two firms than in the first three.

As implied already, the critical and central activity of large batch and mass production was production itself, and it was in the organization of production that differences between firms were most marked. The differences will be described in more detail in the following chapter; briefly, firms varied not only in the extent to which their production processes were rationalized and the administration of production separated from the supervision of production operations, but also in the effectiveness of their programming and control procedures. Shortages of parts, tools, and materials, and failures to get orders out on time occurred more frequently in some firms than others.

The importance of the production function conferred status on the managers and supervisors concerned with production, but they were not an *élite* like research managers in unit production firms. This was because the situation was complicated by the separation of the 'brainwork' of production from the supervision of production operations. Those concerned with the administrative element in the production functions were increasing their status at the expense of those responsible for production supervision. The managers responsible for financial control and for production engineering formed two high-status groups. In the two firms where production engineering was associated with product development, the latter function had acquired a higher status than the production function.

The draughtsmen working in large batch and mass production firms did not occupy the critical communicating position occupied by their counterparts in unit production firms. They did a variety of jobs and provided a service. Their drawings were translated into manufacturing instructions and programmes by production administration departments; draughtsmen working in the firms studied were seldom in contact with the workshops.

Marketing was the final phase of manufacture in this type of industry. The relationship between production and marketing, like that between production and research, was an uneasy one. Many of the managers and supervisors interviewed on the production side were on the defensive in discussing their relationship with sales personnel. Here again the relationship tended to be worse when the two groups saw a lot of each other. This was mainly because in most firms they came into contact only when things were going wrong. Apart from routine exchanges of information, their main common concern was the meeting of delivery dates. Where production administration was efficient, or production mainly for stock, sales managers had very little to do with production managers. The firms in which they had most to do with each other placed great emphasis on quick customer service, and consequently the sales department put pressure on the production department to get work out.

The primary task of the sales departments of large batch and mass production firms was to persuade the customer that he wants the goods the firm produces. This required relatively little technical knowledge of either the products themselves or the production processes. The proportion of staff with scientific or engineering qualifications in the sales departments of the large batch and mass production firms was smaller than it was either in other departments of the same firm, or in the sales departments of the firms in the other two production categories. A few of the sales staff interviewed had economics or psychology degrees, but they tended to occupy staff rather than line roles, responsible for ancillary activities such as sales forecasting, advertising, and market research, rather than for the marketing of the actual products.

Although not so highly qualified technically as their counterparts in other types of industry, sales managers were more specialized. A larger proportion had attended special courses or obtained special qualifications. They were also more interested in the activities of the professional management associations. Only a very small proportion of the people interviewed had moved into a sales department from another department of the same firm. The majority had either been trained and upgraded in the department in which they were currently employed, or came into the firm at middle management level from a sales department of another firm. One result of this was that in the firms without operational contact between production and sales staff there was little social contact. In two firms, the middle managers on the sales side did not even know the names of the managers at a similar level in the production and research departments. One of these was a firm employing over 10,000, size alone making inter-departmental contact difficult, but the other employed only 2,000; and as all the middle managers used the same canteen, the lack of contact between sales and other staff was particularly surprising.

It was interesting to find that, generally speaking, the people most involved in the affairs of professional management associations were least involved in the internal politics of their firm. The increasing professionalization of society is reflected in the growth of management associations; this growth may well be encouraged by the isolation of the various departmental groups inside the factory. Participation in the activities of management associations may provide compensation for inadequate contact or unsatisfactory relationships at work; and as rationalization and technical development make the co-ordination of industrial activities less and less dependent on inter-personal contacts, professional management associations may gain in strength and importance.

The greater independence of the basic functions of manufacture in large batch and mass production meant that the senior executives resonsible for development, production, and marketing were more autonomous than their counterparts in unit production. They rarely became involved in each other's operational or organization problems. On the sales side, for example, policy decisions about how far the sales function should be decentralized, or whether a territorial sales force should be built up, were usually taken by the senior executive in consultation with the chief executive. Other managers were only brought into the discussions where they were directly involved. In one firm each sales manager was associated with a particular production unit; the firm had a number of units scattered throughout the country whose products were similar. Here a proposed change in the organization of the sales department was going to affect the production schedule in the various units, and the production manager had therefore to be consulted.

Organizational structure being much more segmented in large batch and mass production than in unit production, the total picture was of a less homogeneous management group. Managers and supervisors were more closely identified with their functions; they were in different reference groups and concerned as much if not more with their own sectional interests than with the overall objectives of their firms. These sectional interests were sometimes in conflict, and as a result functional departments were hostile and suspicious in their relationship with each other.

Large batch production resembled unit production, however, in that organization has to serve both technical and social ends. In the firm in which changes in products were rare and manufacturing processes highly rationalized, the control system provided a mechanism for the co-ordination of work. In the other four firms the provision of this mechanism was the main function of organization.

These studies showed that in large batch and mass production the technical and the social ends of organization can conflict. Doubt was also thrown on whether they can ever be completely reconciled. It was evident, as we have seen, that the network of relationships best for production is not necessarily the best for people. If technical ends are well served the result will be commercial success; if social ends are well served the result is likely to be a satisfactory and co-operative staff. Technical ends may best be served by conflict and pressure. Many of the conflicts that occurred in the firms studied seemed to be constructive by making a contribution to end results, and it was certainly not true to say that the most successful firms were those with the best relationships and closest identification between the staff and the company. So in large batch and mass production the organization planners have a twofold problem: they have to consider not only how to reconcile technical and social ends, but also how end results will be affected if they try to do so.

PROCESS PRODUCTION

In process production the sequence and weighting of the manufacturing functions were different again. Moreover task functions were more widely separated from each other; in the case of two firms the research workers had to go outside the area to complete the picture. One process firm, omitted from this part of the analysis, had its main development laboratories overseas and its marketing done by a separate company.

But there is a danger of presenting an over-simplified picture, for one characteristic of process production is that product development breaks down into three distinct and almost autonomous stages. Not only did all the process production firms have their research laboratories under separate control from their development laboratories, but they also had a department called the works chemical or technological department responsible for the final stages of product development. The relationship with other manufacturing activities differed at each of these stages of product development.

In every case the first two stages came at the beginning of the manufacturing cycle. Research laboratories were almost entirely occupied with pure research; from what they said, the staff in these laboratories regarded their objective as being more the extension of knowledge in the field in which the firm was operating than the development of any specific new products. They were remote from the day-to-day activities of the factory, knew very little about what managers and supervisors in other departments did, and certainly did not involve themselves in factory politics. The atmosphere was very like that in university research laboratories or other research organizations. What they said about their firm indicated that they regarded it more as a provider of research funds than as their employer in the accepted sense. The senior executive operated as the functional leader of a research team. There was very little co-ordination even in the exchange of information between this stage of product development and other factory activities. In some cases it was positively discouraged; the research workers were told that 'a firm needs to be very discreet about its fundamental research as competitors can benefit from information that leaks out'.

Managers and supervisors in other departments seemed to know very little about the research laboratories and what went on there. In most cases they were not interested, although a few references were made to the fact that secrecy was exaggerated. They had a respect for the higher qualifications of the research staff, and seemed to regard research of a more fundamental kind as a prestige activity. A number of people laid stress on the contribution the firm was making to social welfare generally. This was particularly the case in the pharmaceutical chemical firms studied. It was interesting to find that in all the firms included in this group, the number of people employed in the research laboratories had more than doubled during the ten years 1946–56.

The development laboratories on the other hand were responsible for applying knowledge acquired at the pure research stage to the development of specific products. The relationship between them and other manufacturing activities was based on co-ordination of the exchange of information kind and in this respect they could be compared with product development departments in large batch and mass production firms.

On the whole, however, relationships were better. Several factors contributed to this comparative harmony. In the first place (as the background survey had already shown) pressure on people was less in this type of industry than any other, and what pressure there was tended to be evenly distributed between departments. This made the development of satisfactory inter-personal and inter-departmental relationships easier at all levels.

A second factor was that managers and supervisors employed on development work seldom became involved in plant problems. This involvement was reserved for the works chemical or technological department responsible for the third stage of development, about which more will be said later; it was these departments which were the trouble spots as far as relationships with production were concerned.

Thirdly, the education and training background of the managers and supervisors in process production employed on product development was similar to that of the production managers. Managers and supervisors were interchangeable between development laboratories, and production departments; and were not only aware of each other's difficulties and problems, but also of the fact that one day they might find themselves tackling these problems.

In all four firms, the research laboratories and the development laboratories were brought together in organization at the second level down, the department being responsible to a senior executive, who himself was directly responsible to the chief executive. In two cases this senior executive had been promoted from research and in the other two from development. The background of the senior executive had a bearing on the relationship not only between the departments under his control, but also on the development-production relationships. In the two firms where he had a research background, those employed in the development laboratories seemed to have a feeling of inferiority and were more remote from their research colleagues. The effect of this was to bring them closer to the production and marketing departments.

In the two firms where the senior executive had a development background, the relationship between research and development was much closer, the two departments regarding themselves as equal in status. This meant that there was a wider gulf between development and other manufacturing activities. In both these firms reference was made by some of the marketing personnel to the difficulties they experienced in getting information from the development laboratories, and to the fact that development staff paid little attention to suggestions coming from the production side.

It was between the second and third stages of product development that the main marketing activity fitted into the manufacturing sequence. The disposal of products after manufacture was largely a routine matter, the most important task of the marketing department being to find an assured market for new products. The decision to proceed to the third stage of product development and to manufacture in bulk depended on the finding of a market. Taking the fine and pharmaceutical chemical industry, for example, only in exceptional cases is there a market waiting for a new drug. Penicillin and polio vaccine were in demand before they were produced commercially, but the vast majority of new pharmaceutical products are sent out and tested by representatives of the medical profession. Large-scale production begins only when the chances of selling the new medicines seem to be good.

The oil industry too has to be sure of a market for a product before capital is invested in a new plant. Drucker (1956) gives an example of the lengths to which a firm will go in order to create a market.[2] He tells how at the beginning of this century the Standard Oil Company of New Jersey distributed kerosene lamps, free of charge, to Chinese peasants in order to obtain a market for kerosene, the by-product of a new refining process. Nothing as dramatic as this was encountered during the research, but the research workers heard a great deal about efforts being made to find markets for the products of the rapidly developing petroleum chemicals industry.

This securing of markets was important not only because of the heavy capital expenditure involved in plant installation, but also because it is on the steady absorption of its products that the efficient operation of a plant depends. In all process production firms studied, either the products themselves were difficult or impossible to store, or the storage capacity was extremely limited; production flow was therefore directly and immediately determined by the market situation. This is also true in large batch production, of course. But unlike large batch production, a drop in output in process industry does not have an immediate effect upon the labour required; a plant not working to full capacity requires its full labour complement and is more difficult and expensive to run. This means that a drop in sales does not, in the short term at least, create anxiety among the labour force.

The importance of securing a market put the marketing function into a dominant position. Marketing was the central and critical activity of process production, and in all the process production firms studied, the marketing departments were high-status departments; a lot of effort was put into making them efficient. A large proportion of the managers and supervisors employed in them had university degrees or professional qualifications, and there was less ambivalence in attitudes towards the selling function than in other types of industry. Few people interviewed appeared to feel that there was any social stigma in being associated with selling.

As far as the technical knowledge required was concerned, the emphasis was on how the products could be used rather than on

[2] Peter Drucker, *The Practice of Management* (Heinemann, London, 1956).

how they could be made. There was therefore a high degree of identification with the customer. It also meant that the marketing personnel, although as well qualified as their counterparts on the production side, had qualifications of a different kind. In the marketing department of a firm making fine chemicals, for example, there were people with medical, pharmaceutical, and veterinary qualifications; the production personnel, on the other hand, were mainly chemists or chemical engineers. The different backgrounds of the people concerned seemed to widen the gulf between the two functions. Professional groups do not appear to find it easy to work closely together in industry. It was found for example that one result of the increasing tendency to package drugs was that problems of relationships arose when pharmacists were brought into association with chemists in the production departments of chemical firms.

The gulf between the two functions, although exaggerated by the different backgrounds of the people concerned, was in any case inevitable. The independence of the basic functions in the process firms meant that those who were involved in the important job of finding markets were in normal circumstances completely dissociated from the day-to-day operation of the plant. Only in one firm studied was there any operational co-ordination between production and marketing, and even in this case only one product was involved. This firm made bitumen, and the special problems of storage and delivery made it necessary for the plant manager concerned to keep in close touch not only with those responsible for disposing of the product but also with the customers.

Thus, although the marketing departments had high status, the people employed in them were not sufficiently well-known to be an *élite* like the development engineers in unit production.

One of the most interesting characteristics of the social structure of the process firm studied was that it consisted of a social system within a social system. In each firm a very close network of relationships had been built around the operation of the plant. This network will be described in more detail in the following chapter; it had its own status system, system of communication, and authority. The people who were in any way concerned with the operation of the plant satisfied their social needs in relation to work entirely inside this network of relationships. The plant chemist, for example, was very concerned about his status in relation to that of the plant engineer, but not at all interested in his relative position in the wider social system of his firm, or in where he stood in relation to the marketing managers.

But although they were excluded from the network of social relationships centring round the plant, few marketing personnel sought compensation by associating themselves with professional management associations. They showed much less interest than their counterparts in large batch and mass production firms. This may have been because their status was unquestioned and their job a critical one from which a great deal of satisfaction was derived. Or, because of the critical nature of their function, they were working under greater pressure than their colleagues in other departments. It must also be remembered that they had close ties with their customers; in this they were like their counterparts in unit production, and these ties probably helped to compensate for lack of social contacts at work.

The third stage of product development, the stage covered by the works chemical or technological departments, was more closely linked with production than with research; these departments were an intrinsic part of the inner social system of that plant. Their responsibilities included setting up and operating pilot plants, supervising the installation of new plants, and operating either the newly installed plants, or any existing plants making new products during the experimental stages. In two firms they were also responsible for increasing the efficiency of existing plants, being actively and continuously involved in production routines.

The relationship between these departments and the production departments was not unlike that between product development and production in the large batch and mass production firms, where product engineering was linked with product development. There was a similar confusion of roles and the situation was further complicated by the fact that they also fulfilled the functions of a product development department providing a bridge between development and production. In two firms the works chemical or technological departments were responsible to the senior executive in charge of research; in the other two to the senior executive responsible for production. The place on the organization chart did not appear to affect the relationship with other departments. In all these firms the production managers and supervisors interviewed were more hostile to these departments than to any of the others. Quarrels between their staff and pro- duction managers were not, however, as intense as inter-depart- mental quarrels in large batch production. The reasons for this were probably those mentioned already; the more harmonious relationships existing in process industry generally and the greater homogeneity in the background and training of the different managers. Staff were interchangeable, and as all the process firms studied were developing rapidly at the time of the research, there was a lot of movement between the production and either the works chemical or the technological departments.

As in unit production, production itself came at the end of the manufacturing cycle. The controllability and predictability of production results made the organization of production a relatively simple matter. There were variations in production schedules. In three cases these were worked out by production managers on the basis of information supplied by the marketing division; in the fourth firm the technological department acted as intermediary. This gave the technological department yet another function: it was responsible for passing all communications between produc- tion and other departments. It was therefore a very powerful and high-status department; it operated as the nerve centre of the production organization and was actively involved in such matters as estimates and budgeting. But production schedules could vary only within fixed limits, and planning was much longer-term than in other types of industry. While the research was in progress a butane plant was installed in one firm and it was thought that it would take twenty years to recover the capital expended, assuming that the plant would work at full capacity. The long-term plan- ning, together with the fact that there was no direct relationship between output and either effort or the amount of labour required, made employment very much more secure in process production than in other types of industry.

The basic tasks of manufacture in process production firms, the development of a new product, the finding of a market, and production, are more independent of each other than in any other system. The result, however, is not so much a segmented structure as a two-dimensional one. There is an inner ring centred on the plant itself and between the people in this ring and the peripheral departments such as the research laboratories and marketing departments, there is very little co-ordination. As we have seen, in unit production and large batch and mass production, organization has to serve both technical and social ends; the co-ordination of basic activities depends upon organization, the difference between these two types of production being that whereas in unit production there is no conflict between technical and social ends, in large batch and mass production such conflict can and does arise.

Process production is different again. This is the type of industry where organization does not have to provide a mechanism for the co-ordination of work; its main purpose is therefore social. Inside the inner ring the plant itself provides a framework of discipline, control, and co-ordination. As far as commercial success is concerned, the form of organization is comparatively unimportant. There is therefore no reason why the organization planner should not concentrate on building an organizational structure which meets the needs of the people employed. The fact that organization does not provide the mechanism for the co-ordination of work may be the fundamental reason why relationships between development, production, and marketing were more harmonious in process firms than in large batch and mass production firms, even though roles were in general less clearly defined.

9 The Planning and Control of Production

Turning from the general overall organizational structure of the firms covered by the research, to the more detailed examination of the way in which the production operations themselves were planned and controlled it was found that there was considerably more data on which to draw. All the firms in which these follow-up studies were made were production units, either self-contained or associated with larger organizations, and as the emphasis of the studies had been on the examination of manufacturing processes, much of the time in each firm had been spent in discussing the planning and control of production and the problems of production personnel.

The analysis of these data was based on the assumption that the production task breaks down into elements, each having the same means-end relationship to it as to the overall objectives of the firm. The main element functions associated with production are planning, execution and control, and closely related to planning are the service elements concerned with the maintenance of plant and machinery and the supply of materials, tools, and personnel. Planning denotes the activities which precede execution and control. The object of the analysis was to see how the firms studied varied in the extent to which they differentiated between element functions, what the relationship was between them, and their relative importance. Here again, an attempt was made to relate these variations to differences in technology.

The picture that emerged was rather different from the one obtained earlier. A link between organization and technology was not always apparent. Production organization did not appear to be as closely related to the scale of technology illustrated in Fig. 11 as other aspects of organization. In the categories at the extremes of the scale there were no problems. Three firms dealt with special orders one at a time in chronological sequence; in these firms production organization was identical. The four process production firms of the single-purpose plant type[1] were also alike organizationally in most respects. But between these two extremes a relationship between production organization and technology was difficult to establish. The general impression obtained from the background survey—that there was greater variation in the way production operations were planned and controlled in firms in the middle ranges of the scale—was confirmed by the follow-up studies.

A partial explanation of the differences could be found in the inadequacy of the scale by which technology had been measured. The classification was admittedly a very crude one, and on closer examination it was found that firms put into the same categories were not always as technically alike as had originally been supposed. The dangers of breaking down the technical spectrum into categories were apparent: the problem of placing boundaries between categories, for instance. In particular such factors as batch size and product diversity overlooked in the original classification were now seen to be important.

But even allowing for the inadequacy of the measuring instrument, the impression was confirmed that, as far as the organization of production was concerned, situational demands impose themselves more rigidly and obviously at the extremes than in the middle of the scale. Those responsible for organization planning have less room for manœuvre. There are few alternative ways of organizing production in a special order production firm, and an unsatisfactory structure seems to show itself immediately in a decline in business success. As has already been pointed out, in the less technically advanced firm organization provides the basis for the co-ordination of work. In the process firm, on the other hand, organization serves primarily social ends and any failure to satisfy these ends is immediately reflected in confused and conflicting role relationships. Situational demands therefore are largely related to social control.

[1] Category IX of Fig. 11, p. 39.

In the middle ranges of the technical scale there seemed to be not only a greater choice for organization planners, but an unsuitable form of organization had little immediate impact on business success. Thus, although technology remained an important variable, other variables were equally important.

Before going on to suggest possible reasons for this, or to discuss the technical and structural variations between the firms studied in the middle ranges of the technical scale, a brief description is given of the production organization characteristic of special order production and single-purpose plant production, to provide a basis of comparison.

SPECIAL ORDER PRODUCTION

The first characteristic which unit production firms dealing with special orders one at a time, in ordered sequence, had in common was that the chief executive rather than the board played the major part in determining objectives as well as manufacturing policy. The board did little more than define the field of operations and review results. This was because the formulation of policy involved the making of numerous decisions, all relatively short-term and of almost equal importance. A policy decision was made each time an order was accepted, but it committed the company only for the period the order took to complete. This period could be several years. In one firm studied, for example, large and complicated transmission equipment was being made; nevertheless, the time span of decision in special order production was short in comparison with other types of production.

Because policy decisions were made in relation to specific products, they were frequently modified in the course of production. As seen in the last chapter, a crisis arising at any stage in the manufacturing cycle quickly involved all basic functions and often led to changed specifications. Thus, policy decisions were not only numerous and short-term, but also tended to emerge out of problem-solving decisions. The distinction between crisis and policy decisions was in no way clear-cut.

Another characteristic of this type of production was the lack of differentiation between the functions of planning, execution, and control. There was little specialization, the man responsible for operations being generally responsible for the other elements in the production process. Moreover, it was difficult to distinguish between these three functions on a time basis. Planning continued after execution had begun, and control was exercised from the moment the work was put in hand.

The planning element (the translating of objectives into an activity sequence) was relatively simple, although each order had to be planned individually for production. There seemed to be a closer link between the determination of objectives and planning in this type of production than in batch production. It will be seen later that in some of the batch production firms studied, vagueness and inconsistency in the determination of objectives made the task of those responsible for planning extremely difficult at times. The fact that the chief executive of the special order production firms played so large a part in the determination of objectives probably ensured that they were based on a realistic assessment of available facilities. Moreover, if problems did arise the modification of policy was a relatively easy matter.

In all three firms the production manager's office was the centre of information. This flowed in from the chief executive or from the research and development organization via the drawing office. The production manager was usually quite clear about what he was trying to achieve and was responsible for making the most effective use of his resources to evaluate performance and take any corrective action required.

The linking of the responsibility for planning and control with the responsibility for execution persisted right down the line. The foremen looked to the production manager's office for specifications and bills of material, and for advice about methods of manufacture and the general sequence in which the work was wanted. The detailed organization of the work was left entirely to them, and as the division of responsibilities was based on product rather than on type of operation, there were considerable planning and control elements in their jobs.

The same was true of the production operator's job. In many firms he was responsible for determining the method and sequence of operations, as well as for the quality of the finished product. This linking of production operations with production administration meant that at every level of the hierarchy a wider area of discretion was allowed to the individual than in other types of production.

There appeared to be no sense of urgency in the production departments in any of the unit production firms. Reference has already been made to the protection from pressure which is afforded by a large development content in the process of manufacture. The close association between the individual salesman and the customer, another characteristic of this type of production did, however, lead to the application of some pressure. A salesman trying to satisfy a customer would do his best to get his particular job speeded up. When any enquiry was initiated, someone from the production office would tend to go out into the shops and search for that particular order or its component parts. When it was found an attempt would be made to persuade the foreman concerned to give it precedence. If he agreed, the other orders would be thrown out of sequence. The situation could get out of control; in one section of a firm studied, one order after another had been chased; the end result being that all the work had been labelled urgent—and the original sequence of jobs re-established.

The strengths and weaknesses of special order production as a system of technology are obvious. Its great advantage—flexibility —carries with it the corollary of inefficiency in the sense that it is extravagant in its use of facilities and that the highest level of efficiency cannot be achieved in relation to any single operation. Technical inefficiency does not necessarily result in commercial failure; as the background survey showed, the chances of success in this type of production were much the same as in others. The important part played in the successful operation of the special order firm by the skill and ingenuity of those responsible for research and development, has already been noted. This does not mean that the effectiveness of the production operations is entirely irrelevant. It is important to draw a distinction between the technical inefficiency which is intrinsic to special order production and management inefficiency in the broader sense. Management efficiency in the special order firm depends entirely on the efficiency of individuals. Each order handled in the production shops of the firms studied created a new problem and demanded individual attention. There was no automatic rhythm of production to keep output flowing. The difficulties of measuring the tasks involved meant that the line supervisor had to act intuitively when trying to balance requirements against production capacity. The difficulties of measuring also created problems of control, and as a result the exercise of self-control was essential to successful operation. As far as production organization was concerned, it was the line supervisor's skill in making wise clinical judgments on which the strength of the special order firm rested.

The research workers were unfortunate in not having the opportunity to study an unsuccessful unit production firm; all three firms have been classified in the 'average' or 'above average' success categories. They were not able to compare the calibre of management and supervision in successful and unsuccessful firms. Those interviewed in the unit production firms were impressive in comparision with their counterparts in batch and mass production. They did not lag behind in their outlook, and were very concerned that methods and equipment were kept up to date. There was a high degree of involvement in the affairs of the company, and a responsible attitude to work was noticeable at all levels in the hierarchy down to and including the operators themselves. Although there was a lack of pressure and little sense of urgency in the production shops studied, the impression gained was of hard and consistent work.

Special order firms rely on the effectiveness of individuals, and individuals appear to respond. The nature of the work itself, and the sense of responsibility associated with it, is obviously an important factor. The satisfactory situation cannot be explained in terms of individual motivation alone, however; theories of group behaviour are also useful in its analysis. As we have seen, there was no conflict between the technical system and the social system in unit production. The network of relationships demanded by production was satisfactory to the people involved, because role conflicts and cross-pressures were at a minimum and there were no mutually inconsistent demands.

The research workers found that in all the firms studied in this category there was an alignment of formal and informal organization. Those employed seemed to have little difficulty in accepting management's definition of their primary task. Selznick (1956)[2] suggests that alignment of this kind which makes it possible for the constituent groups of an organization to work well together depends on the making of administrative decisions which define

[2] Philip Selznick, *Leadership in Administration* (Ron Peterson, New York).

aims and values, and create a social structure to embody them. He says that this can only be done by paying special attention to decisions affecting the basic character of the enterprise. Rice (1958) says something similar, pointing out that groups which find it difficult to accept management's view of their primary task tend (consciously or unconsciously) to redefine it.[3]

The appreciation of aims and values characteristic of special order production which leads to a satisfactory social structure seems to depend upon the close link between policy making and planning, the definition of objectives, and their translation into an ordered sequence of actvities. This ensures that means and ends are kept in balance and that the relevance of primary tasks to organizational objectives is always apparent.

Unit production may be technically inefficient, but from the point of view of social organization it is undoubtedly the most effective system of production. This effectiveness is a compensating advantage often overlooked by production engineers concerned with the rationalization of manufacturing processes: in particular, with extending rationalization to a wider area of technology.

SINGLE-PURPOSE PLANT PRODUCTION

Reference has already been made to the two dimensional structure associated with process production. In the process firm, therefore, a study of production organization involved a study of the inner social system centring round the plant itself. Technically and economically, process production is at the opposite end of the scale from unit production, but from a social organization point of view this inner system was surprisingly similar to the social system of the special order production firms studied. There was the same identification of formal and informal organization, and although instances of role conflict were found, the general impression in all the process firms studied was of a satisfying social group life.

It was interesting to find that where role conflicts did occur, they did not lead to stress situations of the kind encountered in the large batch production firms. The higher level of sophistication and education of those employed in this type of production may

[3] A. K. Rice, *Productivity and Organization* (Tavistock Publications).

have enabled them to deal with role conflicts intellectually rather than emotionally. As Bion (1961)[4] points out, the sophisticated group tends to respond to situations of stress by 'working through' to a solution of its problems and dealing with the realities of the situation, whereas the less sophisticated group tends to 'act out' its response; one way of doing this being to attack or blame individuals, groups, institutions, or ideas to which the stress can be attributed.

Allowing for the fact that the high standard of relationships revealed could have been due in part to a more sophisticated approach, the technology of process production did in itself appear to provide a mechanism for the satisfaction of social and psychological needs. It had two important characteristics in common with special order production: a definition of the primary task not only clear-cut but acceptable to those employed, and a close association of the planning, execution, and control elements in the production function.

This clear definition of the primary task did not depend (as it did in unit production) on the close association of the chief executive with policy making and planning. As far as the inner social system of the process firm was concerned, the making of manufacturing policy was a remote activity. Policy decisions were fewer than in batch or unit production, but committed firms further into the future. The meetings attended at the headquarter's organization of firm C—one of the firms in which the intensive studies were made—were concerned with the erection of a plant to produce petroleum gases which was likely to take three years to build and twenty years to give an adequate return on the investment. Not all policy decisions were as long-term as this. Nevertheless, most decisions were too long-term to be the responsibility of one individual and the organizational structure had to allow for joint decisions by senior management. More policy decisions were made at board level in process industry than in other systems of production.

For the purposes of the background survey, the chief executive had been defined as the highest level of authority operating full-time on the spot. Only in two of the process firms was this the head of the organization, as the other four were units of larger

4 W. R. Bion, *Experience in Groups* (Tavistock Publications).

organizations. Even in the self-contained process firms, however, the chief executive was outside the inner social system and—as in the other four process production firms—the highest level of operating and identifiable authority for those concerned with production was the senior production executive. These works or refinery managers were rarely involved in the determination of objectives, except as members of the board or other policy-making bodies. They had no individual responsibility for policy making, and were rarely required to translate policy into action.

Nevertheless there was a close link between policy making and planning. This was because the sequence of activities was usually built into the plant or equipment at the construction stage. This meant that objectives had to be clearly and precisely defined at that stage. In process production of the single-purpose plant type there was little danger of means determining ends. The research workers became aware during the second stage of the research that a framework of discipline and control provided by the plant controlled not only those who operated it, but also those responsible for making policy decisions in relation to it. When embarking on the construction of a new plant, management were forced to be precise and consistent about what they were trying to achieve.

The incorporation of much of the planning function into the construction of the plant ensured that the management's objectives were obvious to production personnel. The stage was set; all the production personnel had to do was to maintain the established sequence of activities by keeping the plant running as near to full capacity as possible. Everybody interviewed in process industry showed that they understood and accepted this as their primary task. The chief executive of one of the firms studied, when asked how he would assess the capabilities of his plant managers, or measure their success, replied without hesitation 'by the number of days in the year they can keep their plants running'. He went on to say:

> I would obviously be concerned with the effective use of resources, materials, manpower, steam, etc., but the cost of having a plant shut down is so great and the effect of delays in production so far-reaching, that I would be prepared to accept a certain amount of inefficiency in these respects in the interests of keeping the plant

running. The effective use of resources is not an end in itself and I have to be careful not to let the tail wag the dog.

It seems, therefore, that a mechanism for management control is also built into the plant. This was true in a general sense in all the process firms studied, individual performance being evaluated in terms of the satisfactory operation of the plant. In the recently erected plants it was also true in a more particular sense. Mechanisms for process control, evaluating performance, and initiating corrective action were being increasingly incorporated into the plants themselves.

The reduction of independent planning and control activities to a minimum threw increased emphasis on production itself. It was found, for example, that inside the inner social system of the process firm the *élite* consisted of the people responsible for plant operation. This was true both of management and operator level. The status of the plant manager was enhanced by his responsibility for the safety of anybody coming into his plant. Such independent planning and control activities as did exist were the responsibility of production management in most of the process firms. They were also responsible for labour planning and control. There was also a growing tendency for routine tests of quality not incorporated into the process itself to be undertaken by process operators, under the supervision of plant managers.

The most difficult problem in all the process firms studied was the establishment of satisfactory relations between operating personnel and the personnel of maintenance departments and works chemical or technological departments. There was considerable conflict and hostility in these relationships. This was partly due to the high status given to operating personnel; staff of other departments were jealous of their position. This did not provide a complete explanation, however, for it was found that although the status of the operating departments was similar in all firms, the quality of relationships varied from one firm to another.

Strangely enough, the difficulties seemed to be greatest in the firms with the most highly developed organization-consciousness, in which most thought was given to relationship problems. This seemed to be so because conscious planning usually implies an acceptance of the line-staff convention and an organizational structure of the departmentalized kind. As already indicated, this is a form of organization less appropriate to process than to other types of production. In the firm in which conscious planning of organization was most developed, with a responsible organization department, a very complicated structure based on a differentiation between functions had been built up and superimposed on the natural framework of discipline and control provided by the plants themselves. Following the Urwick principle of specialization, a very large maintenance organization had been set up, all the repair and construction work being brought together under a single control. Moreover, the breakdown within this maintenance organization was also based on the nature of the work. The instrument department, for example, was responsible for all the instrument fitting throughout the firm, the object being to ensure the efficient and economic use of labour by bringing together the people with similar knowledge and skills. The effect of this form of organization was to separate the task of maintaining the plant from the task of operating it. Maintenance had become an end in itself rather than a means to an end, and a secondary system of technology set up. The maintenance organization had many of the characteristics of the jobbing and small batch production firms studied; the attitudes and behaviour of the maintenance personnel being different in many respects from those of the operating personnel.

The fixing of priorities in routine maintenance and emergency repairs was the responsibility of the senior executive on the maintenance side. This meant that he was at loggerheads with many of the plant managers. Every plant manager interviewed regretted the fact that there was no one with special responsibility for the maintenance of his particular plant.

The fact that there were two primary tasks and two cultures inside the organization made conflicts between operating and maintenance personnel, difficult to resolve. As Coser (1956)[5] points out, internal conflicts in which the contending parties do not share the basic values on which the legitimacy of the social system rests and see their primary task in different terms, tend to disrupt the structure itself. The research workers came to the

[5] Lewis A. Coser, *The Functions of Social Conflict* (Routledge, Kegan Paul).

conclusion that it was only the high level of sophistication, characteristic of process industry, of the people concerned, and the tolerance of conflict resulting from it which made the organization viable.

At the other extreme, as far as production organization was concerned, was a firm in which the operation and maintenance of each plant or section of plant was brought together under a single control. Plant managers had their own maintenance teams. This arrangement was more the result of historical development than of conscious planning. The firm was one of the oldest in the area and like other firms in the heavy chemical and oil industries, had employed less highly qualified men on the engineering than on the production side before the 1939–45 war. Even at that time a large proportion of the plant managers had been graduates, whereas the people responsible for maintenance had mostly been ex-ship engineers. Thus the higher status of the operating personnel had been accentuated by educational differences; the engineers had been made subordinate to the plant managers and had had relatively little chance of being promoted to top management.

This firm had its problems too, but there were far fewer disruptions than in the firm described above. One difficulty had arisen from the recruitment of graduate engineers after 1946 and the emergence of chemical engineers. The more highly qualified maintenance personnel resented their subordination to the operating managers. The position had become even more difficult, as technical developments and highly automatic plant meant that keeping the plant running was more a maintenance than an operating task. The research workers listened to a number of heated arguments as to whether a chemist or an engineer was better qualified to take charge of a chemical plant. An attempt to solve this problem was being made; when vacancies for plant managers occurred, some were filled by engineers. This broke down the barriers that had kept the engineers out of top management positions. It was decided not to departmentalize the organizational structure in the way described above.

Another problem was the organization of maintenance personnel on a plant basis, which meant that craftsmen sometimes had to accept men as supervisors who had served apprenticeships in trades other than their own. On the other hand there were far fewer demarcation disputes than in the firm described above, where organization was on a craft basis. Thus it was difficult to decide where the balance of advantage lay as far as industrial relations were concerned.

From time to time the senior executives in this firm became worried about whether they were using labour extravagantly. Sometimes the maintenance men on one plant were slack while those on another were working overtime. But the proportion of total turnover allocated to wages and salaries in this firm was much the same as in other process firms. If the system was extravagant, therefore, this was relatively unimportant when set against a wider background of cost structure. The system certainly seemed far more economical of management time; there were fewer 'crisis' meetings and arguments about priorities of work between one plant manager and another. The advantage of this form of organization seemed to be that it concentrated more attention on the primary task and involved people more in the firm's objectives than the form of organization described above.

The production organization of the other process firms fell between these two extremes. There was a separation between operating and maintenance, but the two departments were organized on a similar basis; the unit of organization was the plant itself, each operational manager having a counterpart on the engineering side. Relationships between the plant managers and plant engineers seemed to be better when they were located together in a plant office than when one or both of them were housed in a more remote administrative headquarters. Plant loyalties developed, cutting across inter-departmental loyalties. These firms naturally had some of the problems and some of the advantages of each of the other two.

The relationship between the works chemical or technical departments and the operating departments also seemed better where it was organized on a plant basis. In the firm with the most harmonious relationships the plant technologist and his staff shared an office block with the operating and engineering management. Conflicts between works chemical and operating departments were usually resolved more easily than conflicts between maintenance and operating departments. The people concerned had similar backgrounds and experience, and in most firms there was interchange of staff between these departments.

The main function of the works chemical departments was development. They were involved in the only phase of research activity represented inside the inner social system of the plant. Their main responsibilities were to bring new plants into operation and to modify older plants. The conflicts were functional and similar in character to those found in unit production and in the batch production firms whose development engineers were involved in shop floor problems. One bone of contention was material losses—the inability of operating departments to get the quantity of finished products from the raw materials which the works chemical department had managed to get during the pilot runs. These conflicts were functional, in that they usually led to an increased effectiveness in operations.

Other less constructive conflicts occurred from time to time. One problem was that this department tended to acquire additional responsibilities often unrelated to its primary purpose. In one firm, for example, the technological department was responsible not only for development work, but also for production scheduling, the quality control laboratories, and plant budgets. The planning and control activities of this department complicated its relationship with the operating department; a functional empire had been built up with high status and prestige. This made the relationships with the operating department particularly difficult, as the latter felt that it had been pushed out of its proper place in the status structure.

It will be seen therefore that in the operation of a plant it is impossible to draw any real distinction between executive and advisory roles. The high status conferred on operating personnel sometimes gives the impression that theirs is the line role, but the work of the maintenance and technical departments is certainly not advisory.

Fortunately, the higher level of sophistication of the people concerned makes it less necessary for them to reply on the line-staff convention as a mechanism for resolving conflict. They appear to understand and accept the concept of joint accountability, and the relatively clear-cut definition of the primary task makes it easier for them to see the end results for which they are jointly responsible.

In view of the fact that this type of production is likely to become more common in future, it seems important to increase our knowledge of the organizational problems associated with it, and to develop a new set of concepts on which to base organizational planning. It seems that too rigid an adherence to the traditional rules can do positive harm to the process production firm.

BATCH AND INTERMITTENT PRODUCTION

The remaining sixteen firms were heterogeneous, both in respect of their technology and of their organizational structure. As far as technology was concerned, the only thing they had in common was that they all operated within the batch or intermittent production field. Some of them shared technical characteristics in common with the firms in the first category described; in particular, the initiation of production on a basis of firm orders only. Standardized production was handled in this way by one firm, and it was the most common system in firms where standardized parts were assembled diversely. The main difference between these and the unit special order firms was that a large number of orders were dealt with simultaneously. This led to extremely complex control procedures and to uneasy relationships between those responsible for the administration of production and those responsible for the supervision of production operations.

There were also some firms within this group with characteristics like the single-purpose plant process firms. These were the mass production firms in which work moved automatically through a standard sequence of operations, and the process production firms making several products in the same plants. In both types of production the plant or machinery provided a framework of discipline and control; large quantities were involved; there was no direct relationship between output and effort; and production control was relatively simple. Even in a multi-purpose plant only one chemical can be made at a time. The main differences between these firms and the single-purpose plant process firms were that plant and machinery were more flexible, and products could be modified with relatively minor plant modification. This had an important effect on behaviour and relationships, as decisions about production did not have to be made in such detail when plant was planned and erected. This left more decision making to the senior executives.

There were a number of significant technological differences between the firms in the residual group. This suggested that if more firms had been included in the second phase of the research, it might have been possible to evolve a more precise and meaningful classification. The differences included batch size and whether a batch was produced only once or repeated at regular or irregular intervals. Another variation was the number of different articles or components produced. At one extreme was a firm in which several thousand components were made, any order being accepted which the machines available could be adapted to produce, and at the other a firm whose only product variation was colour. The nature of the products also varied; some were technically complex and subject to rapid change and development, others were stable and simple. While these firms could not be divided up into discrete sub-categories, it was possible not only to see whether they had characteristics in common or differed in any significant respects from the other two groups, but also to isolate some of the technical variables and relate them to organizational and behaviour characteristics.

The first significant difference between these and the other firms was that managers and supervision found it very much more difficult to say how they would judge their own performance or that of keeping a plant running. They discussed their work in terms of 'maximization of profit', 'quick customer service', 'adequate standards of quality', and as 'high an output as possible'. Precise definition of objectives appeared to have been replaced as a stimulus to action by a management ideology.

There seemed to be a number of reasons for this relative lack of precision. First there was the element of uncertainty already referred to as a characteristic of batch production. Because the ultimate extent to which production can be controlled and its physical limitations pushed back is unknown, managers and supervisors have to think about their objectives in terms of 'maximization', 'quick', 'adequate', and 'as high as possible'.

The respective roles of the board and the chief executive in relation to policy making and planning being less clear-cut also caused uncertainty. In process industry the board was responsible for the determination of policy as well as for the major part of the planning activity, whereas in special order production both policy making and planning were the responsibility of the chief executive. In neither group was there a dichotomy between policy making and planning; they were integrated processes. As far as policy decisions were concerned, the boards in these sixteen firms came somewhere between their counterparts in the other two groups; they not only identified the field of operations but were responsible for the planning of facilities and the general determination of activity levels. They did not make detailed decisions about the 'how', 'how much', 'where', and 'when' of production. As far as formal organization was concerned these decisions were the responsibility of the chief executive; he was responsible for translating objectives into sequences of activity.

The situation became even more uncertain when the chief executive, who was nominally responsible, delegated the making of the 'how', 'how much', 'where', and 'when' decisions to subordinates. The growth of specialist departments fragmented the planning process. In all these firms decisions about quality, quantity, time, and cost were taken by different people at different times. In theory they were operating inside a master plan and their decisions were integrated by the chief executive. In practice specialist departments operated independently and in extreme cases in complete isolation, their independence having been encouraged by the increasing professionalization of management activities. Each specialist put his own interpretation on the general policy directives emanating from the board. The result was a series of control systems operating simultaneously, subsidiary objectives being established in relation to such factors as cost, quality, and customer service.

This fragmentation of the planning process created problems of two kinds. In some of the firms studied it was possible to trace the way in which subsidiary objectives over a period of time had become primary objectives; the purpose and aims of the firm had changed without any specific policy decisions being taken at board level. This tendency for objectives to change in a purposeless way was exaggerated by the fact that (in contrast to the other two groups of firms) they were not set in relation to a time scale.

In both special order and continuous flow production, plans were made for fixed periods. In special order production these periods were relatively short. In process production they were much longer, but in both types of production there had to be an appraisal and redefinition of objectives at the end of each fixed period. In batch and intermittent production even the consciously planned policy changes came about spasmodically in response to various pressures and stimuli. In these circumstances the primary objective became the survival of the firm rather than the production of specific goods or the provision of services, and decisions taken about production became part of the strategy of keeping the firm alive.

The second kind of problem resulting from the fragmentation of the planning process was that the subsidiary objectives so created were sometimes difficult or impossible to reconcile with each other. In most of these firms the master plan was more of a myth than a reality. In some firms it did not seem to exist at all, and in others it was an unreal plan, consisting of a series of targets set in relation to various criteria which could not be met simultaneously. Many of the senior executives responsible for the production function, and also in theory responsible for integration and reconciling conflicting subsidiary objectives, seemed to be unaware of the problems—or unwilling to commit themselves.

During the course of the research a number of line supervisors found it impossible to meet schedules and still maintain the required quality standards, or keep within the standard costs. Which was the most important therefore became a frequent question. In more than half the firms studied the first-line supervisors had to find the answer for themselves and to reconcile conflicting objectives in the light of current circumstances. They had to make up their minds, for example, whether they would get themselves into more trouble by stock-piling components than by failing to meet delivery dates. This often meant interpreting the mood and balance of power in the senior management group, as the relative importance of subsidiary objectives varied from time to time. It seemed to the research workers that a foreman's reputation depended a good deal on his ability to interpret moods. The 'good' foreman was the man who always made his schedules when this was important, who could cut down his stock if 'inventory reduction' became the key phrase, and who concentrated on quality if the grape-vine told him that there was an alarming increase in customer complaints.

Perhaps it should be re-emphasized at this point that the firms studied in more detail were all rated as 'average' or 'above average' in success. As far as results were concerned, the basic uncertainty of this type of production may have made this *ad hoc* reconciliation of conflicting objectives a functional process. As far as human relationships were concerned, however, the picture was not such a happy one. A considerable strain was put on the first-line supervisor; indeed, this uncertainty seemed to cause more stress than any other aspect of his job, and to be the basis of his insecurity. It complicated his relationships with staff departments. For example, the information about the relationship between line supervision and inspection personnel was in line with that obtained by McKenzie and his colleagues,[6] but undoubtedly the tensions were greatest in firms where the importance of maintaining quality standards varied in relation to the urgency of getting the work out.

Additional evidence of the importance of this uncertainty to the quality of line-staff relations was found in one exceptional firm. Here the works manager had become aware of the problem, and to overcome it had instituted what he referred to as a six-monthly objective. He called meetings of all line supervision and staff personnel at six-monthly intervals and told them the aspect of production which was to be given priority over the next six months. For example, the target for the period of field work was scrap reduction. In the previous six months the main concern had been meeting schedules. There was a slight atmosphere of unreality about this process, and some doubt about whether the objective was consistently pursued throughout the six-month period, but line-staff relationships were more harmonious in this factory than in the other fifteen batch and intermittent production firms studied.

Associated with the lack of integration between policy making and planning, and the uncertainty to which it gave rise in the definition of aims and values, was the difficulty experienced by groups and individuals in identifying or accepting the manage-

---

[6] See, for example, R. M. McKenzie and D. S. Pugh, 'Some Human Aspects of Inspection', *Institution of Production Engineers Journal*, June 1957.

ment's definition of the primary task. This applied to managers and supervisors as well as the operators themselves. If a research worker asked an operator what his or her job was, the reply usually came in terms of the details of the operations; reference to the wider purposes of the organization, to the product, or even to the objective of the department concerned was rarely made. This was in contrast to those employed in special order firms, in which such a question always brought a reference to the product, or in process firms, where the relevance of the job to plant operation was usually stressed.

The main reason for this difference in attitude appeared to be the fact that in the special order and process firms identification of the primary task did not depend upon the management's definition. The work broke down in such a way that the relevance of a job to the achievement of the overall objective was obvious to the person doing it. They identified through experience; little conscious effort was required. Any conscious effort made by the top management to communicate a sense of purpose or to put across the firm's aims and values only had a marginal effect. As far as identification of the primary task was concerned, there was little to choose between people working in firms with no formal communication mechanisms and those in communication-conscious firms. Indeed, in one firm in the process production group, the management's preoccupation with communication techniques was disruptive, as it cut across the automatic process of identification through experience.

In batch and intermittent production, work seldom breaks down in such a way as to enable those doing the various jobs to assimilate the aims and values of the firm through experience. An important variable here was the manufacturing layout; the firms in which the identification was closest were those in which there was layout by product rather than by process: the purpose of the work was better understood and the relationship between individual effort and group objectives was more clear-cut.

But in batch and intermittent production, on the whole, the identification which develops spontaneously in other types of production can only be brought about through conscious and deliberate effort by the top management.

This area being progressive, not only in technical development but also in ideas about personnel management, the fact that a deliberate effort was required to communicate aims and values was generally accepted. A considerable amount of time, thought, and money had been spent on communication techniques. The greater part of this effort had been put into communicating information about the firm itself to the employees. In one firm studied, for example, there was a newspaper—well produced, attractive and easy to read—giving information in general terms about future plans. It was frank about the firm's failures and jubilant about its successes. A survey had been made showing that this paper was widely read; people appreciated being given the information and found it interesting. There was no evidence to suggest, though, that it helped to give the sense of identification already referred to. It was interesting for the operator to know that the firm was going to spend several million pounds on development, but it did not help him to understand the significance of his own particular job, or change the frame of reference in which he did it.

As far as the definition of primary tasks and the development of a sense of purpose in relation to these was concerned, it was much more important for the operator to know why a belt was being speeded up or slowed down, how delays and shortages occurred, and why work which had passed inspection yesterday would have been unlikely to get through had it been examined today. The operators always seemed to be aware of the foreman's dilemma in seeking to satisfy conflicting objectives; thus, the fragmentation of the planning process had repercussions on the shop floor.

The research workers felt that in many firms much less thought was given by personnel and public relations managers to the nature of the information required to make work meaningful to the people concerned than to actual techniques of communication. Acceptance of management's definition of the primary task seemed to depend upon the purpose of each man's job being made explicit, clear-cut group and departmental objectives, and an understanding of the way production was planned and controlled. Important as the projection of an attractive and benevolent company image may be, it is an inadequate substitute for the identification through work experience characteristic of other types of production.

We have seen that the elements of production management,

planning, execution, and control were separated from each other in the batch and intermittent production firms. The relationship between planning and control departments and producing departments varied from firm to firm (and so did the relative status of the three elements); but in every firm formal organization was based on the line-staff concept. The departments concerned with various aspects of planning and control were considered to be staff departments, and they were attached to the line organization at a point above the first-line supervisor level. The point of attachment varied; in some firms it was immediately above the first-line supervisor, in others at senior executive level. In two firms planning, execution, and control were co-ordinated only at chief executive level. As might have been expected, the higher the point of attachment, the greater the degree of centralization in the planning and control activity.

In several firms interesting discussions took place as to whether planning was a staff function in the normally accepted use of the term. Theoretically the schedules and the job instructions issued to the supervision were advice rather than executive orders. There was a minority of firms in which the line supervisor could reject this advice; he was allowed a certain amount of discretion and could modify both programmes and methods. The changes were sometimes made after the work had started, so that in effect the planning and execution phases of production overlapped. The extreme case of this was a firm in which the foreman got his instructions orally from senior line supervision and on paper from the production control department. The result was that he often had the work completed but was unable to pass it out of his department and into the despatch department because the documents were missing. It was not surprising that the production control department was usually referred to as the 'paper mill' by other managers and supervisors. But in the majority of firms the directives prepared by planning and related departments were not advice but executive orders which could not be ignored by line supervisors even if they had wanted to do so. In practice, therefore, line supervisors received instructions from one source of authority and were responsible to another for the results achieved. In every firm studied this created difficulties. Where poor departmental performances were due to inadequate planning, line supervisors were afraid of being unjustly blamed. On the other hand, planning personnel often seemed to feel that they were being made scapegoats for failures of line personnel.

The variations in the relationship of the planning and control functions to the execution function, in the degree to which these were separated, and in the relative status of the three functions, depended in part on technical considerations and in part on the freedom of choice already referred to as characteristic of this type of industry.

In general it was true to say that the larger the batches and the lesser the product diversity, the better the relationship between planning personnel and line supervision. The planning and control tasks were in themselves easier, and they involved line supervision in less recording and reporting. Plans were also longer-term, and in the majority of the larger batch firms the senior managers were able to go over orders and schedules before they were given to the workshops. This meant that first-line supervisors were operating under directives which, if not issued by were at least approved by, their own immediate superiors. Thus, the responsibility for the plans was accepted by the more senior production managers, and if things went wrong they shared the blame. Moreover, there was a better chance of the inconsistencies being noticed and conflicting objectives reconciled before the orders reached the shop floor. The lot of line supervisors seemed to be a reasonably happy one; they seemed more secure and less on the defensive in their relationship with planning and control personnel than their counterparts in the small batch production firms.

The most difficult problems to solve were in the small batch special order firms making a wide variety of different components. This was the point on the scale of technology at which freedom of choice was most evident and at which there was the greatest room for organizational manœuvre. It was also the type of procedure for which the planning process was most complicated and control most difficult to effect. Thus, the process of establishing norms called for a complex and high-powered planning and control organization, and in some firms of this kind the personnel concerned with planning and control were more able, better qualified, and of higher status than line supervision.

The alternative way of organizing this type of production

seemed to be to integrate planning, execution, and control, replying almost entirely on the clinical judgments of the line supervisors, who retained the major responsibility for the entire production process. In these firms the planning and production control personnel were little more than clerks who serviced the line supervisors, often operating from their offices. Plans could be changed either before or during the course of operations. The control information was also fed back to the line supervisors, who evaluated the performance of their own departments and initiated any corrective action necessary.

It seemed that compromise between these two extremes of organization was seldom possible. Of all the production control departments and techniques studied, both the most and least highly developed were found in the small batch diverse product firms. As far as the rationalization of production processes was concerned there could be no half-measures in this type of industry. Both forms of production organization had their advantages and disadvantages. The high-powered production control departments in firms with the first form of organization made nonsense of the line-staff convention. It was in these firms that most resentment was shown to the activities of planning and production control. Another problem was the reduction in the status and authority of the first-line supervisor. This impaired his ability to make decisions —with the result that his usefulness as a trouble-shooter was diminished. The complexity of the planning and control tasks, and the fact that even high-powered and well qualified planners can go wrong, make the trouble-shooting function an important facet of the line supervisor's job. It seemed too that the insecurity of the first-line supervisor took away his confidence in dealing with subordinates, and made it more difficult for him to communicate with them. It was possibly more than coincidence that the firm with the least harmonious shop floor relations was that with the most highly developed production control departments.

Small batch production firms with the second type of organization (in which the major responsibility for production remained with the line supervision) had fewer human relations problems, the atmosphere being very much the same as in the special order production firms. There was greater acceptance and identification of primary tasks and less fragmentation of the planning process.

Management efficiency depended entirely on the first-line supervisor's skill in making clinical judgments and on the personal performance of the operators, and any failure on the part of a supervisor had serious repercussions. This was a disadvantage.

The history of planning and control functions and of their separation from the execution function suggested that, in many of the sixteen firms studied, the rationalization process had been set in motion in order to safeguard against such failures. The setting up of production control as a separate function was regarded merely as making use of the principle of specialization. The difficulties of the small batch, diverse product firms suggested to the research workers that there is a danger of extending the rationalization of production processes and the specialization of functions over too wide an area of technology. In the fringe area between unit and batch production, the increased efficiency derived from rationalization is minimal because of the uncertainty in the production processes and the probability of error in the setting of standards. The increased tension in human relationships, and the greater difficulty experienced in identifying primary tasks resulting from rationalization probably cancel out any benefits accrued. Discussions with production engineers and others responsible for production planning showed they were aware that human and social factors could and did limit the advantage obtained from any increased rationalization of a production system; but as they were unable to analyse these factors or predict their effects they tended to ignore them in their calculations. Taking their cue from text books on production control they tended to assume, when making decisions, that everybody affected by them would behave rationally.

A possible alternative to rationalization as an aid to efficiency in this technological area might be a sustained effort to increase the decision-making skill of the first-line supervisor. All the small batch production firms studied had supervisory training schemes in operation. But these schemes were of a conventional kind; they consisted of lectures about the firm and its organization, and discussions in which participants exchanged experiences. Decision-making was not included as a subject and relatively little use was made of case studies or business games.

Another factor influencing the relationship between the planning, execution, and control functions has already been referred to: manufacturing layout. Here again there was freedom of choice. In special order production and continuous flow production layout was dictated by technical factors alone, but in many of the batch and intermittent production firms, work could be broken down on a basis of either type of operation, or type of product or component. The compensating advantages of layout by process and layout by product had to be considered and decisions taken as to where balance of advantage lay.

In the conscious planning of company organization, there was a trend towards divisionalized or product-centred organization. There was a similar trend in the planning of production organization; layout by product was returning to favour, superseding layout by process. A change of this kind had taken place in one firm about six months before the research started, in another a similar change was about to be made, and in two more it was under discussion.

Effecting the change had apparently created a number of problems. The highly specialized foremen who used to look after one kind of work only had found it difficult to assume responsibility for a wider area of operations. For instance, long-established working groups had been broken up, people were disturbed, and resisted the changes. Being unfamiliar with some of the jobs now being done under their control, the supervisors were also at a disadvantage in their dealings with work study engineers and a spate of price disputes, many of them 'try-ons' on the part of the operators, had followed the change-over.

Things seemed to have settled down surprisingly quickly, however, and when the research interviewing was done, the general feeling amongst both supervisors and operators was that the new system was better than the old. The only problem for management as far as the line supervision was concerned, was the small minority of the foremen who had not been able to assume the additional responsibility owing to lack of qualifications and a too inflexible approach. But like product-centred organization, layout by product increases the power and status of the line supervision at the expense of staff departments. Management's greater problem at the end of six months was the resentment and frustration in the planning and production control departments.

Layout by process of the kind previously in operation in this factory involves a complete separation of the planning, execution, and control activities, the administration of production being completely out of the hands of those responsible for the supervision of production operations. The co-ordination of work depends entirely on the planning and control procedure, and is affected at a remote level through the reciprocal relating of the various factors in the situation. Thus the procedures formed a framework of discipline and control not unlike that formed by the plant in process industry. Formal organization may allocate staff roles to planning and control personnel, but they have a considerable power and are executive except in name, and accountable for end results.

The change to product layout had altered their roles in a number of ways. First, planning on a product basis was a simple task; the work itself had become less interesting. Secondly, it was no longer possible to separate planning from execution. The line supervisors were in a better position to modify plans if they did not like them, both before the job started and while it was in progress. Finally, great stress was laid on the fact that line supervisors were in future to be held responsible for end results. Planning and production personnel felt that they were no longer important and many of the abler and well qualified men were beginning to look for jobs elsewhere. Another effect of the growing professionalization of managers is the tendency of specialists to identify first with the job and only secondly with the firm. This makes personal adjustment to organizational and role changes more difficult.

Recalling the results of the background survey, it will be remembered that a link had been disclosed between business success and conformity with the organizational rules of management theory. The follow-up studies confirmed this; the firms studied were successful, organization-conscious firms with a structure based upon the line-staff concept and the principle of specialization. In spite of their success, however, employment in these firms was characterized by stress and anxiety. Whatever aspect of organization was being studied, the result always seemed to be the same. The intractable problems of human relations were concentrated in the technical area where production control procedures were most complex, and sometimes more rigorously applied; in batch production where products were manufactured intermittently, and in the standardized production of a large number of parts subsequently assembled into a variety of products. This is the area in which production objectives cannot be assimilated through work experience, and so a separate control system has to be established to ensure that these objectives are met.

It was in uncovering the facts about production organization in firms in this technical area, and trying to make sense of them that the research workers were most acutely aware of the inadequacy of existing organizational theory. The line-staff convention and the principles of administration were useful by providing definitions when organizational problems arose. In the firm described above, for example, the change in the control system was put across to the people concerned as an attempt to restore executive responsibility to the line supervision.

But as a basis for analysing and understanding the behaviour and relationships associated with complex production processes, these concepts were of little value. The changes in role associated with the change in the control system suggested that it is the control system which furnishes the key to organizational relationships. Conventional ideas about line and staff add little to our understanding of the relationship between the element functions associated with the production task. More detailed study of control systems as components in their own right might suggest ways in which some of the human relations problems associated with them might be overcome.

Part Three

THE FOLLOW-UP
INVESTIGATIONS

10 Problems in Studying Change

Going step by step through this long and complex series of investigations shows that the existence of a link between technology and organizational characteristics emerged from a survey almost by chance. Subsequently case studies were undertaken to deepen the research, a limited number of manufacturing situations being analysed in more detail.

These case studies not only confirmed the link but demonstrated that it was causal rather than coincidental. They also threw more light on the situational demands associated with various technologies. Relationships between organization and technology were now seen to be more complex than the survey had suggested. At the extremes of the technical scale the physical work flow restricted organizational choice, with the result that firms in the continuous-flow and jobbing production categories tended to be homogeneous as far as organization was concerned. Between these two extremes, however, in the batch production area, the physical work flow did not impose such rigid restrictions, with the result that technology did not so much determine organization as define the limits within which it could be determined. The separation of production administration from production operations, rationalization of production processes, and attempts to push back the physical limitations of production resulted in the emergence of a control system that depended in part on the physical work flow and in part on top management policy. In batch production, therefore, organization was not so much a function of technology as a function of the control system, the latter depending partly on technology and partly on social and economic factors.

Another problem arising from the case studies was that the original system of classification proved to be too crude a measure as a basis for the analysis of production organization. It became clear that a better instrument for classifying technology and relating one production system to another would have to be found before the interaction of technical and behavioural factors could be completely understood.

REPORTING BACK

When the field work of the case studies was completed and the intensive studies of firms A, B, and C nearing completion, a series of meetings was held at the South East Essex College of Technology to report back the results of the research project to representatives of the firms which had participated. These meetings took place immediately before the publication in 1958 of *Management and Technology*,[1] a summary of the research. Considerable interest was aroused among those present at these discussions by the idea of a link between organization and technology. The readiness with which the idea was accepted was no doubt due in part to the deep-rooted feeling some managers have that their own firm is not only unique but isolated, and that problems and solutions found by other firms have no relevance. It was also comforting for some of the firms represented to be told that problems of industrial and inter-management relations can arise from the circumstances of the environment, and are not always, as the press so often seems to imply, the result of lack of skill on the part of managers and supervisors. But even allowing for this immediate reaction, it was obvious that many of those participating felt that the analysis and presentation of the research findings did provide a meaningful explanation of organization and behaviour in their firm, and helped them to compare their present environment with situations they had experienced in the past or heard about from others.

The discussions also led to a much greater understanding and appreciation by the managers present of the social scientist's approach to organizational studies. A similar relationship to that

[1] Joan Woodward (H.M.S.O., London, D.S.I.R. series, *Problems of Progress in Industry*, No. 3).

which had been established in the three firms studied in depth began to develop over a wider area. Several firms, including some that had not hitherto co-operated in the research beyond the background survey stage, now wanted to go further. Pressure was put on the research team to pay return visits, either to make a deeper study or to examine changes that had taken place or were likely to take place in the immediate future. The research workers were told that some of these changes were directly attributed to the earlier researches. The resurgence of interest demonstrated a fact well known to all social scientists who do research in closed groups. The discussion of research findings is a stage in, rather than the end of, a project, for the research workers are left with new ideas and unsolved problems.

Unfortunately this resurgence of interest created a dilemma: as the research unit at the South East Essex College of Technology had no permanent existence, it was difficult to see how anything further could be done. The detailed studies of factories A, B, and C, nearing completion, were bringing to an end the programme of research financed by the Joint Committee of the Department of Scientific and Industrial Research and Medical Research Council, and the research team was already disintegrating. There was no reluctance on the part of the College to continue with these activities, but there were difficulties in obtaining both staff and resources.

At about this time, however, the Imperial College of Science and Technology began to teach industrial sociology in association with its production engineering and management studies. The data obtained in South Essex were taken there and worked on for a further period. Thus it also became possible to follow up some of the ideas that had emerged and to carry on the research on a limited scale.

THE ANALYSIS OF TECHNICAL VARIABLES

As a first step, three post-graduate students of the Production Engineering Section of the Mechanical Engineering Department tackled the problem of the measurement of technical variables, trying to find a better way of classifying and comparing systems of manufacture than that used in the original studies.[2] As will be

[2] Brewer's account of this work is given in Appendix II.

seen, only a limited amount of work was done and the study cannot be regarded as more than a pilot investigation in this field. Nevertheless, the findings have interesting implications; an attempt was made to identify a number of parameters, each representative of a technical characteristic, and capable of numerical expression which could be used together to produce an adequate picture of a firm's technology, and so provide a framework for the study of related organization and behaviour. One of the parameters identified can loosely be described as the density of production. This was also the basis of the system of classification used in Fig. 11, and the vertical scale on the diagrams given in Appendix II is an elaboration of this classification, showing how the different systems of production are related to each other.

When the production density of some of the firms included in the background survey was measured by using this scale, an interesting fact emerged. Firms that had been classified as unit and small batch were grouped closely together at one extreme, and those classified as process were grouped at the other. The remaining firms were distributed over a wide area in the middle of the scale. As far as production density was concerned, therefore, some firms within the original batch and mass production category differed more widely from each other than from some firms in one of the other two categories. This could imply that variations in organizational and behavioural characteristics revealed by the case studies in batch production firms might be explained by variations in technology rather than by reference to the notion of an independent control system.

Appendix II also shows that firms within the same industry can differ both in production density and order time. Firms in the motor industry, for example, are not as alike technologically as is commonly supposed. There has been considerable press speculation about the reasons for the differences between car firms in the climate of industrial relations. While it is not suggested that there are no other important variables, the difference may be partially explained by reference to technical variables.

Although this work on the analysis of technical variables has not yet progressed very far, it has demonstrated both the need for a more refined measure of technology to facilitate the prediction of industrial behaviour and organizational characteristics, and its use.

THE STUDY OF CONTROL SYSTEMS

In February 1960 the Production Engineering and Management Studies Section of Imperial College, as part of this expansion in the field of industrial sociology, accepted a contract to supervise the completion of the second of the 'Cases in the Application of Work Study' begun by the Department of Scientific and Industrial Research as a direct project. The results of this study were interesting in relation to the data that had been obtained from the South Essex project; in particular, to those describing the emergence of the independent control system in batch production firms, and the way the control system complicates both organizational and management-worker relationships.

Klein (1964)[3] found that in the firm under review, work study had at least as important and far-reaching an effect on behaviour as part of a control system as it did as the basis of a system of wage determination. Her investigation into work study led her into problems of production, quality, and cost control, and into the ways in which control information was used. This concentration of interest in the control area suggested that a next logical step would be to try and find out more about control systems, their relationship to technology, and the behaviour associated with them. Several firms which had participated in the South Essex project had expressed interest in such a study. A proposal was therefore made to the Human Sciences Committee of the Department of Scientific and Industrial Research, and with the help of this Committee a start on the new project was made in October 1962.[4] An idea of the way in which this study is being approached is given by Eilon (1962).[5] Briefly, the project is based on the assumption that when the management of a firm makes a decision to manufacture a product or series of products a control system is automatically brought into existence. Objectives have to be determined in relation to the product and a sequence of activities planned in order to achieve those objectives. Plans then have to be executed and information generated to enable the results to be assessed. If the activities are to be repeated, corrective action may

[3] Lisl Klein, *Multiproducts Ltd.* (published for D.S.I.R. by H.M.S.O.).

[4] See *Register, etc., of Research in the Human Sciences 1960–63* (H.M.S.O.).

[5] S. Eilon, 'Problems in Studying Management Control', *International Journal of Production Research*, Vol. 1, No. 4, December 1962.

have to be taken or the objectives modified in the light of the result obtained. For those concerned with the product at all levels of the hierarchy, the control system is the framework in which they operate, determining the amount of discretion they have in the organization of their own activities. It is hoped that a way of describing control systems in terms of such parameters as degree of formalization, complexity, and fragmentation will be found, and the behaviour associated with them analysed.

FOLLOW-UP

Finally, in the period between the completion of the field work in firms A, B, and C, and the beginning of the management control project, it was found possible to do a limited amount of the follow-up work which had been suggested by those present at the discussions held at the South East Essex College of Technology. Return visits were made to seven firms in the area in which technical changes were taking place of particular significance either to the original study of the relationship between technology and organization, or to the new project, with particular reference to the effects of formalization on control procedures. These studies can therefore be regarded as a bridge between the two research projects —follow-up of the original work and pilot research for the new studies.

Studies of technical change undertaken by social scientists, or by research workers using social science methods, have been of three kinds. Most of them have concentrated on the actual initiation of change, and on what happens either at managerial or at working group level while changes are being assimilated. Here the results have indicated an almost universal resistance to change, and consideration has been given to the reasons for this resistance, the extent to which it is rational or irrational, and to the strains and stresses in personal and role relationships associated with it. Other studies have concentrated on the longer-term effects of changes in the organization of work, these effects being directly attributed to the nature of the change and persisting after the initial period of upheaval has passed. Finally, there are studies of the kind already referred to: Burns and his colleagues[6] were concerned with

[6] T. Burns and G. Stalker, *The Management of Innovation* (Tavistock Publications Ltd., 1961).

technical changes of a particular kind; they were interested in the problems of organization and management that can arise where change is rapid and continuous, and where products are progressive, subject to development, and of considerable variety.

The three kinds of studies have overlapped, however. In earlier investigations—the Hawthorne experiments being the classic example—social scientists did not find it easy to distinguish between the effects of involvement in a process of change and the effects of the changes themselves. In some cases the distinction was not even recognized, and this led to a tendency to ascribe reactions and responses to the change itself, which were more likely to have arisen from involvement in the process of change. Similarly, there is a tendency for some social scientists to identify the management of change with the management of innovation, in the sense in which the word was used by Burns, and to generalize on the basis of his results.

In the follow-up studies done in South Essex, it was particularly difficult to distinguish between the three phenomena. The main emphasis of the studies was on the long-term organizational effects of the changes observed. The long period of association with the firms concerned made it possible to compare the organization before the changes had taken place with that which had emerged after its immediate impact had been forgotten. Nevertheless, it was impossible to ignore the changes themselves—to turn a blind eye to what was happening in a firm while a process of change was actually taking place. For example, as a number of firms were being studied simultaneously comparisons could be drawn about how changes were initiated, how decisions were made and communicated, and how any resultant problems of industrial relations were handled.

INVOLVEMENT IN CHANGE

We have seen that the managers of the firms in South Essex were not only progressive in outlook themselves, but had succeeded in building up a readiness to accept change among their employees. This had probably not been too difficult, as both supervisors and operators had derived considerable benefit from technical changes in the past. The industrial history of the area suggested that people had done well not only from a pay but also from a promotion point of view. Thus, the apparent readiness to accept change was probably based on prevailing expectations.

Involvement in change might therefore be expected to create few problems. Unless management made obvious mistakes in introducing changes, the chances were that they would get going with the minimum of disruption. This did not prove to be the case, however; in some of the firms studied, mistakes were made, and there were several failures of communication. But even where the situation was handled well and all the rules adhered to, the introduction of change was not as smooth sailing as the research workers had predicted. In particular, there were two problems arising in every firm studied. First, the length of time taken to introduce changes: the initiation and implementation of change turned out to be an extremely slow process. Secondly, no matter how carefully and slowly the idea of change was introduced, the immediate reaction of lower supervision and operators was to resist. Changes seemed to be opposed as a matter of course—a conditioned reflex.

Considering first the time lag, the information obtained from these follow-up investigations certainly supported Dubin's (1962)[7] argument that the time scale of decision is much longer than the formalistic analysis of the decision-making process suggests. In the case of some of the firms covered by the investigations, four years had elapsed since the original contact had been made in connection with the background survey. Nevertheless, none of the changes being put into effect were completely new to the research workers; all had been mentioned as possibilities during the earlier stages of the research. It seemed that intentions had taken four years to materialize into plans and harden into decisions. Only in two of the seven firms had a substantial part of the intervening period been spent on the fabrication of the new plant or machinery. By far the greater expenditure of time had been on meetings and discussions. The function of these meetings had been to reconcile the conflicting interests of individuals and departments, and to effect compromise.

An interesting point was that, except when thinking specifically

[7] Robert Dubin, *Business Behaviour Behaviourably Viewed* from the *Social Science Approach to Business Behaviour*, Argyris *et alia* (Homewood Inc., Dorsey Irwin).

about formalized delivery dates or control periods, many of the managers seemed to be unaware of the passage of time, and what it costs. For example, in one firm it took nearly eighteen months (or twelve meetings held at four- to six-weekly intervals) to solve a bottle-neck problem by changing the manufacturing layout. The problem was first raised at a routine production control meeting, and one of the managers present was asked to get information about it. The information could have been obtained within a few hours, but those present could not arrange a mutually convenient date for the next meeting until about six weeks later, with the result that the matter lay dormant for six weeks.

It was interesting to observe how the fixing of the date for the meeting became an end in itself, and when everyone involved had been successfully accommodated, there was almost as much satisfaction as there would have been if an immediate solution to the problem had been found. Everyone felt that something had been done, and relieved of responsibility. The problem was therefore forgotten, and even the manager who had been asked to get information did very little about it until the day before the meeting.

When the meeting did take place a similar process occurred. It was decided that the problem was a serious one, and that it would be a good idea to appoint a sub-committee to investigate further. The election of the sub-committee also became an end in itself. After this a number of sub-committee meetings were held, interspersed with reporting-back sessions, before any positive action was taken. Even then discussions about the problem were not at an end, for another six months elapsed before the decisions were put into effect. During these six months attempts were made to analyse, and accommodate where possible, the conflicting interests of the various departments and individuals.

At no time during this process did the research workers feel that there was any deliberate procrastination or sabotage. The managers concerned seemed committed to the idea of increased efficiency. It seems therefore that even in firms where resistance to change among the upper echelons is minimal, and where the reputation for being progressive and technically up-to-date is valued, the planning of change is a slow process.

These follow-up studies not only supported the contention that it is impossible to develop any valid theory of decision without taking the time dimension into consideration, but also that the value of social science research is enhanced if it can be carried out inside a 'real time context'.

It had to be admitted that as far as resistance to change was concerned, observed behaviour in the situations studied in the final stage of the research was at variance with attitudes expressed in the earlier stages. Thus the usefulness of attitude surveys as predicted instruments was challenged by the course of events. That the labour force in South Essex thrived on change and development seemed to be more of a myth than a reality.

But a closer look at some of the incidents during the course of the investigations revealed that the discrepancy between attitudes and behaviour was not as great as appeared on the surface. Significantly, the greatest opposition to change came from the most self-assured and successful individuals and groups. On the shop floor it was the working groups that Sayles (1954)[8] described as 'strategic' and 'conservative' rather than the less secure 'apathetic' and 'erratic' groups which started to pressurize management as soon as they heard that changes were under way. These groups were composed of people whose work was relatively important to the firm in the eyes of both management and fellow workers. Moreover, they were the *élite* of the labour force. Certainly the men in the 'conservative' groups would have been able to obtain comparable employment locally if they had lost their present jobs. It soon became obvious that what appeared to be resistance to change was in reality a firm determination to get something out of the change. The political consciousness and sophistication of the labour force in the area has already been referred to. Much of what the operators said and did reflected their awareness of the fact that the basis of their employment was an effort-wage bargain; and through their representative either at local or national levels, they wanted to make quite sure that any technical change introduced would improve their relative position. Thus, the resistance was rational rather than emotional. One of the changes studied involved the introduction of shift work into a production department. Obviously, the men concerned did

[8] Leonard R. Sayles, *Behaviour in Industrial Work Groups, Prediction and Control* (John Wiley and Sons Inc., New York).

not like the idea of working shifts, but it was equally obvious that they were prepared to do so if the price was right. In general, therefore, technical changes were seen as opportunities to re-open the effort-wage bargain negotiation in an attempt to obtain either a reduction of effort or an increase in wages. Moreover, the operators always seemed to be successful up to a point; even where they did not get all they asked for they managed to get something, and resistance evaporated as soon as terms were agreed. It was amusing to find that within weeks they were talking about the changes in the boastful or tolerant way they had done in the earlier interviews.

A similar bargaining process was carried on at middle management and supervisory levels. Here, however, the bargaining was about the distribution of power rather than the effort-wage equilibrium. But like the bargaining at operator level it was the secure rather than the insecure who became deeply involved and vociferous, thus appearing to be more resistant to change. Those who had appeared, in previous interviews, to be most confident in their relationships with higher management demonstrated this confidence by making their feelings known right up to the chief executive level if necessary. Their resistance was not based on their fear of losing power but on their determination to get what they could out of the change. Like the operators, the managers did seem to gain from this agitation. Even if they failed to increase their relative power positions, their reaction made top management increasingly conscious of the critical role of middle management and supervision in the successful implementation of change. In at least two cases, this increased awareness had practical and material results when annual assessments of performance and salary review were made.

PRODUCT DEVELOPMENT AND VARIETY

As Appendix I shows, the research workers collecting information for the background survey had divided the products being manufactured in the firms they studied into three categories; stable products, firmly established, subject to a minimum of variety and slow to develop; progressive products, subject to considerable variety and rapid development; and specification or made-to-measure products.

Two of the firms included in the final stage of this research manufactured products of the second kind, and the studies involved consideration of the way that new or modified products were brought into the production lines. This was also the technological area studied by Burns and his colleagues, and the data obtained was therefore directly comparable with that presented in *The Management of Innovation*.[9] These two studies corroborated his findings in a number of respects. The fact that an organizational change of the kind he had observed had taken place in both firms since the completion of the background survey, was particularly interesting.

A special department, called the engineering department, had been set up to bridge the gap between development and production departments, and to iron out the design problems that arose when new products were being transferred to the production lines. In both firms there had been consequent changes in the organization and functions of drawing office, methods department, and development workshops, and these departments were put under the control of the new department.

The problems arising were also very much the same as those described by Burns, but it was interesting to find that one firm succeeded in overcoming these problems much better than the other. In the former, the new department did eventually succeed in establishing a place for itself as a channel of communication between the development and production function; in the other firm there was complete failure; various pressures combined to make the services of the new department redundant, and it lasted for only nine months. The difference could not be explained in terms of technology either, for the technologies were similar, or, in terms of Burns's hypothesis, both firms tended to be organic rather than mechanistic in structure. Thus it was interesting from the point of view of organizational analysis as it highlighted some of the other variables on which organization and behaviour depend.

The firm in which the new department ultimately became established was less then ten years old, whereas the other firm had been in existence before the 1939–45 war. Thus roles had not become so set or functions so clearly established. It was also one of the few firms studied in which the director of research was not

[9] Burns, op. cit., p. 190.

merely an executive who had been given the title for status reasons or to support an external image but a full member of the board involved in policy making as well as executive action.

The firm was unusual, too, in having almost as high a proportion of graduates among the staff on the production side as on the development side of the business. The development engineers worked in small groups on particular types of products, these product groups corresponding with the main product divisions of the manufacturing organization. The product divisions were also profit centres and there was already a well-developed communications network between departments with which the development engineers were linked. The project engineers staffing the new department were drawn from the development and the production departments, with the result that the personnel of the new department had links with both production and research. These project engineers fitted neatly and naturally into the existing organization, and after a few teething troubles they settled down to make a positive contribution to the smooth transference of new products to the production lines.

The other firm had manufactured stable products for a number of years before being forced to change its policy. Its organizational structure had, however, been flexible and democratic in comparison with other firms studied. When the policy changed and new products were introduced, a research and development department was set up, staffed from outside the organization. There were no graduates on the production side of the business and the managing director himself had risen from the lower ranks of line supervision. While seeing the need for the expansion, he found it difficult to accept completely. His attitude affected that of his subordinates, with the result that the production supervision tended to look on the laboratories as unnecessary luxuries. Production and development remained apart, and although communications followed easily inside each department there was a minimum exchange of information between them. The bone of contention was change in design. The production supervision with their background of stable product manufacture resented the modifications in design which the development engineers insisted on introducing after production had started.

The engineering department had thus been set up to solve a

very serious problem for this firm, an urgently needed bridge between the development and production functions. But it was not adequately recognized that to be effective the new department would need high status and considerable power. In fact, it was given little prestige and adopted an apologetic attitude from the start. Moreover, as the project engineers were newly appointed from outside the organization, they had no links with either production or research personnel. The result was that they were soon squeezed out of the picture by the two powerful departments they were trying to serve; they either left the factory or were transferred to the development department.

It is obviously dangerous to generalize from two cases, but these studies suggested that the success of bridging departments is related to the size of the gap that has to be bridged; in the firm where the gap was small and communication was already taking place, the department was able to perform a useful function. But the setting up of the engineering department in the second firm was not an adequate organizational device to establish a communications link between departments hostile to each other.

CHANGING TECHNIQUES BUT NOT TECHNOLOGY

Coming now to the main purpose of the follow-up investigations— the study of the longer-term effects of technical change on organizational structure—the three case studies already completed formed the starting-point. These had shown that far less organizational disturbance and modification had resulted from technical change in firm C than in either firm A or firm B. This might have been expected in view of the character of the technical changes being studied, for those in firm C had had relatively little effect on the character of the production system. All that had happened in fact was that more highly automated continuous-flow production plants had been introduced into a firm which was already in the process production category. The case studies appeared to confirm that technical changes involving a change in the nature of the production system have the greatest effect on organization and behaviour.

Firm C was therefore less interesting as a study of technical change than as an opportunity to study at depth the organization and behaviour associated with process industry. It showed how the technology of process industry and the situational demands associated with it establish conditions particularly conducive to the development of harmonious and contributive social relationships.[10] The firm was a stereotype in the sense that all the characteristics of process industry already described were present in an extreme form.

As far as the newer plants were concerned, production facilities were inflexible and the commercial success of the venture depended on there being an assured market for its products for at least the next twenty years. In this setting objectives had had to be very clearly and precisely defined before the plants were built, with the result that as far as plant operation was concerned, imponderables were relatively few, and the consequences of taking a particular course of action could be predicted with a reasonable degree of certainty. Thus, the managers and supervisors responsible for plant operation worked within the rigid framework of a highly formalized control system; departments virtually ran themselves. Moreover, as this was the process firm already referred to in which the organization of maintenance activities was closely linked with plant operation, with formalized routine maintenance, maintenance personnel too were brought into the same framework of control.

The study confirmed that the development of harmonious relationships between individuals and departments is facilitated by a common reference point, the reference point being the operation of the plant in this case. Managers from different departments, responsible for different functions, spent far more time together than in any other firm studied. The pattern of management interaction was noticeably different in firm C from that observed in firms A and B. Nearly 70 per cent of the contacts recorded were with other managers at the same level, the remaining 30 per cent being superior and subordinate contacts. In firm A the percentages were reversed.

The rationalized production process in firm C led to a set routine, the working day fell into a pattern and interaction between managers was linked more with this routine than with pressure

[10] This has been confirmed by Flanders's description of the Esso refinery at Fawley. See A. Flanders, *The Fawley Productivity Agreements* (Faber and Faber, London, 1964).

arising from the job itself. This was also true of the contacts up and down the hierarchy; although fewer in number than the horizontal contacts, they were also brought about through work routines rather than through the difficulties and problems which occurred.

The general effect of all this was an atmosphere of calm and absence of pressure in comparison with other firms studied. Occasionally, however, the calm was shattered by a crisis, generally of a technical nature. Such crises had an important function, generating energy, providing the stimulus needed to keep managers alert, and increasing their satisfaction in their jobs. As we have seen, when things were going smoothly the area of discretion was limited. In time of crisis it was very wide. Moreover, responsibility for making the problem-solving decisions was delegated down the hierarchy. The technology made delegation inevitable, for decisions had to be made quickly and as close to the plant as possible, but other circumstances also favoured delegation. For example, it had been observed during the field work that the chief obstacle to delegation in an industrial firm was the fear of supervisors that decisions made by their subordinates would embarrass them or threaten their position. Where a superior felt confident that his subordinates were likely to make much the same decisions over a wide area as he would himself, he delegated more readily. In firm C, most of the managers above the level of first-line supervisor had similar qualifications and background training: a good degree in science or engineering, followed by a formal period of training with the firm. This homogeneity meant that, given the same facts, all managers tended to make the same decisions, and the delegation necessitated by the technology at a time of crisis was achieved without anxiety.

The homogeneity of this management group had other interesting effects. It was found, for example, that fewer decisions were reversed than in any other firm studied in depth. Even where time and circumstances would have allowed senior managers to intervene, they rarely did so. Moreover, junior managers seemed to find it easier to subscribe to and identify with the decisions made by their superiors than their counterparts interviewed elsewhere. This was because they knew they would have made similar decisions in similar circumstances. Thus, the homogeneity of the management group facilitated identification upwards as well as delegation downwards. This identification, together with the freedom of action in time of crisis, seemed either to compensate for or to conceal the fact that in normal circumstances the managers operated within a rigid framework of control. In this firm there were fewer complaints than in any other that the authority of the managers and supervisors was too limited. Managers seemed to feel freer and more responsible than they did elsewhere.

The predominantly horizontal pattern of communications and the relatively few superior-subordinate contacts did not result in a stratified status hierarchy with each level of management forming a discrete social group. The internal communications pattern was offset by external social contacts. Out of working hours there were more contacts between subordinates and superiors than in the case of any other firm studied in depth. The homogeneity of the management group, based as it was on similar educational backgrounds and common experience of training, led to social equality. Social status was less closely linked with occupational status in process production than in any other production system.

Reference was made in the previous chapter to the role of the chief executive in process industry. The rigid framework of discipline and control provided by the plant, together with the fact that crisis decisions have to be delegated for technological reasons while policy decisions are too long-term to be the responsibility of any one man, mean that he spends less time on purely technical matters than do his counterparts in other systems of production. The result as observed in firm C was that he emerged more clearly as the ritual head of the firm; he was the key figure in its social organization, spending almost half his time on the formal social functions so important to its corporate life. Technically he seemed to be in a decision-making vacuum, the decision-making in which he was involved being of the subjective non-programmed type mainly associated with human relations. Organization, industrial relations, and public relations were his primary concerns, and any problems relating to these aspects of management were quickly communicated to the top of the hierarchy. A record was made of the main activities of the chief executives in all the firms studied in depth throughout this research, and it was in firm C that the chief executive spent the most time with trade union officials and other visitors to the factory, and in discussing labour and staff problems, promotions, and organizational changes.

The personal involvement of the chief executive in the routine of industrial relations had several interesting effects. It demonstrated to outsiders, particularly to trade union officials, that the company valued its reputation for good industrial relations. Internally it set a pattern of involvement of line supervision in industrial relations problems. The personnel department was small in relation to the size of the firm and not high-powered, demonstrating that a firm can have not only a good industrial relations atmosphere but also a reputation for industrial peace without a strong professional personnel department. Moreover, the fact that decisions about industrial relations could be obtained from the chief executive with the minimum of delay gave the impression that the management was prepared to take the initiative in these matters. There were fewer complaints about the length of time taken to get an answer to a query in this than in any other firm studied.

Another characteristic of firm C was that the managers interviewed thought promotion was a less chancy and less political business than it was in many other firms; nearly 90 per cent said that they were satisfied with the progress they had made, and only 5 per cent felt they were entirely dependent on the goodwill of their immediate supervisor for their success. There had been a good deal of staff movement, but it seemed to have created very little insecurity. The greater involvement of the chief executive in promotion matters was a contributory factor to this satisfactory state of affairs, but there were other important factors. In the first place the formalized system of control facilitated an objective assessment of performance. Every manager interviewed said that his success would be judged by his ability to keep the plant operating as near to maximum capacity as possible. Therefore the managers were able to appraise their own performance to a very large extent.

The rapid turnover of staff also affected attitudes to promotion. No one interviewed in this firm above the grade of foreman had been in his present job longer than three years. This was not only an obvious manifestation of the fact that promotion prospects were good, but also threw emphasis on role as opposed to personal elements in management behaviour. The continuity in the operation of the plant depended on one manager behaving in very much the same way as his predecessor had done and as his successor was likely to do. There was very little in the way of written job descriptions or instructions, so this consistency in behaviour depended on the long formal training period which each potential manager went through at the outset of his career.

The existence of a formal management training scheme had an interesting effect on attitudes to promotion. Of the firms employing graduates studied in depth, about half had a training scheme, and the majority of the management trainees interviewed were disgruntled. Many of them felt they were ready to take responsibility long before being given it, and much of the wastage in the trainee group was said to be due to a graduate's desire to get down to a real job. A number of the young graduates in firms without any formal training schemes said that they had in fact chosen their particular firms because they knew they would be put straight into a job rather than given more training. During the immediate post-graduate stage, people seemed to get more satisfaction from working in firms where there was no training scheme. The attitudes of those who had had about five years' working experience were very different. Graduates in the 25–29 age group who had received a formal training looked back on it with appreciation, while those who had gone straight into a responsible job now seemed to regret this. In general, they had found that their promotion opportunities had been limited to the department or function in which they had started work. The result was that they had either become disgruntled or had identified themselves closely with the success of their department. They were less conscious of themselves as managers and less involved with their firms than their counterparts in firms with formal management training.

Another characteristic of process production seen in its most extreme form in firm C was effective management by committee. Committees met to make decisions through an exchange of information and an appraisal of known facts. In the highly rationalized setting of process production joint decision-making is a practical possibility, and management committees can make a direct and positive contribution to the achievement of both technical and social objectives. In the other firms studied, the various management committees—executive, policy, and production—were not joint decision-making bodies in the same sense; their main function seemed to be to allow an opportunity for the operation of the political factor in the decision-making process. They were part of the political rather than the technical system of the firms concerned.

Firm C, although undoubtedly the most peaceful and least tense of all the firms studied, was not Utopian, nor completely free of organizational problems and tension. Administrative problems had resulted from the fact that it had not been possible to build the new plants less than two miles from the older ones. This had led to communication difficulties and administrative duplication. At the time of the research the administration headquarters were on the other site, giving the two sites almost equal status. The newer plants had status in their own right while the older plants retained their status because of their close proximity to top management. It was, however, planned to build a new administrative headquarters on the new site and a gradual deterioration in the status position of the older plants could be foreseen, creating problems in the future.

Interestingly enough from the point of view of the research, some of the tension was the legacy of older and more far-reaching changes in technology. In its early days this plant had merely been an installation, purely concerned with the storage and distribution of petroleum products. The introduction of refining had reduced the status of those concerned with the installation activities, and as the volume of production grew, installation personnel were forced into positions of continuously decreasing status. Those still involved in installation work were resentful of this, and becoming increasingly insecure.

Finally, there were promotion problems among the nongraduates. Plant operators who in most cases had left school at about fourteen or fifteen years of age accepted philosophically that they were unlikely to get beyond the chargehand or plant foreman level. Their horizon was defined, and in staying with the firm they had accepted its limitations. It was not so easy for grammar school entrants to do this. In the main these were employed in the drawing offices, laboratories, and offices. Opportunities for promotion were limited, and the fact that senior appointments were in the main reserved for graduates created resentment.

It would be unfair to give the impression that the high quality of organizational and personal relationships in firm C was entirely the result of technological circumstances. The calibre of management was high, and when difficulties arose the sophistication of the people involved resulted in a swifter and greater awareness of what was happening; a real effort was made to work through the problems by dealing with the realities of the situation. There is no doubt, however, that the technology of oil refining, an extreme example of process production, does provide a fertile soil for the seeds of progressive staff and labour policies. The comparative lack of routine pressure makes it possible to approach the problems of the job intellectually rather than emotively.

CHANGING TECHNOLOGY

In firms A and B, the technical changes had a more dramatic effect on the production system. Although different in kind their results were similar, leading in both cases to standardized production of the large batch type. Firm A, which for many years had been operating entirely in the unit and small batch production field, had begun to produce standardized components, and firm B, which until after the second world war had been a process firm with all the advantages described above, had established production lines to package drugs and prepare them for sale.

A recurrent theme of this book has been that the most recalcitrant problems of organization and behaviour are likely to be found in the batch production area of technology. Firms A and B, in moving into this area from opposite extremes of the technical scale, were therefore more vulnerable. It seemed likely therefore that the period of readjustment would be difficult and costly, and that the duration of the period of tension and the ultimate degree of adjustment achieved would be influenced considerably by top management's awareness of the problems likely to develop and their realization of the relationship between technology and organization. The speed with which organizational changes could be made was bound to influence the course of events.

A number of difficulties did occur and in both firms the general impression given by those interviewed was that the firm was a less calm and less pleasant place to work in than it had been before the changes took place. One methodological problem of the studies carried out in firms A and B was that the research workers had known neither firm before the changes took place. The earlier organization charts, departmental memoranda, and other available documentation did not give a complete picture; they were dependent to a large extent on the memories of those interviewed. It was impossible to assess how far involvement in current problems made the past seem rosier in retrospect than it had been in reality. In choosing firms for the final studies, therefore, two criteria emerged. First, it seemed advisable to concentrate on changes involving a movement into the batch production area from either unit or process production, because it was in these cases that the effects on organization and behaviour were likely to be most profound and most revealing of the link between technology and organization. Secondly, it was important to choose firms about which the research workers already knew a good deal, so that the investigators could make their own assessment of the before and after situation.

Four firms fell into both categories; three were engineering firms in which either products or parts had been standardized, and one was similar to firm B in that it had introduced new packaging departments into what had previously been a process production firm making chemicals in bulk.

It was decided to look also at three firms involved in technical changes that were taking them out of the batch production area; in one of these automated packaging lines had been installed, the effect being to incorporate the final stages of production into the main process. Another was a firm in which products originally made in batches were now produced on a continuous-flow production line. The third was a process firm changing over from multi- to single-purpose plant.

Because information was available about both the before and the after situation, these follow-up investigations probably came as near to controlled experiments as it is possible to get in social science research. The studies were controlled in the sense that major variables other than technology remained constant; in particular, most of the managers remained in post. There were some

changes among the senior executives but these were insufficient to
have accounted for all the organizational and behavioural changes
observed.

A subtle change had, however, taken place in the relationship
between the research workers and the firm, and it was essential to
take this into account in evaluating the information obtained. It
was found, for example, that information was even easier to get
than it had been previously. Thus, although the methods used
were basically the same as in the earlier case studies, i.e. intensive
interviewing and direct observations, more ground was covered
in a shorter space of time. The discussions held at the South East
Essex College of Technology at the end of 1958 were probably the
main instrument of the change of attitude. The relaxed atmosphere
that developed during the six weeks in which they were taking place
had made it possible to discuss information that implied criticism
of individuals or firms without awkwardness and embarrassment.
This had led to a greater understanding by the managers present
of the way social scientists use and interpret the information they
obtain.

The discussions had also led to a greater interest in social science
research itself, concepts had been discussed at a fairly high level
of abstraction, and the follow-up studies had been suggested by
the firms themselves because some of the senior members of their
management groups had become interested in the ideas put
forward.

The danger was, of course, that another variable was now
introduced into the situation. It was impossible to tell whether the
long association some of the firms had had with research workers,
and their participation in the research project, were influencing
the course of events being studied—in particular whether any
decisions made in relation to change were different from what
they would have been had the earlier research not been undertaken.

There were indications that this might be so. The managers and
supervisors interviewed a second time talked about their jobs in
what appeared to be a different frame of reference; they were more
sophisticated in discussing their problems and seemed more
sensitive of other peoples' reaction to their behaviour.

In the earlier stages of the project, the research workers had found (like other social scientists studying industrial situations) that when changes are taking place, the people concerned find it difficult to describe what is happening. They talk about what has happened in the past, or what the firm is likely to do in the future, but avoid discussion of the present situation.

This was not so in the final studies; not only did people talk about the present situation but they talked about it in terms of role and personality. They seemed aware of the importance of the concept of role in resolving the conflicts and relieving the tension associated with technical change. It is unlikely that this increased awareness would have had no effect on the course of events.

It seems that the sociologist cannot win in his attempts to establish a rigorous experimental framework for his research. The advantages of being able to study a before and after situation may be outweighed by the fact that the behaviour observed in the study of the after situation may have been influenced by participation in the study of the before situation. The following chapter must be read with this possible bias in mind.

11 *The Effects of Change*

The main conclusion emerging from the final group of case studies was that the effects on organization and behaviour of the technical changes investigated were much as had been predicted. The studies certainly confirmed that the most recalcitrant problems of organization and behaviour arise in firms moving into rather than out of the batch production area of technology. Moreover, differences in the ease with which the firms concerned adapted to technical change could be explained in terms of the senior managers' ability to anticipate these problems, and the initiative shown in the simultaneous planning of organizational and technical change.

As has been said, the circumstances under which the research was carried out unfortunately made it impossible to be absolutely sure that the behaviour observed was not being unduly influenced by the research workers' expectations, which were known in advance to many of the people involved in the investigations. But assuming for the purposes of argument that this was not the case, the outcome of the follow-up studies was extremely satisfactory. It provided a further demonstration of the main thesis put forward in this book, i.e. that meaningful explanations of behaviour can be derived from an analysis of the work situation. It seemed that in identifying technology as one of the primary variables on which behaviour depended, a step forward had been made in the determination of the conditions under which behaviour becomes standardized and predictable.

Moreover, confirmation that the situations arising in firms A and B were not unique increased the research workers' confidence in the results they had obtained from the studies of these two factories. It appeared that in talking about the past, distance had not lent enchantment to the view of the people interviewed in these two firms to the extent that might have been expected. They seemed to present to the research workers a fair picture of what their firm had been like before the changes had taken place. But although from the point of view of the theoretical framework of the research, the results of the follow-up studies were satisfactory, their confirmatory nature tended to make them less exciting and their presentation more difficult. In all essential respects what happened in firms A and B also happened in the other firms where similar technical changes had taken place. Thus to describe each case study in detail would be merely to repeat what has already been said. Had it not been for the fact that the methods used in the research project became more detailed and sophisticated as time went by, it is doubtful whether the final phase of the research would have added anything to the previous argument.

The greater detail in which the firms were studied did mean, however, that new light was thrown on some aspects of organizational behaviour, and a greater understanding was reached of the social processes involved in adaptation to change. The focus of this chapter is on this new material. A brief résumé will be given of the problems which arose in firms A and B, supplemented where appropriate by the information obtained during the final phase of the research.

FROM UNIT TO MASS PRODUCTION

(a) *The changes studied*

The study of firms A and B had shown that although both had problems arising from their movement into the batch production area of technology, these were different in kind. In the short term at least, firm B had the more potentially difficult situation to deal with. In this firm the entry into the batch production area of technology had been brought about by the grafting of a batch production operation on to the original process organization. In effect, this meant that a new section of the firm had to be built up. New people were brought in to do this and it was only when the new section had become established that its relationship with the other sections of the firm became a problem, and difficulties arose in fusing the older and newer activities into a single organizational structure.

In factory A, new departments were ultimately set up and new personalities were introduced as a result of the technical changes, but the immediate problem was that people at all levels who had worked for many years under the old system of production had to adjust to the new. The standardization of parts resulted in a total reorganization of production operations, the biggest change being a breakdown into feeder shops and final assembly, and within a very short space of time all sections of the firm, including both research and marketing divisions, found themselves affected in one way or another by the reorganization.

In the three engineering firms studied during the final phase of the research (referred to as firms A/1, A/2, and A/3 in this chapter) the situation was similar. The technical detail of the changes varied to some extent from firm to firm. In firm A/1, as in firm A, the changes involved a complete standardization in the production of components. In firm A/2, some products were also standardized and made in very much larger quantities than they had been previously. In firm A/3 the standardization was applied to parts for some but not all products, a few kinds of product still being completely custom-built. Firm A/3 therefore was moving not only from unit to batch production but also from a unified to a mixed technology. Thus it had to face short-term problems of the kind which had occurred in firm A, as well as some of the longer-term problems occurring in firm B. Moreover, this particular kind of mixed technology was also susceptible to problems of production scheduling, resulting in the development of highly formalized control procedures. This was the only one of the firms studied at this stage of the research which used a computer for production scheduling. Indeed, the changes in production processes were probably the result of using the computer for this purpose. The board, persuaded by good sales technique and encouraged by a desire to 'keep up with the Joneses' had bought the computer and then began to consider the use which could be made of it. One field of application was production control, and the consideration of what was involved in this led to a complete review and reorganization of production operations.

Although in every case the technical changes led to a breakdown into feeder and final assembly shops, there was an interesting difference between firms in the layout of final assembly. In firms A and A/2 the layout continued to reflect the original product divisions. Groups of assemblers concentrated on types of product under specialized supervision. In firms A/1 and A/3 the manufacturing layout was of the process kind described in Chapter 9,[1] there was complete breakaway from any form of product specialization. Operators and first-line supervision dealt with different kinds of products in rotation, but the operations were so broken down that there was little variation in the knowledge and skills required to handle each kind.

Firms A/1, A/2 and A/3 were smaller than firm A. The latter was one of the few firms in the South Essex area employing between 2,000 and 4,000 people. Two of the other three firms employed between 1,000 and 2,000 people, and the third employed just under 1,000. Thus difference in size did not appear to affect the speed with which adjustment was made to technical change.

It will be remembered that the technical change that had taken place in firm A had been initiated by a change in ownership; this was also true of firm A/2. From the point of view of the research, it was a lucky chance that the organization which took this firm over had also been studied during the previous stages of the research; thus the research workers already knew a good deal about the traditions and culture to which firm A/2 became exposed as a result of the change in ownership.

In firm A/1 the technical change was triggered off by an extension being built on to the factory. Consultants had been brought in to advise on the design and specification of the new building, plant, and equipment. Production methods also had to be examined, with the result that a reorganization of work was associated with the move into the new building.

The changes that took place in firm A had resulted not from any change in objective but from an attempt to achieve the original objective in a more effective way. This was also true of firms A/1, A/2, and A/3. In the case of firm A/2, however, the ultimate result of the technical change was a modification in objectives. The increase in batch size and subsequent introduction of a standardized

1 See p. 154.

Table VI. *Differences Between Firms Moving from Unit to Batch Production*

	Original classification	Size category	Technical Change	Change in circumstances	Change in objective	Assembly layout
Firm A	Unit production	2,001–4,000	Standardization of most components	New owner-ship	Nil	Product layout
Firm A/1	Unit production	501–1,000	Standardization of components for all products	New buildings	Nil	Process layout
Firm A/2	Small batch production	1,001–2,000	Standardization of some products only	New owner-ship	Modification in market	Product layout
Firm A/3	Unit and small batch production	1,001–2,000	Standardization of components for some products only	Computer for production planning	Nil	Process layout

product made it necessary for the firm to gain an entry to a new kind of market. This was not anticipated when the original plans were made, but the change in ownership led to changes in marketing techniques as well as in technology, and the new market was successfully penetrated.

Summarizing what has been said above, Table VI shows the main differences between the four firms, and it will be seen later how significant these differences were in influencing adjustment to change.

(b) *Patterns of interaction*

Clues can be found in earlier chapters of the book (particularly in those concerned with the relationship between development, production, and marketing, and with the organization of production) to many of the problems encountered in firms A/1, A/2, and A/3 as they tried to adjust to a new system of production.

The differences between unit and batch production which proved to be most significant in this respect were those relating to patterns of communication and status relationships. The separation of production administration from the supervision of production operations, and the emergence of a separate and more formalized control system, which were inevitable consequences of the change in methods also gave rise to a number of problems.

As had already been observed, one characteristic of the communications network associated with unit production is that the emphasis tends to be on bridge rather than on line communications. Communications are as much inter- as intra-functional, and those employed at every level of the hierarchy have as much to do with colleagues in other sections of the firm as they do with superiors and subordinates inside their own departments. In large batch production, on the other hand, contacts between managerial and supervisory personnel are mainly contained within each task function. It must be stressed, however, that there was no complete breakaway from unit production in any of the firms studied; in every case, either some of the manufacturing processes or the manufacture of some of the products remained as before. This meant that the network of bridge communications already in existence had to be maintained while a much more complicated network of communications had to be built up inside each of the main functions of development, production, and marketing at the same time. The network inside the production function was much more complex than it had been before the changes took place, because it had to take account of the separation of production administration from the supervision of production operations. The practical result of the increasing complexity was likely to be that managers and supervisors would be brought into contact with a larger number of people than they had been before the changes took place.

The managers and supervisors interviewed in firm A had laid great stress on one result of the changes: they were much busier, and more conscious of pressure. They felt that they had less time to themselves than in the past, and spent more time on trouble-shooting activities of one kind or another.

In the studies of firms A/1, A/2, and A/3, an attempt was made to get more precise information about the increase of pressure. Approximately three months before the changes were actually put into effect, a research worker spent a week with the production superintendent in each firm, observing and recording what he did and whom he contacted. The same thing was done approximately three months after the changes had taken place. In each case the production superintendent had one level of supervision below him and one or two levels above; thus, he could be regarded as at middle management level in a literal as well as a figurative sense.

During the time that elapsed between the first and second periods of observation there had been no changes in either the status or the manifest functions of the people concerned. The lay-out and methods in the workshops over which they had control had changed, there had been a breakdown into feeder shops and final assembly, but they still had the same total area of responsibility. At the time of the first period of observation the changes had already been decided on; the production superintendents knew in detail what was going to happen, and were beginning to replan. The initiation of change being a time-consuming business, involving a lot of preliminary discussion and decision, it is probable that even at the time of the first period of observation life was already less calm for these production superintendents than it had been in the past. Even so, as Table VII (summarizing the changes that had taken place in interaction patterns) shows, there were considerable differences between the two periods.

Table VII. *Patterns of Interaction (Production Superintendents)*

	Firm A/1 Before change	Firm A/1 After change	Firm A/2 Before change	Firm A/2 After change	Firm A/3 Before change	Firm A/3 After change
1 (a) % of time spent alone; in office, on machines, etc.	30	28	36	18	33	20
(b) % of time spent in face to face or telephone communication with others	70	72	64	82	67	80
2 % of interaction time (i.e. (b) above) spent with:						
(a) Superiors and equals inside the production function	30	58	34	47	24	54
(b) Subordinates in the production function★	26	16	24	14	33	16
(c) Staff from development and marketing functions or administration	44	26	42	39	43	30
3 Average number of daily contacts (telephone calls, discussions, meetings etc.)	34	52	28	54	33	40

Several points of interest emerge from Table VII. First there is the consistency from one firm to another; the figures show differences of degree but trends are similar. All three production superintendents spent less time alone after the changes had taken place, and the average number of daily contacts increased. They spent more time in contact with people senior to themselves, and less with colleagues from other departments. They also had less to do with their own subordinates.

★ Included in these percentages is the time spent discussing subordinates' affairs with the staff of such departments as personnel, wages, accounts, and surgery.

These more detailed observations thus confirmed what had been said by the people interviewed in firm A. The production superintendents in firms A/1, A/2, and A/3 had certainly been made busier by the changes, and the fact that they spent more time with their superiors probably accounted for the greater consciousness of pressure.

The fact that the production superintendents spent less time alone was significant, for one result of the changes in production methods was an increase in the amount and complexity of the paper work associated with production. Thus, there was more reading, writing, and filing to be done and less time to do it in. This again linked up with what had been said in firm A; a good deal of resentment had been shown by those interviewed to what was referred to as the 'paper mill'. In every firm efforts were made to short-circuit the procedures and to find ways of producing the required data with the minimum of effort. Accuracy was sometimes sacrificed in the process, but as the people concerned had only a confused idea of the control function, and did not fully understand the purposes for which the data was being collected, there was very little incentive to record carefully.

The least reduction in the amount of time the production superintendent spent alone was in firm A/1. This was the firm in which the changes had led to a complete standardization of components and there had also been a move into a new building. The process of adjustment here took a different course. There was a brief period of complete chaos as people found their way around in their new surroundings. Subsequently, however, the changed environment seemed to make it easier for people to accept other changes, particularly those in methods and layout. By the time of the second period of observation there was a more settled atmosphere than in the other firms studied, and this affected the pattern of the production superintendent's day. This was also, of course, the firm referred to in the last chapter, which had previous experience of standardized production. The new methods were not as unfamiliar to the production superintendent as to his counterparts in the other firms studied, and his routine was more quickly established.

The main reason for the increase in the number of upward contacts seemed to be the separation of production operations

from the administration of production. In every firm new departments were set up to cover certain aspects of planning and control.
The production superintendents were therefore brought into
contact with senior planning and control personnel as well as with
their own immediate superiors. Furthermore, when problems
arose, as they frequently did in the course of these new contacts,
the superintendents tended to refer back to their line managers.
The fact that in firm A/1, although more settled than the other
firms, this increase in upward contacts had occurred, suggests that
this was a basic characteristic of the new technology.

But as standardization was not complete in any of these firms,
bridge communications with marketing and development functions still had to be maintained. Looking back to Table VI it will
be seen that in contrast to the other two firms included in Table
VII, the layout of the assembly shops in firm A/2 was on a product
basis. This is probably the reason why the proportion of time
spent with development and marketing personnel decreased less.
The product specialization theme, cutting across the functional
organization, was still dominant.

The amount of time spent on inter-functional contacts dropped
most in firm A/1, where by history and tradition the relationships
between the development and production departments had never
been as close as in other unit production firms studied. In both
firm A/1 and firm A/3, the reduction in bridge communications
created problems (these were the two firms in which a special
department was subsequently set up to close the gap that had
developed). It will be remembered that this experiment was more
successful in firm A/3 than in firm A/1.[2] In the circumstances it
was probably inevitable that interaction downwards was reduced.
In general the new problems were not of the kind that required
the production superintendents to go on to the shop floor, and
they spent less time there than they had done before the changes.
To keep in touch with foremen and operators as closely as before
would therefore have required a conscious effort.

This change in pattern had serious implications from the point
of view of good industrial relations. At a time when these firms
were especially vulnerable, partly because they were involved in
a process of change, and partly because their new technology was

[2] See p. 198.

less conducive to the building of harmonious and contributive industrial relations than their old, there was a drastic reduction in the amount of time spent by middle management on the shop floor.

Table VII shows that before the changes took place, the production superintendent in firm A/3 had been more downward oriented than his counterparts in the other two firms. Even in unit production it is unusual to find a middle manager spending more of his time with those below than with those above him in the hierarchy. He was interested in industrial relations problems outside as well as inside his own firm and had himself been a shop steward before his first promotion to foreman. He was also very skilful in dealing with the operators, taking an active part in the resolution of disputes.

It was interesting to find, therefore, that more labour disputes followed the technical changes in this than in any of the other firms studied. There were several stoppages of a few hours' duration, culminating in a three-day strike about six months later. The main reason seemed to be resentment at the withdrawal of the production superintendent from his close involvement in shop floor affairs. The shop stewards found it much more difficult to get hold of him and became increasingly disgruntled at the delays in getting their grievances dealt with. They were unaware of the fact that even under the changed circumstances the disputes procedure operated much more speedily in this than in most other firms studied, and could therefore only compare the present with the past.

Another contributory factor to the deterioration in industrial relations was the fact that the foremen were inadequately equipped to fill the gap left by the increased involvement of the production superintendent with his superiors. For several years his skill and interest in industrial relations, and his personal intervention in incidents that occurred on the shop floor, had taken from them the burden and responsibility of direct exposure to the operators—with the result that his withdrawal left them as well as the operators anxious and insecure.

(c) *Status relationships*

The technical changes which took place in firms A/1, A/2, and A/3 led to modifications in the status structure similar to that observed in firm A. The position of the development engineers who, as in most unit production firms, formed the *élite* and set the pace, was threatened by the rise in status of those responsible for the production function. There was also a re-alignment inside production itself; in particular the power, status, and area of discretion of the line supervisors and middle managers were reduced as the result of the increasing separation of production administration from the supervision of production operations. The staff responsible for production administration grew rapidly in number and in influence, and a number of specialists were brought in to organize production planning and control, work study and methods engineering, and cost accounting. There were changes too in the role and functions of the inspection departments and drawing offices. There was nothing new or revolutionary in the new approach to manufacturing; it is all familiar enough in large batch production and the problems likely to arise in organization of this kind have been described in earlier chapters.

The earlier investigations had shown that in the commercially successful firms status structure was closely linked with the criteria on which success depended, the people with the highest status being those concerned with the critical function. Thus, in all the firms where the first tentative move into batch production was being studied, the high status given to development engineers was a reflection of a determination to produce the latest or the best in a particular field of engineering. Even in firm A/1, where the mores of batch production had lingered as a result of an earlier phase of development, and where a considerable amount of hostility was shown towards them, the development engineers had managed to get themselves into a dominant position.

Had the change-over to standardized production been complete, therefore, with a new set of objectives emphasizing the importance of production and, in particular, the importance of the progressive reduction of production costs, the gain in status of production personnel, although it would have been painful for the development engineers, would have restored the balance between status structure and objectives, essential to commercial success. But in none of the firms studied was this the case. As Table VI showed, the change-over was partial and had resulted not from the setting of new objectives, but from an attempt to achieve original objectives in a more effective way. Even in firm A/2, where the changes led to a modification in objectives, this was incidental and had not been foreseen when the changes were initiated.

The underlying conflict of objectives may therefore have been the reason why the status struggle in these firms was so bitter, so disruptive, and so permanent. In each case the firm's reputation was still dependent on its development activities, and the development engineers still regarded themselves as the top people in the organization and their contribution as vital to the continued success of the business. But to the new administrators the main aim was cost reduction, with the most economic use being made of the firm's resources.

Conflict inside industrial organization is by no means unusual and not always destructive, but it seemed to the research workers that in these firms the new methods had been introduced without sufficient consideration of whether they would really achieve the original objectives more effectively. Another firm operating in the same type of industry had been visited during the earlier research where a similar attempt to modify techniques in order to increase production efficiency had been made and subsequently abandoned. Standards of performance were said to have deteriorated at all levels of the hierarchy, so that the firm's reputation for 'the best', on which its success depended, had been endangered. The status struggle showed itself in a general deterioration in relationships and in re-alignments inside the political systems of the firms concerned. It also had a practical significance in relation to changes in design and modifications in assembly routines after production had actually started.

Under the old system such changes could be accommodated relatively easily; they led to a minimum of wastage and disturbance. But even the partial standardization introduced into the firms studied made them a much more serious problem; they were the main cause of friction between development engineers and production planning and control staff. Not only did they lead to wastage of parts and materials but they also created delays that made a mockery of the attempts being made to schedule and control production.

The problems arising from design changes had first come to the notice of the research workers when studying firm A. They therefore tried to get more detailed information about them in the final studies. One interesting and unexpected fact emerged: it was not only found that design changes caused more disruption after the new methods had been introduced, but that they occurred more frequently. It is possible, of course, that differences in the complexity of the products in the pipeline accounted for the increase, although this was unlikely to have been the case in all three firms studied. Moreover, because design changes did cause so little disturbance, the research workers studying firms A/1, A/2 and A/3 in the period before the new methods were introduced might have failed to notice some that did occur. But there is another possible explanation of the increase; the very fact that a design change became an issue under the new system could have provoked the development engineers into making it. Such changes provided the design engineers with an opportunity to reassert themselves and to regain control of the situation. Those responsible for production control protested because of the disruption of their plans, but the modifications were always ultimately accepted. The firm's reputation for 'the best' put the development engineers in a strong position when arguing with higher authority. In two of the three firms studied the chief executive himself had previously been a member of the research and development staff.

The suggestion that design changes were a manifestation of the development engineers' desire to reassert themselves is supported by the fact that the biggest increase in their incidence occurred in firm A/2, where the new methods were associated in people's minds with the new owners. Here the impression was given that the struggle for status and supremacy was not only between the development and the production function, but also between the firm and the organization taking it over. The new owners represented the traditions and mores of large batch production, and as they had transferred from their own staff most of the people concerned with the rationalization of production, resistance to the new methods also meant resistance to the new owners. Even here, an argument about a design change was usually won by the development engineers, not so much because the new owners were committed to producing 'the best', but because they had relatively little experience of this type of engineering and had to

accept that if the design was not changed there was a chance of
the equipment failing to work and becoming a total loss.

(d) *Reactions of other departments to design changes*
It was interesting to find that those employed in other sections and
departments tended to be sympathetic to the design engineers and
to take their side when disputes with production planning personnel arose. Their most enthusiastic supporters were the departments who felt that they too had lost out as a result of the new
methods. As expected in view of what happened in firm A, the
drawing offices in the other three firms put up a lot of resistance
to the changes. The draughtsmen resented the fact that they were
no longer the main communicating link between development and
production, and felt that as the methods engineer rather than the
production supervisor now came to discuss their drawings with
them, their status had been reduced. In the crisis and confusion
that followed a design change, however, the new procedures
tended to be short-circuited or forgotten, and as a result the
draughtsmen temporarily reverted to their former role, enjoying
the renewing of old contacts.

The attitudes and behaviour of inspection personnel were
similar. They too appeared to enjoy the confusion caused by
design changes for much the same reason. In all three firms before
the changes took place the inspection department had been
responsible for commissioning and testing the finished equipment.
Thus the inspectors, like the draughtsmen, worked very closely
with development personnel. They usually collaborated with
them in working out the final test specifications. If a piece of
equipment failed to work the inspector concerned went straight
to the development engineers and they tried to analyse and solve
the problem together. As the inspection personnel indicated in
interview, they considered themselves close to the development
engineers in outlook and training, and regarded the contacts they
had with them as one of the major satisfactions of their job.

This happy relationship had been disrupted by the modification
in methods that changed the role and functions of the inspection
department. In the first place the production of standardized
parts created a need for a certain amount of physical or mechanical
inspection, and as this type of inspection is a lower-status activity

than the testing of products all the inspection personnel felt they lost status as a result: the inspection departments grew in size but not in prestige. Even more important, however, was that the close links with the development function were weakened by the intervention of methods engineers and planning staff. The firms varied to some extent in the procedure they adopted; in one case the methods department was made the main inspection contact in the formal communications network, this department becoming the bridge between development and production. In the other two firms, formal organization still allowed some direct communication between inspection and development in respect of test specifications, while the inspection standards for the standardized parts became the responsibility of the methods department. Thus, the inspectors had to get their instructions from the new methods engineers at whom they were inclined to scoff.

Thus design changes were welcomed by inspectors as they were by draughtsmen as excuses to re-establish their contacts and to short-circuit the methods department.

(e) *The control system*

It was the line supervisors in production departments whose attitude to design changes was most affected by the changes in methods. Before the new methods were introduced, design changes were resented by production personnel, and were the chief source of friction between them and the development engineers. Although design changes could be accommodated fairly easily, they made the line supervisors' job more troublesome, and the line supervisors made vigorous protests from time to time. After the changes had taken place, however, they were quick to realize that those responsible for production administration and control now had more to lose from design changes than they themselves.

In changing technology, managements had hoped to be able to improve the efficiency of production operations and to exercise greater control over the physical limitations of production. This meant an increasing formalization of the control system and greater emphasis being placed on supervisory failures. The line supervisors, therefore, soon began to see changes in design as loopholes in the control system. In the past such changes had made life more difficult; now they made it easier, as they provided good excuses for failure. In the six months between the first and second periods of observation, the production superintendents became much more tolerant of what they had previously regarded as the irritating idiosyncrasies of development engineers.

Changes in design after production had started certainly complicated the task of the production planning staff. In firms A/2 and A/3, they tried to modify their plans as necessary and to keep the situation under control. In firm A/1 however, circumstances soon got the better of them, and within a few months the new procedures and paper work of production became completely divorced from the reality of production operations. The paper work assumed an identity and momentum of its own, was created for its own sake, and was almost valueless as a technique for measuring the actual results of the operations of the firm against the results planned for. In some cases works orders appeared on the shop floor bearing delivery dates that had already passed. In others, work was completed on the shop floor and then had to be held back until the relevant paper work arrived. In practice, the advance planning was still carried out as it had been previously by rule of thumb and informal exchanges of information.

In firm A/3 the attempt to rationalize the production system created less friction between those responsible for production administration and those responsible for the supervision of production operations than elsewhere. Two factors contributed to this state of affairs. The first was the use of the computer for scheduling purposes. The introduction of the computer did create problems for the firm, particularly in relation to the staffing and skills required in the office. It was not possible within the scope of these investigations to follow up these problems; the research workers were more concerned with the effects of the new method of scheduling on production organization. Here the computer seemed to make things easier. It had an almost hypnotic effect on line supervision who accepted its decisions much more readily than they would have accepted the decisions of production planning staff made in the more conventional way. An element of 'theirs not to reason why' crept into their attitude and the number of disputes between production administration and those responsible for the supervision of production operations was considerably reduced.

The existence of the computer also made it easier to accept the changes in organization, and in particular the greater degree of centralization which had resulted from the introduction of the new production methods. Federal decentralization on a product type basis is not always compatible with the effective use of modern information technologies. What Follett (1927)[3] called the 'law of the situation' made it obvious to the production supervisors that the computer had made it impossible for them to go on in the same self contained way as before.

The second factor was that many of the new production administration staff, particularly in the work study and methods engineering sections, were skilled craftsmen promoted from the shop floor. This not only gave great satisfaction to the people concerned—as one of them said 'I didn't think I'd ever be coming to work in a white collar'—but it had a stimulating effect generally, as it was felt that the changes in methods were improving the chances of promotion. Moreover, the new production administration staff knew the older supervision well and were therefore better equipped to deal with problems that arose.

(f) *The success of the new methods*

These three studies, like the study of firm A, provided the research workers with examples of the continuous and increasing efforts that are being made in industry today to rationalize production systems in the interests of increased industrial efficiency. The furthering of this rationalization process, not only by speeding up and intensifying it but by extending its range to a wide area of technology, is the concern both of progressive managements and those working at a more academic level in the production engineering and operational research fields.

The studies showed that this rationalization process has wide human and social implications; it affects not only the content of the work done by operators, supervisors and ancillary groups, but also the context in which that work is done. It leads to a reduction in the area of discretion of individuals and replaces co-ordination through direct contact between individuals with co-ordination at a more remote level, through the reciprocal relating of the various factors in the situation. Some of the problems arising as a result

[3] Follett, op. cit., p. 35.

have been described in this chapter. It remains to consider whether in spite of these problems, the firms did achieve the increased production efficiency at which they were aiming. In firm A there was evidence in the form of control data to suggest that benefit had been derived from the new methods. The reasons for success appeared to be the fund of good inter-department relationships, which made it possible to get over the disruption caused by the changes, and the fact that men of exceptional drive and ability were associated with the new methods.

In the firms studied subsequently the results were less certain. In firms A/1 and A/3 the stimulus of the new building and the introduction of the computer facilitated adjustment to the changes. In all three firms the large number of components or items of equipment going through the production lines simultaneously made the task of those responsible for production planning and control a difficult one. To achieve their targets they required a close and continuous collaboration from line supervisors prepared to act as trouble-shooters as and when the need arose. This the line supervisors were often not prepared to do. The extra pressure put upon them and the targets they were set made it necessary for them to concentrate on getting out of their own troubles rather than letting themselves become involved in the troubles of others. This, together with the confusion in objectives resulting from the technical changes and the fact that the reputation for producing 'the best' was put in jeopardy, may have outweighed the advantages derived from the new and more rational production techniques.

Thus, these studies led to the conclusion that there may be limitations in the range of technology to which the new techniques of rationalization and analysis can successfully be applied. While their value is not questioned in the more traditional batch production fields, it was felt that in this type of industry efficient production might have been achieved more successfully by a systematic attempt to improve the calibre of line supervision and to increase their skill in the making of hunch decisions than by the introduction of rationalized production techniques.

FROM PROCESS TO BATCH PRODUCTION

Firm B/1, like firm B studied earlier, had been drawn into the batch production area of technology as a result of a decision to package and prepare for sale products which had hitherto been sold in bulk. This happened to be the only firm in South Essex which started to package its products in the period under review, but as the background survey had shown, nine firms in the area were already doing this. Moreover, in view of the increasing enthusiasm for packaged goods of all kinds, the problems associated with this particular technical change will be commonplace to managers up and down the country.

The background survey had shown that most of the firms in this category organized the packaging activity independently of the process. Each activity was the responsibility of a senior executive who (sometimes on paper, and always in practice) had a considerable amount of freedom in determining his relationship with the other parts of the organization. It was found that there were longer lines of command on the process than there were on the packaging side of the organization, and similar differences were seen in many of the other facts and figures collected about organization. The organizational structure required by the process did not seem appropriate to the packaging activity and relatively little thought had been given to deciding whether or how the two types of production could be welded together into a single social system. This was certainly the case in firm B. Here the new activities had brought in new personnel, many of whom had spent all their working lives in batch production industry. An organizational structure, typical of large batch production, in which there was a separation of production administration from the supervision of production operations, was set up. From what was said, in the initial stages there were apparently few problems arising from the readjustment of existing personnel to a new set of circumstances. The new functional specialists had had their hands full in setting up a planning and control system for the new activities, and they felt that it was only when they needed information or scheduling modifications from the plant supervision that the problems of establishing a more comprehensive communications network were revealed. The most serious difficulty appeared to be that of reconciling the related roles of line supervision and functional specialists in a standard operating practice to cover all the firm's activities.

Differences in tradition between process industry and large

batch production became exaggerated when the two systems were brought into contact. It was found that there were considerable differences in the managers' and supervisors' dress, behaviour, routines, and attitudes to work between the two sides of the factory; references were made to the 'wall' dividing the process from the packaging end. The process managers spent most of their time on the plant itself, the duffle coat being their uniform. The packaging managers spent most of their time in their offices, in white collars and neat suits. There was rivalry between the two groups not only about their relative importance to the success of the enterprise, but also about their relationships with the chief executive and board. Although this conflict had repercussions throughout the hierarchy, it created most problems for the people at the top. From what happened in firm B it seemed that the introduction of packaging activities is the kind of technical change which makes life especially difficult for the chief executive and his immediate subordinates.

In studying firm B/1, therefore, the focus of attention was on the top of the hierarchy. The main interest of the study lay in seeing whether the senior managers were able to find a way of effecting the integration of the new with the older activities. In this firm, before and after studies of the role and routines of the chief executive were made, in much the same way as those of the production superintendents had been studied in firms A/1, A/2, and A/3; the chief executive being sufficiently interested in the research to subject himself to detailed investigation.

The study confirmed that the changes had increased the pressure under which he worked. Before the changes, he had spent only 5 per cent of his time in discussing technical problems and making decisions about technical matters. By the time of the second period of observation, this had risen to 28 per cent. The other big increase was in the time he spent in dealing with disagreements between members of senior management and in organizational problems generally. Here the figure increased by 17 per cent. In this firm the plants were mainly of the multi-purpose type. He not only had problems of plant utilization resulting from the need to provide adequately for the new packaging operations, and the resultant complication of programmes and schedules, but also such problems as losses of raw materials during the chemical processing becoming more difficult to deal with. It is doubtful whether plant performance had actually deteriorated, but as more people were now interested in performance levels, more time was spent discussing them.

This increase in both technical involvement and trouble-shooting activities meant that there was less slack in the chief executive's timetable. He therefore found it necessary to cut down the time he spent on other management activities, for example routine visits to the plants; this reduction was from $12\frac{1}{2}$ to 5 per cent. The effect of this on the standards of tidiness and house-keeping on the plants, was soon apparent, and it was not surprising to find that six months after the new packaging departments started to operate the factory accident rate had increased. This was due not only to the higher rate at the packaging end but also to an increase in accidents on the plant.

The other big reduction was in the time spent on the ritual duties of the chief executive. Moreover, the amount of time spent interviewing or talking on the telephone to trade union officials went down in the six months between the two periods of observation from 18 to 7 per cent. This meant that more decisions about industrial relations matters were made either by middle management or by the personnel department. The effect of what appeared to be a withdrawal on the part of the chief executive had a similar effect on the attitudes of the trade union officials as the withdrawal of the production superintendents had had on the attitudes of the shop stewards in firm A/3. There was resentment at the increased delay in dealing with grievances and a feeling that the climate of industrial relations had deteriorated. The technical change in this firm not only created problems of industrial relations but impaired the effectiveness of the existing procedural arrangements. This study, like those of firms A/1, A/2, and A/3, also showed how detailed changes in routines arising out of technical changes can in themselves provide an explanation of some of the human relations problems associated with these changes

The study of firm B/1 also threw more light on the long-term problem of building up harmonious and contributive relationships between those responsible for the process activities and the staff brought in to deal with the packaging end of production operations.

The following table shows the interviewers' assessment of the effect on attitudes to other departments brought about by the changes. This table was compiled from answers to a series of questions about relationships between production and other departments.

Table VIII. *Attitude to Other Departments—Firm B/1*

| | Before changes | | After changes | |
	No	%	No	%
Good	42	77	41	65
Average	10	18	12	19
Bad	3	5	10	16
TOTALS	55	100	63	100

When first studied the social structure of firm B/1 was typical of process industry generally. There was the inner social system centred around the plants themselves. Marketing and research activities were too remote to be a cause of anxiety as was the making of manufacturing policy. In the operation of the plants, planning and control were closely associated with execution. The relationships built up around the new packaging activities, however, were typical of large batch production; closer collaboration between production and marketing and the separation of the element functions within production, was required. There was a breakdown into production supervision and production administration, unfamiliar to those concerned with plant operation.

While as in firm B the two technologies operated with a 'wall' between them, things went reasonably well. But in this firm the production specialists did not take kindly to staying on one side of the 'wall' for ever. When they had the immediate situation on the packaging side under control, they began to feel that they could do their job more effectively if they could extend their activities to plant operations. The plant supervisors resented this intrusion, and made it as difficult as possible for them to obtain control information. This behaviour was regarded by the production specialists as completely irrational and merely an expression of resistance to change. They looked to the chief executive to give them more power to deal with the recalcitrant plant managers. The reluctance he showed was regarded as weakness.

The most difficult problems arose in the personnel management area. The firm had recently appointed a new personnel manager. This appointment was coincidental with the technical changes that had taken place, but the two things were not casually related. It so happened, however, that the previous experience of the new personnel manager had been in large batch production industry, and he was therefore unable to recognize the special problems arising on the plant as a result of the technical changes. He realized that he was performing a very useful function in helping to iron out the industrial relations problems arising in connection with the new activities. Much pressure was being exerted on the operators by the line supervision and the personnel manager was acting as a safety valve. The line supervisors themselves accepted this, and although they maintained the myth of line-staff friction they were really very relieved at having someone on whom they could unload their problems. Indeed, the tendency to make industrial relations a loophole in the control system was recognizable from the outset as part of the behavioural pattern of the line supervision. But the plant managers took a different view: they were jealous of their relationship with their operators. They felt with some justification that as they had known them well for a long time they were better judges of the validity of their complaints than the personnel manager. The personnel manager failed to recognize that the situation on the plant was basically different from that on the assembly lines. His formal training in personnel management had laid emphasis on the importance of applying personnel policy, and operating industrial relations procedures at a uniform level throughout the firm. Like the other functional specialists who had to deal with the plant managers as well as the packaging managers, he was unable to understand or accept the duality of role which was imposed upon him by having to deal with the two different technologies.

It seems that it is this lack of understanding encouraged by the emergence of management specialization and the growth of specialist mores and ideologies which make it so difficult for even the most enlightened and sophisticated top management to weld together different technologies into an integrated organizational structure. Technical advance will make these mixed technologies more common, and it will be increasingly important to build the ability to recognize the needs of different technologies into the training of functional specialists, personnel managers in particular.

TOWARDS AUTOMATION

The technical changes so far described in this chapter were not interesting in themselves; as already indicated, there was little that was new in the techniques introduced. From a technical point of view their main interest lay in the attempt to apply the rationalization and production techniques of standardized production to a wider area of technology. Probably the greater number of technical changes introduced into British industry in the next decade will still be of this kind. This will mean that there is likely to be an increase rather than a decrease in industrial relations and organizational problems.

But in the other three firms studied, the technical changes were of the kind to which the term 'automation' is usually applied. They were therefore of particular interest in providing clues to the future and in making it possible to put to the test the conclusion to which the whole of the research programme described in this book had consistently pointed: that as far as internal relationships are concerned, both at inter-managerial and at management-worker level, automation is likely to resolve more problems than it creates.

We have seen how in the building up of harmonious and contributive human relationships the technically advanced firm of the process industry type starts with a number of advantages. As far as can be foreseen, the automatic factory will have these too. To sum up: in the first place the low proportion of total turnover allocated to labour costs encourages a more flexible approach to bargaining and wage negotiations. Small primary working groups, supervisors with limited spans of control, high ratios of managerial to hourly paid workers, of administrative and clerical to industrial workers, and of indirect to direct workers are all conclusive to the building up of strong loyalties and close associations at every level between superior and subordinate. Personal relationships develop which blur the edges of role relationships and make both role conflict and innovation easier to deal with.

Another advantage of this type of industry from the industrial relations point of view is the negative relationship that exists between productivity and effort, people having to work hardest when things go wrong. Human beings respond almost automatically to crisis situations and on these occasions can work hard without experiencing the pressures associated with the continuous and routine efforts of batch production workers.

Moreover, technical advance is usually associated with more sophisticated management; the managers concerned tend to have a better educational background, form a more socially homogeneous group and approach their problems more intellectually and less emotionally than their counterparts in batch production. There is greater awareness of the nature of risk and uncertainty in the making of decisions.

In the last three case studies, therefore, the research workers were looking for an improvement in the long term as a result of the changes. Their predictions about the worsening of conditions in the firms already studied proved to be correct; it was going to be interesting to see whether the predicted improvement would come about as obviously and speedily as the deterioration in the other four firms.

The improvement was almost immediate in the first firm studied —this was the firm changing from multi-purpose to single-purpose plants. Industrial and inter-managerial relations were already of a high standard in this firm, and the way the changes were handled made them better. New plant had to be built and existing plant modified; thus there was a time lag of nearly two years between the decision to change and the commissioning of the new plants. The firm wisely used this to plan in advance the organizational and labour policy modifications demanded by the new situation.

The firm was fortunate in that although the new plants required less labour than the old, the difference in labour requirements was accommodated within the normal labour wastage during the building period. The operators responded to any labour crisis during this period in the way they normally do in process industry. They worked double shifts and additional overtime to keep things going in the last few months when the plants were seriously undermanned.

Concern had been expressed at the outset about whether the

existing plant operators would be able to cope satisfactorily with the more complicated continuous-flow plants. It had also been decided to transfer the routine testing of the products hitherto carried out in the laboratories to the plant itself in order to speed up the feeding back of control information. It was therefore necessary to carry out an intensive operator re-training programme. This led to a re-examination of the wage structure and the adjustment of wage differentials to fit a new job evaluation scheme.

Re-training and reorganization were also necessary at the management level. The change-over meant a considerable reduction in the scheduling and programming activities. Less attention had to be paid to plant utilization, and the maintenance work was simplified. In reorganizing, the firm was helped by the fact that process industry tends to recognize specialisms but not specialists. The people who had been responsible for the activities whose importance had decreased also had a wide variety of other experience, and they were soon re-absorbed into other jobs.

The only serious problem that arose during the change-over period was finding alternative employment for the laboratory assistants who were no longer needed on routine testing. They were offered work on the plant, with the promise that after training they would be considered for junior supervisory posts as operating assistants. Most of them felt, however, that this was a reduction in status even although staff status for hourly-paid operators was at that time under consideration; they preferred to look outside for laboratory assistant or junior administrative jobs. This reflected a problem discussed in earlier chapters of this book: the inadequacy of the traditional industrial status structure to accommodate the work roles of technically advanced industry. This technical change went smoothly throughout, with little disruption, and no press publicity. Relationships being already good, there was a sound basis on which to build. Another possible reason for success was the intellectual approach to the analysis of the problem which in return stimulated a rational response from the people involved. Only in the case of laboratory assistants was an issue debated with high emotional content. But perhaps the most important factor in the situation was that managers and operators got to know the new plants during the building stage. They looked very much like the old plants, and therefore created little anxiety in the minds of the people who were going to operate them.

The technical changes that took place in the other two firms studied were manifested more dramatically, and this may be one of the reasons why the adjustment to them was a longer and more painful process. The automatic packaging plant with inbuilt inspection and counting mechanisms, and the automatic assembly line of the transfer machine type with its uncanny mechanical handling devices created feelings of anxiety even in the research workers themselves, although they were not directly involved.

Nothing came out of these two case studies to suggest that in the long term the calm and harmony characteristic of technically advanced industry would not prevail; indeed, there were indications that this was beginning to happen before the research workers completed their investigation. But these two cases certainly provided empirical evidence of Festinger's (1957)[4] thesis that longer-term satisfactions are not necessarily incompatible with real dissatisfaction at the time of change. Mann and Hoffman (1960)[5] in describing the effects of technical advance in power plants, showed how initial resistance to change was broken down as the operators began to get some compensations in the form of enhanced status and increased security for the decrease in satisfaction they got from the work itself. They also found that the organizational framework in which their work was done had become more congenial.

This suggests another explanation of why the changes went so smoothly in the first firm. By chance or design—probably the former—the management took advantage of the long building period to make the people concerned aware of the compensating advantages they were getting from the changes almost before they experienced the disadvantages. There are practical implications here for the future. Where the advantages of technical change are likely in the long term to outweigh the disadvantages, it is in management's interest to ensure that the people concerned become aware of this through day-to-day experience as soon as possible.

As implied in the last chapter, the research workers got the

[4] L. Festinger, *A Theory of Cognitive Dissonance* (Tavistock Publications, London).

[5] F. C. Mann and C. S. Hoffman, *Automation and the Worker* (R. Hall and Co., New York).

impression that some of the resistance to change they observed in their two final case studies resulted from a positive determination to get as much as possible out of the changes, rather than from insecurity. From a bargaining point of view, therefore, it was unfortunate that in both firms the situation immediately preceding the changes was an abnormal one from the operator's point of view. The decision to instal the new machinery had been made in the first place because of bottlenecks due to inadequate production capacity. In both firms this had resulted in an excessive amount of overtime and high bonus earnings. The immediate effect of the changes as far as the operators were concerned, therefore, was a drop in take-home pay, and it was not until the passage of time had taken the sting out of this and they had got used to lower earnings again, that they could appreciate the advantages of their new situation. Management, on the other hand, because it had been forced to pay what it considered to be inflated rates on the new plants to provide partial compensation for loss of overtime, was in no mood to overlook failure on the part of the operators or to relax pressure in the way they might have done in the new technical situation.

This may all seem very down-to-earth and obvious in comparison with much that has been said and written by social scientists about resistance to change, and it may be that if these practical problems had not arisen, there would still have been disturbances which were not so easily accounted for. But as Lupton (1963)[6] found, industrial behaviour tends to be more rational than has sometimes been supposed. There may be two worlds in the factory but there is usually only one logic. The management and the operator worlds are affected differently by the way in which organizational goals are set and the work organized, but in both cases behaviour tends to be a function of the circumstances appertaining in the factory.

In these two firms, it may have been inevitable for pre-change conditions to develop which made the change-over itself more difficult. It did seem, however, that if more of the problems had been foreseen, and the technical changes planned for in the thorough-going way that they had been in the first firm studied in this group, there would probably have been less disruption,

6 T. Lupton, *On the Shop Floor* (Pergamon Press, Oxford).

and a state of equilibrium would have been reached more speedily.

THE RELATIONSHIP BETWEEN FORMAL AND INFORMAL ORGANIZATION

As has already been made clear these investigations covered a wide range of research methods. The background survey was based on the collection of factual information during the relatively short visits to firms, and the earlier case studies on interviewing and longer periods of association. The changed relationship between the research worker and the firms studied, and the facilities offered in the final stages of the project, made the methods of social anthropology easier to apply. It obviously would not have been practicable for the research workers to pitch their tent on the factory floor or in the managing director's office, but they were able to spend long periods of time in both workshops and offices without becoming directly involved in what was going on, and without conducting a formal interview.

It was interesting to find that from these different approaches, different pictures of the same firm were obtained. The picture emerging from the background survey was not always in accord with that emerging from the more detailed case studies carried out later. One reason for this has already been noted: as analysis deepens, differences between firms tend to stand out more clearly than similarities. In the main, however, the discrepancies were related to the depth at which it was possible to study the way in which informal organization operated. Even from the relatively superficial enquiries made for the background survey, some light was thrown on this aspect of organization. But in both the background survey and the earlier case studies, the research workers could only rely for cues on the conflicting and contradicting accounts of the same organizational characteristics and procedures given by the different people contacted. A limitation of this approach was that it made the appraisal of formal organization and informal organization as separate parts of social structure almost inevitable; these two major concepts of organization could only be related on a basis of discrepancy and deviation. The emphasis had to be put on the way that organizational goals were modified and organizational patterns distorted by the behaviour of managers and supervisors, either as individuals or as members of groups. The new approach led to a greater appreciation of the functions of formal and informal organization as parts of a whole, and of the complexity of the relationship between them. It was found, for example, that organizational objectives were frequently achieved through the informal rather than the formal organization. A disfunctional formal organization could be compensated by contributive informal relationships. This was particularly noticeable in relation to technical change.

In three of the firms studied during the last phase of the research, organizational changes were planned and put into effect at the same time as the technical change; here technical change had a direct impact on organization and the interest for the research team lay in the adaptation of informal organization, not only to the technical changes themselves, but also to the decisions that had been taken in the formal organization context. In the remaining firms technical changes were made independently of formal organization, it having been taken for granted that the existing organizational structure would prove adequate for the new technology. In every case this proved to be not so. The first thing that happened was that informal organization began to respond to the new situational demands imposed upon it. The result was a serious discrepancy between formal and informal organization, and the achievement of organizational goals almost entirely through an informal network of relationships. In general, senior management were sophisticated enough to be aware that this was happening, and after a varying period of time had elapsed changes were made in formal organization. Either the existing informal relationships were defined and formalized or mechanisms were introduced to minimize the discrepancy. For example, in one firm a production committee was set up to allow people to establish contact with those to whom they were not related in the formal hierarchy.

Although this adjustment of formal to informal organization was the more interesting social process, from the point of view of successful adaptation, the balance of advantage appeared to lie with the simultaneous introduction of technical and organizational change. It was true that at the outset the organizational disturbance was more dramatic, and in one firm the disgruntlement caused by the organizational changes undoubtedly increased the hostility shown towards the technical changes themselves. Adjustment was, however, a much speedier process. One reason for this was that the critical organizational decisions were made in advance; there was less occasion or opportunity for political manœuvre and for the power bargaining referred to earlier. Adjustment to technical and organizational change took place simultaneously, informal organization was slowly modified to cope with the new situation, and the process was continuously under control.

12 *Towards an Organization Theory, 1953–1963*

The decade covered by the investigations described here has seen not only a considerable increase in the number of empirical studies of management behaviour being undertaken, but also the emergence of several schools of thought on organizational theory.

Looking back to September 1953 and the setting up of the Human Relations Research Unit at the South East Essex College of Technology, it now seems almost unbelievable that the methodological problems of studying management behaviour loomed so large, or that the theoretical framework for the proposed studies was so limited and orderly.

The phrase 'classical management theory' has been used throughout this book to denote the systematic body of knowledge about organization developed by Frederick Taylor, Henry Fayol, and their successors. The adjective 'classical' has been generally applied to this body of knowledge only in the last few years or so to distinguish it from the more recent schools of thought. At the time the research began there was no other systematic body of knowledge to which the term 'organization theory' could be applied. This does not mean, of course, that social scientists had not by then come into the industrial research field at all. Indeed, one of the more far-reaching effects of the Hawthorne investigations was that they brought the social sciences in an integrated way into the study and analysis of industrial behaviour. But except that Burns's concept of organic and mechanistic systems of organization was applied to the survey data as a separate and subsequent exercise,[1] the analysis of the original data obtained in this research was based entirely on the concepts and ideas of

[1] See p. 23.

classical management theory, with the result that the facts and figures presented in Chapter 2 tend to illustrate the scope and limitations of the classical approach. The four major and related elements in the theory were the division of labour, the scalar and functional organizational processes, and the structure which resulted from them. In the analysis of the information the scalar processes are implied in such aspects of organization as the length and growth of the command hierarchy, the size of the span of control, accountability, and delegation of authority; while the functional processes are represented in the grouping of the specialized activities resulting from the division of labour, and particularly in line-staff relationships. The aim of the pioneers in the management field was to establish management theory on scientific foundations, to formulate laws which would describe phenomena and explain the relationship between cause and effect.

Implicit in their approach was the assumption that the work to be done in an organization can be so divided and the relationships between tasks and between those responsible for tasks so ordered that the effective achievement of the overall objectives of the organization is assured. They also believed that the rules for doing this could be evolved through a process of deductive reasoning. Certain assumptions about organizational behaviour were implicit in this approach. For example, it was more or less taken for granted that people who join an employing organization either accept it and its purposes, or can be educated to do so, with the result that they will behave in the way that advances organizational goals.

The studies undertaken at the South East Essex College of Technology were by no means the first to demonstrate that the rules of classical management theory do not always work in practice. This was the conclusion reached by those responsible for the Hawthorne investigations, and the entry of the social scientists into the field was triggered off by the need to find an explanation of the failure. In seeking an explanation social scientists questioned neither the appropriateness of the rules nor the conceptual framework of the theory, but the behavioural assumptions implicit in it. Their contention was that at neither manager nor operator level do people consistently behave rationally within the same system of rationality as that on which the organizational goals are based. This was the starting point of what might be called the traditional social science or behavioural approach to the study of organization. The earlier social scientists operating in the industrial field regarded organization as springing up almost spontaneously in response to social needs. Their central thesis was that since management involved getting things done through people, the study of organization should be concentrated on inter-personal relationships. Many empirical studies of industrial behaviour have been undertaken since the publication of the Hawthorne results, on the basis of what is fundamentally the same hypothesis: that there are a number of factors other than the formal specifications laid down for the pursuit of organization goals which influence the behaviour of people and groups within an industrial setting. Different social scientists have concentrated on the factors of most interest to them—from the effect of in-dividual personality differences at the psychological end to the cultural aspects of industrial behaviour at the social anthropology end.

At first sight it appears that the approach of the traditional social scientist is in conflict with the approach of the classical manage-ment theorist. Certainly two bodies of knowledge have been built up which to a considerable extent cancel out each other. But classical management theorists and social scientists managed on the whole to live quite happily together. There were dogmatists on both sides always sniping at the other; but as management education got under way in this country, both approaches were represented in the syllabuses of courses, and the contribution of the social scientists came to be regarded as compensatory rather than contradictory to classical management theory. The human relations movement which grew out of the Hawthorne researches did not question the ideas and theories of the classical approach, but took the view that modifications had to be superimposed to allow for the fact that people act in response to other pressures. If the rules of classical management theory failed to work, the failure was due either to imperfections in the way that they were applied or to the capacity of human beings to disrupt even the most carefully laid organizational plans. It was therefore important for managers to know about the factors underlying human interactions and to increase their sophistication and skill in dealing with human behaviour. Management could look to the social scientists for help in making the rules work.

Co-existence at the intellectual level was facilitated in two ways. First it became generally accepted that the phenomena explained by organization theory were different from those explained by social science, and that the former were related to the macro as opposed to the micro approach. Secondly, formal organization came to be regarded as the province of organization theorists, while informal organization became the subject matter of social science research.

It was interesting to find, for example, that as recent a writer on classical management theory as Brech (1957)[2] makes no reference to informal organization. The social scientists of the 1940s, on the other hand, also seemed almost too ready to accept the idea that informal organization was their main field of interest, emphasizing that it was through this facet of organization that the social needs of individuals and groups were primarily met.

This separation of formal and informal organization as fields of study had unfortunate repercussions as far as the development of industrial sociology was concerned. Mayo and his associates at Hawthorne used Pareto's concept of the social system to help them with the analysis of their results. They saw organization as a complex of interdependent but variable factors and identified formal and informal organization as two of these variables; the interdependence of formal and informal organization being basic to the concept. The emergence of these two facets of organization as separate and almost independent parts of a whole confused the issue; the impression was created that each could be looked at in isolation and that the interaction between them could be analysed in the same terms as the interaction between separate organizations or between separate parts of organizations. The relationships between formal and informal organization was one of the recurrent themes of social science research in the late 1940s. This distortion of the original social system concept may be the reason why this period was such an arid one from a theory-building point of view.

The fact that the research at the South East Essex College of Technology started at a time when this separation of formal from

[2] E. F. L. Brech, *Organization* (Longmans, Green and Co., London).

informal organization was almost complete is reflected in the earlier chapters of this book. In formulating the study the research workers regretted that the methods of study were inappropriate to the analysis of informal organization and reconciled themselves to the fact that only formal organization could be included in their examination. But as the research proceeded it became increasingly clear that even the most superficial examination of organizational structure brought them into contact with the patterns and problems of informal as well as formal organization, and as the investigations deepened in character, the dividing line between the two facets of organization became increasingly difficult to draw; they certainly did not interact with each other in the way implied in the original approach.

The controversy that followed the publication of the booklet *Management and Technology* in 1958[3] can only be understood against this climate of opinion. Had the South Essex research merely indicated that in the firms studied, the rules of classical management theory did not always work in practice, or implied that the failures observed were due to human intervention or inconsistencies, all would have been well. The emotion aroused was due to the suggestion that the failure was not human but circumstantial, the underlying assumption being that the principles of management theory were adequate only within a very limited area of technology in providing either solutions to concrete problems or a basis for the examination and interpretation of organizational behaviour. There was also a suggestion in the research results that the phenomena explained by management theory and social science respectively were fundamentally the same.

To many, although by no means all of those concerned with management education in 1958, these assertions were regarded as a threat rather than a challenge. The British Institute of Management, through its Education Officer, sought the views of the teachers of management subjects preparing students for the Diploma in Management, and the underlying theme of much of the correspondence thus initiated was that 'to deny the existence of the management principles of such pioneers as Taylor, Fayol, and Follett, was to strike at the very roots of all that has been done and

---

[3] Woodward, op. cit., p. 186.

is being done in technical colleges and elsewhere in the field of management education'.

This reaction was not altogether unexpected. Management education had been a plant of very slow growth in this country. By 1958 most of the larger firms had taken steps to provide in-company training for their potential managers, but the traditional faith in learning by experience was an obstacle to the development of any enthusiasm for longer-term external courses. Academic institutions were also ambivalent; inside universities and technical colleges, management education outside a fairly narrow technical field was generally regarded as a fringe activity. This not only affected the quantity and academic quality of the students and teachers attracted to this field, but also led to the development of defensive and aggressive attitudes among those who had been so attracted. In this climate of opinion it was not surprising that any ideas which appeared to question the content of management education programmes should be immediately rejected.

Another interesting feature of the correspondence was the emphasis placed on the fact that no good teacher of management subjects continued to put across the rules of management theory as though they were principles in the scientific sense, or as Urwick (1958)[4] said 'no serious student of management has ever suggested that there was one best way of organizing a business'. The phrase 'flexible rules' was also used to describe the way in which management theory was then being taught.

This emphasis on flexibility indicated the change in approach that was beginning to be noticeable in management education about this time. The use of the phrase 'flexible rules', which in itself suggests a dilemma because it is a contradiction in terms, reflected the drift away from the determinism which was characteristic of the classical approach. This can also be seen in the management textbooks published or re-published about that time. Davis (1957), for example, says: 'While Taylor employed certain mechanisms he adopted the applications of his principles to the conditions and requirements of each business situation as he found it.'[5] A similar drift was taking place in the narrower field of

---

[4] L. Urwick, *Times* Review of Industry, December 1958 (London).
[5] Ralph Currier Davis, *Industrial Organization and Management* (Harper Brothers, New York, p. 16).

industrial engineering; in the planning and control of manufacturing operations older methods were giving way to operational research techniques. The philosophy of the 'one best way' was replaced by the philosophy of the better way and deterministic methods by statistical analysis. The collapse of the earlier approach to industrial engineering led to the development of new scientific methods through which it was hoped to understand, utilize, and control industrial operations better.

The main conclusion of the South Essex studies—that the same principles can produce different results in different circumstances although too soon and too crudely expressed for general acceptance was no more than the empirical demonstration of a truth already fundamental to the thinking of many of those involved in teaching and research in the management field at that time. Had they not been so sensitive they would have realized that far from casting away management principles altogether, one of the more significant factors in the research findings was the confirmation that these principles were positively linked with business success in one particular area of technology. But the recognition that the same principles can and do produce different results in different circumstances, although important from a teaching point of view, is obviously not enough. Flexible rules are neither an adequate guide to those who have practical management problems to contend with, nor likely to provide the basis of a valid theory of organization.

The research showed not that the rules themselves were valueless, but as a guide to action their use was limited, the crux of the problem lying in the quotation from Davis given above. In Taylor's work, as in that of all the adherents of the classical school of thought, the process of adaptation is more important than the rules themselves. An analogy can be taken from physics; water does not always boil at 100° Celsius, but as a 'flexible rule' this statement can provide a useful generalization for everyday requirements. But before a serious student of physics can reach any understanding of the underlying scientific processes, however, the exact circumstances under which water fails to boil at this temperature have to be identified and explained.

Analytically the central problem in the development of a comprehensive theory of organization is to determine the conditions under which behaviour inside organizations becomes standardized and predictable. Techniques have to be found to describe systematically, and evaluate quantitatively, complex and intricate manufacturing situations. Such techniques would provide not only a tool for the student of organization but also a method of tackling concrete organizational problems. They would provide an answer to a question so often in the minds of those responsible for organizational planning: how can an assessment be made of the appropriateness of a firm's existing organizational pattern to its needs ?

Probably the most important facet of the South Essex studies was the contribution they made to the solution of this problem. It is not suggested that the research produced anything approaching a general law about the relationship of technology to organizational behaviour. The difficulties of defining and measuring technology made this impossible. It did suggest, however, that technology, particularly at Dubin's (1959)[6] second level, that is the technology involved in carrying out the managerial function, is causally related to the structural and behaviour variations observed in manufacturing situations.

The work that was done concurrently by Sayles[7] at Columbia, and Trist[8] at the Tavistock Institute in London, suggests that this is also true at Dubin's first level of technology, that relating to the tools and machines of manufacture. These researches like the South Essex studies, and the work of Dubin himself all provide demonstrations of the fact that information relating to different kinds of manufacturing situations can be systematized, and uniformities traced among the diversities. Theoretically this means that it might be possible for sociologists interested in organization to build stabilized variable models of the kind used by economists. Organizational structure is the complete product of an unknown number of variables, and appropriate solutions to organizational problems might therefore be found by holding some variables constant and regarding the remainder as mathematically interdependent.

The South Essex studies also helped to identify the areas in which more concentrated empirical work is needed. References

---

[6] Dubin, op. cit., p. 36.   [7] Sayles, op. cit., p. 194.

[8] The latest and most comprehensive account of this work is to be found in E. L. Trist, G. W. Higgin, H. Murray, A. B. Pollock, *Organizational Choice* Tavistock Publications, London, 1963).

have already been made to the lack of a satisfactory instrument for measuring technology. This is needed at both levels. Then there is the problem of the relationship between management control and technology. Is the control system a further dimension of technology? Finally, it is necessary to do a great deal more work in identifying and isolating the variables other than technology on which behaviour inside organizations depends. This constitutes the outline of a lifetime's research.

Scott (1961)[9] has pointed out that organizational concepts have gone through the same process of development as those of both the physical sciences and economics. First came an attempt to discover order leading to the formulation of general laws. Variations in behaviour were then observed which demanded analysis in terms not of the whole universe, but of the smaller units of which it is composed. Next, attempts were made to integrate the results of these intensive studies, and finally, this integration led to new general laws, the older concepts being synthesized with them into a comprehensive theory.

Turning from the problems of analysis and integration to the attempts that have been made in the last ten years to formulate a general theory of organization, the first impression is of complete confusion. Whereas before 1950 there was relatively little writing in this field, since that date the balance has been more than redressed. There has been an increasing stream of literature on organization from engineers, sociologists, psychologists, economists, and mathematicians, which is fast approaching the proportions of a torrent. There have been some outstanding exceptions, but in the main the literature has come from the U.S.A. The impression of confusion arises not only because a number of different disciplines have become involved in the subject, but also because inside each discipline each researcher seems to have his own individual approach, and unfortunately he often finds it necessary to denigrate the work of others in its support. The only characteristics that the various new approaches have in common is an antipathy towards classical management theory.

Even so, inside what Koontz (1961)[10] called 'the management

[9] William G. Scott, 'Organization Theory', *Journal of the Academy of Management*, Vol. 4, No. 1. April 1961 (Garrard Press for Michigan State University).
[10] Harold Koontz, 'The Management Theory Jungle', *Journal of the Academy of Management*, Vol. 3, No. 3, December 1961.

theory jungle', it is possible to trace uniformities among the divergences; at least four separate approaches to organization theory and problems can be identified. The first is the sociological approach from which the conceptual framework for the analysis of the South Essex research data was derived. Basic to this approach is the concept of the social system, and the sociologist approaches the industrial firm as he would any other institution: in his analysis he aims to identify the parts of the system and study their interdependence.

The second is the approach of individual psychology. This approach is exemplified by the work of Argyris (1957)[11] who presents the theory by focusing on a presumed antagonism between individual and organizational goals. In this setting organization is evaluated in terms of its ability to achieve its goals while simultaneously providing means for individual self-realization.

The third approach, developed at the Carnegie Institute,[12] the decision theory approach had its roots in theoretical economics. It concentrates on the rational approach to decisions and analyses the decision process. Initially limited to the economic rationale of decisions, this approach has widened to include all other ingredients of the decision process indicating the social and psychological factors and the value considerations affecting decision-making.

Finally, there is the mathematical approach, which goes much further than the mere advocacy of mathematics as a tool of management or of the other disciplines concerned with organization. It sees organization as a system of mathematical processes. One of the more unfortunate aspects of the cut-and-thrust atmosphere in which organizational theory is now being developed, is that it is almost impossible to take a half-way position in any argument. It is particularly difficult to be neither for nor against the mathematical approach, to reject the idea that mathematics and management are synonymous while accepting it as a useful tool. There can be no question of its usefulness not only to economists

11 Chris Argyris, 'Personality and Organization', *The Conflict between System and the Individual* (Harper Bros., New York).
12 James G. March, Herbert A. Simon, and Harold Guetzkow, *Organizations* (John Wiley and Sons, New York).

and social scientists but also to practical managers in finding solutions to a variety of problems. The formulation of these problems does, however, require the concepts and methods of other relevant disciplines. Moreover, although there is no doubt that a quantitative approach can often sharpen the edge of these other disciplines, the formalization of concepts that are inadequately formulated by the use of mathematical techniques can give an air of false sophistication to a research project.

Exponents of the mathematical school have sometimes been referred to as 'management scientists'. The somewhat exaggerated claim implied brings us back to the question of whether these newer approaches are getting us any nearer to the development of what might be more realistically called 'a management science' than the classical approach was able to do. Have they anything in common and is it possible to synthesize the work now being done by their various exponents? One obvious common characteristic is the emphasis on empiricism, that is, on observation and experiment rather than on theory alone. They are all consciously moving into the final phase of Scott's[13] process of development. Although they draw on the results of intensive studies their main concern is with the extent to which these results can be integrated into general laws.

Even more important from the point of view of ultimate theory-building is the fact that the various schools of thought are all beginning to see themselves as concerned with the study of systems. This means that whether the approach is basically mathematical, psychological, sociological, or economic, the starting point is the identification of a system and the questions subsequently asked are very much the same: what are the objectives and strategic parts of the system under review and how are these parts interrelated and interdependent? One result of this is that those concerned with the study of organization are beginning to develop a common language, on whatever discipline their work is based.

It must not be too readily assumed, however, that they have concepts in common. The idea of a general systems theory is gaining popularity; attempts are being made to develop a universal science using common organizational elements found at all system

[13] Scott, op. cit., p. 249.

levels as its conceptual framework. This approach offers attractive possibilities. It is obvious, for example, that much of the data collected from the firms in South Essex could be analysed on the basis of the concepts and terminology of cybernetics in the way suggested by Beer (1959.)[14] Many of the phenomena observed lend themselves to presentations in terms of feedback, control, and regulation. But it is dangerous to take for granted that organizational elements found at different system levels are of the same nature or operate in the same way. It is impossible to be sure how far the analogy can be taken and it is doubtful whether the description of a social system in cybernetic terms will at this stage lead to a better understanding of it.

Summing up, therefore, the situation remains in essence much as it was in 1953. No complete or systematic theory of organization based on solid research has yet been proved valid, but the chances of reaching this position are infinitely better than they were; the concepts and methods of a number of disciplines are now being concentrated in the organization theory field.

Accepting that some progress has been made in the last ten years in our knowledge and understanding of the management process, the question remains whether the large amount of research and writing in this field has been useful to or used by industrial managers in tackling their practical problems of organization. The answer is unfortunately in the negative. There are several reasons for this lack of impact and for the difficulties academics working in this field and practising managers have in communicating with each other. From a manager's point of view much of what is being written is difficult to read. The lack of any universally accepted vocabulary of organization created difficulties during the field work of this research project. There is also the problem of jargon, about which a great deal has already been said by reviewers and critics of management literature. Moreover, a lot of recent writing is at a high level of abstraction—this is especially true of the work done in the decision theory area. Many full-time students of management both here and in the U.S.A. find much of the literature difficult to assimilate, and for the practical manager at the end of a day's work, with limited time or inclination, the task

[14] Stafford Beer, *Cybernetics and Management* (English Universities Press, London, 1959).

is wellnigh impossible. There is an urgent need for clarity and simplicity in what is being said and written.

The recent publication of collections of papers and extracts such as that edited by Litterer (1963),[15] in which the work of exponents of different schools of thought is brought together under selected themes, may be useful in bridging the gap between the theorist and the practitioner.

The failure of communication is not, however, only a language problem. There is also the problem of synthesis. As long as there is no integrated management science (and this still seems a long way away) managers who wish either to absorb what is being written into their thought processes or to use it to identify the nature of their practical problems need to know enough about the concepts and methods of the basic disciplines to find their way around in the literature. Management problems may be technical, psychological, sociological, or economic in character but sometimes, of course, they are mixed. Thus the manager has not only to understand how he can draw on these disciplines and appreciate what mathematical tools are available to help him, but he may also have to build up the separate elements into a connected whole before he can find a solution to his problem.

In general it is true to say that management education in the past has not given the manager the intellectual equipment he requires for this. Emphasis has been laid on tools and techniques rather than on fundamentals, and more attention paid to alleviating symptoms than on the diagnosis of causes.

If the development of management education contemplated in this country is to be worth while, its basis must be inter-disciplinary thinking. This is as important at teaching and research levels as at student levels. While it must be admitted that research is still likely to be most profitable if concentrated within particular fields—economists, for example, are likely to make their greatest contribution if they continue to regard management problems as economic problems—and that economic, psychological, sociological, and technical relationships cannot yet be brought together into a single model, it is essential for all those working in the management field to be aware of disciplines other than their own,

[15] Joseph A. Litterer, *Organizations: Structure and Behaviour* (John Wiley and Son Inc., New York and London).

and have respect for what is being done. Management must not be regarded as synonymous with economics, sociology, or even mathematics. Students—and this is particularly important at the full-time post-graduate courses level—must be given enough of the relevant disciplines to find their way around in them all. This is a part of management education which does not require prior experience. They must also be helped both at this stage and later to synthesize the different approaches. Here case studies are a useful tool. One of the weaknesses of the case study approach in the past has been that they have been regarded by enthusiasts as the whole of management education, and have been used before students have been provided with an adequate analytical equipment for dealing with the problems under consideration.

In these circumstances discussion of cases consists merely in an exchange of experience and opinion, and although interesting for the participants and regarded as down-to-earth, rarely develops their decision-making skill.

While it is hoped therefore that more and different facilities for management education will help us to improve communications between managers in industry and academics working in the management field, there is another factor that cannot be overlooked. The gulf has unfortunately been widened by management ideology itself.

The period 1953–63 saw a considerable increase not only in management research activities, but also in management's consciousness of itself, and of its economic importance and social prestige. These years saw the final emergence of management as a social institution in this country: a group of people bound together by a common ideology or system of beliefs. The two processes proceeded in parallel rather than in unison.

This evolution of an ideology is an interesting social process in itself. It is a common phenomena in areas where knowledge is limited or unavailable, and its importance must not be underrated. The emergence of a management ideology has helped to establish a common set of values in British industry, holding together people with opposed sectional and private interests. It helps them to feel a unity and perceive these common values and—perhaps most important of all—gives status and security inside the wider social environment. It is the cohesion and persistence associated with this process which has brought about the growth of management associations, and it has played a considerable part in the development of management education.

Management ideology has its own literature. In addition to the books and papers about the study and investigation of industrial organization which have appeared during the last ten years, there has been an equal volume of literature directed towards the propagation of this ideology. Such books have been dismissed as 'orgies of avuncular pontification' by McClelland (1963)[16] but they do fulfil an important social function. They record, communicate, and so help to perpetuate the system of beliefs of the management group and provide a guide to behaviour for the up-and-coming manager.

Social scientists and other academics operating in the industrial field have benefited from the development of this ideology; it has stimulated and formalized interest in management problems, and has provided many of these people with a forum and with entries into industry. But it has created a barrier. This is partly due to the fact that once an ideology has been established the people concerned live it, with the result that they can no longer be analytical about it and become reluctant to accept that it can be analysed, and partly to the nature of the ideology (or rather some of the beliefs associated with it). People living an ideology think and feel about it in terms and values which reflect but do not explain the forces that really control their social behaviour. Its beliefs are not truths or untruths in any absolute sense. There is usually enough truth in them to keep them intact but they are not exact descriptions of the feelings or behaviour of all the people concerned. In the industrial relations field, for example, there is a belief among managers that if they and their supervisors are sufficiently skilful they will be able to create an identity of interests between them and their labour force, and that conflicts can be avoided. There is some truth in this belief; social skills can be increased by sensitivity training; the interests of employers and employees do coincide at various points and some conflicts can be avoided. But it is not absolute truth and the belief does not make life easier for social

---

[16] W. G. McClelland, Review in *British Journal of Industrial Relations*, Vol. 1, No. 2, June 1963 of the book *Management Principles* by Walter Puckey (Hutchinson, 1962).

scientists who are interested in studying the functions of social conflict or trying to point out that it is impossible to solve problems by teaching 'human relations'.

As Galileo found to his cost, it is always difficult and can be dangerous to operate in a field where research results come into conflict with a system of beliefs. Not only does it make it more difficult to gain acceptance for the research, but the adjustment in attitudes and behaviour that has to be made when factual information makes the beliefs of an ideology no longer tenable is a very painful process for the people concerned.

It is recognized, of course, that those engaged in social research in industry have some way to go before they find themselves in the position of Galileo, and are forced to retract because their discoveries are unacceptable. But the abiding impression from the ten years' study of management organization outlined in this book is that some of the beliefs associated with the ideology of management are remote from reality. Moreover, this ideology tends to obscure reality, making it more difficult to perceive and understand what is actually happening.

This is particularly the case in relation to success in business. Important aspects of the ideology of management are the emphasis laid on the personal qualities of leadership and the belief that learning by doing is the only worth-while kind of training, knowledge being acquired almost entirely through experience. It is certainly true that many of our successful administrators and managers, whose example and words carry great weight and become part of the ideology, have been brought up in the empirical school. It is also true that the classical rules of management are so inadequate that the emphasis has to be laid on the process of adaptation already referred to. But the existence of the ideology makes it almost impossible for managers to be detached and impersonal enough to be conscious of the nature of their own achievements. It is much easier to let it be assumed that the explanation lies in the possession of the elusive, almost mystical qualities of leadership, and long experience. These investigations suggested, however, that it is possible to be much more specific about the reasons for a firm's or manager's success. The techniques involved can be described, analysed, learnt, and repeated by comparatively inexperienced people. More detailed study in this field might relieve British industry of its excessive dependence on leadership characteristics.

These two processes—the patient and detailed explanation of what actually happens inside industrial firms, and the building up of management as a social institution with the cohesiveness and energy to maintain itself—are both important but there is undoubtedly a need for them to be more closely associated with each other and kept in better balance than they are at present. If the gulf between academics working in the management field and practising managers is to be bridged—and it must be bridged before the best use can be made of the facilities which are to be provided for management education—academics must recognize that in the present limited state of knowledge, management needs a system of beliefs, and that the propagation of this system of beliefs is a legitimate part of management education, and management must recognize that a system of beliefs becomes less necessary as factual knowledge is extended and must be prepared to modify or relinquish their assumptions as soon as evidence is produced to show that they are no longer tenable.

APPENDIXES

I Schedule of Information Obtained[1]

1. *Classification of Industry (Ministry of Labour)*[2]
   - (i) Bricks, Ceramics, and Glassware
   - (ii) Chemical Manufacture, Oils, Dyes, Paint, Soap, &c.
   - (iii) Metal Manufacture (Blast Furnaces, Smelting, Foundries, &c.)
   - (iv) Engineering, Shipbuilding, and Electrical Goods
   - (v) Vehicles and Accessories
   - (vi) Metal Goods not elsewhere specified
   - (vii) Precision Instruments, Jewellery, Watches &c.
   - (viii) Textiles
   - (ix) Leather, Leather Goods, and Fur
   - (x) Clothing
   - (xi) Food, Drink, and Tobacco
   - (xii) Manufactures of Wood and Cork
   - (xiii) Paper and Printing
   - (xiv) Other manufacturing industries, including Rubber, Toys, Plastic Mouldings, etc.

2. *Nature of Product*
   Is product (i) Counted by numbers?
   (ii) Measured in pounds, gallons, cubic feet, etc.?
   (iii) Mixed?

3. *Is Production Predominantly*
   - (i) Single simple articles?
   - (ii) Prototypes?
   - (iii) Large equipment, built in stage?
   - (iv) Jobbing?
   - (v) Small batches?
   - (vi) Large batches?
   - (vii) Mass production?
   - (viii) Continuous flow?

[1] The information obtained was transposed on to a coding sheet.
[2] See Notes on p. 266.

4. *Type of Product*
(i) Stable products firmly established with a minimum of variety and slow in development
(ii) Progressive products which are fairly new, subject to rapid development and considerable variety
(iii) Specification products 'made to measure'

5. *Programme*
Is programme determined by
(i) Market Research?
(ii) Sales Forecast?
(iii) Analysis of incoming orders?
(iv) Firm orders only?

6. *Is any Measure of Capacity and Production Used?*
(i) Yes
(ii) No
(iii) Any other reply

7. *Technological Change*
(a) Have any major technical changes taken place in the last six months or are any such changes contemplated?
(b) If so, is the nature of the production system affected?

8. *Labour Costs as Percentage of Total Costs*
(i) Under $12\frac{1}{2}$
(ii) $12\frac{1}{2}$–25
(iii) 26–50
(iv) Over 50

9. *Turnover and Profit Trends Over Recent Years*
(i) Unsatisfactory
(ii) Satisfactory
(iii) Good

10. *Output*
(a) Is volume of trade in the industry increasing?
(b) Is the firm's proportion of the volume of the industry increasing?

Analysis of Organization

1. *Is an Organization Chart Available?*
(i) Yes
(ii) No
(iii) Any other reply

2. *Type of Organization*
 (i) Self-contained firm
 (ii) Unit of larger manufacturing organization

3. *Chief Executive*
 (i) Chairman
 (ii) Managing Director
 (iii) General Manager (member of Board)
 (iv) General Manager (not a member of Board)

4. *Number of Executives Responsible to the Chief Executive*

5. *Number of Levels in the Hierarchy*

6. *First-Line Supervision*
 (a) Number of first-line supervisors (in charge of production depart-
    ments)
 (b) Number of direct production workers

7. *Sales Organization*
 (a) Is there a Sales Manager?
 (b) Is he a member of the Board?
 (c) To whom is he responsible?
      (i) Managing Director
      (ii) Another less senior official

8. *Research Organization*
 (a) Is there a research manager?
 (b) Is he a member of the Board?
 (c) To whom is he responsible?
      (i) Manager Director
      (ii) Another less senior official
 (d) Is production capacity planned for new products when they have
    completed
      (i) The research stage?
      (ii) Development stage?
      (iii) Market tested stage?
      (iv) Methods planning stage?

9. *Planning or Production Control Organization*
 (a) To whom is the Head of the Planning or Production Control
    Department responsible?
      (i) Managing Director
      (ii) Another less senior official

(*b*) Which of the following departments does he control?
  (i) Programming
  (ii) Scheduling
  (iii) Works Order Issue
  (iv) Materials Requisitioning and Control
  (v) Progress
  (vi) Internal Transport
  (vii) Industrial Engineering
  (viii) Methods
  (ix) Work Study
  (x) Production Control
  (xi) None

10. *Inspection*

(*a*) Is there an Inspection Department?
(*b*) To whom is Head of Department responsible?
(*c*) Which of the following forms of inspection are used?
  (i) Shop floor
  (ii) Centralized
  (iii) Mixed
  (iv) None

11. *Personnel Management*

(*a*) Is there a Personnel Department?
(*b*) To whom is the Personnel Manager responsible?
  (i) Managing Director
  (ii) Another less senior official
(*c*) Are there any of the following departments?
  (i) Employment
  (ii) Training
  (iii) Welfare
  (iv) Employee Relations or Industrial Relations
  (v) Medical
  (vi) None
(*d*) What is the quality of the industrial relations in the firm?
  (i) Difficult—frequent labour disputes
  (ii) Average
  (iii) Very good—the firm has an outstanding reputation in this regard

12. *Accounting*

(*a*) Are cost accounts part of the financial figures?
(*b*) Is a cost or works accountant employed?
(*c*) If so, is he responsible to
  (i) Chief Accountant?

(ii) General Manager?
(iii) Anyone else?
(*d*) Is there a system of budgetary control?

13. *Maintenance*
(*a*) Who is responsible for maintenance of Plant and Machinery?
(*b*) To whom is he responsible?

14. *Purchasing*
(*a*) Who is responsible for Buying?
(*b*) To whom is he responsible?

Labour Analysis

1. *Total Personnel*
  (i) Less than 100
 (ii) 100–250
(iii) 251–500
(iv) 501–1,000
  (v) Over 1,000

2. *Labour Statistics*
Is a breakdown of labour by departments or by degree of skill available?

3.
(*a*) Number of industrial hourly paid workers
(*b*) Number of direct production workers
(*c*) Number of maintenance workers
(*d*) Number of other indirect workers
(*e*) Number of clerical and administrative workers
(*f*) Number of managerial and supervisory staff

4. *Qualifications*
(*a*) Are there any graduates employed in the firm
    (i) in line supervision?
   (ii) in specialist departments?
(*b*) Number of graduates
(*c*) Number of professionally qualified staff other than graduates

5. *Promotion*
  (i) Mainly from within
     (Formal management development programme)
 (ii) Mainly from within
     (No formal management development programme)
(iii) Mainly from outside
(iv) Mixed

NOTES FOR RESEARCH WORKERS

Analysis of Production

1. This classification has been taken from the Standard Industrial Classification of H.M. Central Statistical Office (reprinted 1953, H.M.S.O.) to which reference can be made.

2. Measured Products will be such things as gases, liquids, crystalline substances.

Give a brief description in 'remarks' column of the coding sheet of the main production process; indicate if it is a single-purpose or multi-purpose plant.

A mixed product is something like soapflakes produced by the lb in a plant and subsequently packaged.

3. If the predominating system is batch or mass production, indicate if it is of the assembly line type, in which the pace of working is determined by the speed of the belt.

6. If so, state in 'remarks' column whether it is in terms of unit of production, unit of cost, man/machine process hours.

7. It would be useful to find out how many technical changes that have taken place have affected the nature of the production system and if possible to code the change in accordance with the definitions given under questions 2, 3, 4. It is essential here to also give a brief description of the technical development in the 'remarks' column.

8. This information will arise from the breakdown of total turnover into labour, materials, and overheads generally.

9. If obtainable without pressing the firm. These classifications may require more exact definition. Comment in the 'remarks' column would therefore be useful here.

Analysis of Organization

1. If so, please attach to coding sheet.

2. If 2, state in the 'remarks' column how many more factories there are in the group and where they are situated.

3. The chief executive is defined as the senior official in residence at the factory, to whom decisions can be regularly referred.

4. Insert the number in the 'code' column, and list the titles of the people concerned in the 'remarks' column.

5. Insert the number in the 'code' column, and list the titles of the people concerned in the 'remarks' column, e.g. foreman, superintendent, manager, general manager, managing director.

6. First-line supervisor is defined as the lowest level official who spends more than half of his time on the supervision of production operations. Working chargehands are not included. The classification 'production operators' includes the total staff of all production departments including labourers and others not necessarily on direct production work.

7. (*c*) Enter the title of the person concerned in the 'remarks' column.

8. (*c*) Enter the title of the person concerned in the 'remarks' column.

9. (*a*) Enter the title of the person concerned in the 'remarks' column.

   (*b*) Add any others in the 'remarks' column; also say if any of these departments exist but are responsible to someone else.

10. (*b*) Enter the title of the person concerned in the 'remarks' column and leave the 'code' column blank.

11. (*b*) Enter the title of the person concerned in the 'remarks' column.

   (*c*) All these departments may not be under the control of the personnel manager. Note in the 'remarks' column those that are.

12. In the remarks column give a brief description of the cost reports produced, how product is costed, etc.

13. (*a*) Enter title of the person concerned in the 'remarks' column.

   (*b*) Enter title of the person concerned in the 'remarks' column.

14. (*a*) Enter title of the person concerned in the 'remarks' column.

   (*b*) Enter title of the person concerned in the 'remarks' column.

Labour Analysis

1. Enter the exact number in the 'remarks' column.

2. If so, please attach to coding sheet. It might then be unnecessary to answer Question 3.

3. Give the exact figures in the 'remarks' column, leaving the 'code' column blank for the time being.

   (*b*) This figure should correspond with that given in the answer to Question 6 of 'Analysis of Organization' section.

   (*d*) This means $a - (b + c)$.

   (*e*) Weekly and monthly paid staff as opposed to hourly paid workers.

   (*f*) This will include all those in what are considered by the firm concerned to be supervisory grades. There will be some borderline cases, in all of these, follow the line taken by the firm. Total personnel given in answer to Question 1 will be made up of $a + e + f$.

4. This information may be difficult to get, if so, do not press this question but make a note of any remarks made. If the information is available, give the exact figure in the 'remarks' column, leaving the 'code' column blank.

II The Measurement of Technical Variables

By R. C. Brewer

Reference was made, in Chapter 10, to the problem of delineating the position of a given technical situation within the spectrum which ranges from unit production at one extreme to mass production of very simple small components, or of dimensional products, at the other.

Anything which varies continuously from a minimum to a maximum value may be classified in two ways:

(1) according to a system of division into sections or categories;

(2) by deciding upon some parameter which is both representative of what is being classified and capable of numerical expression.

It may be helpful at this stage to consider the salient features of the two approaches. Of the system of division into sections, it may be said that:

(a) it is simple, provided the number of sections is not too large. (In this connection, it may be noted that the second method is the limiting case of the first method as the number of sections tends to infinity.)

(b) it is arbitrary; this is, in general, a weakness but if there is real difficulty in ascribing a numerical parameter, it may be better to adopt an arbitrary division into sections than use a numeric which is un-representative, since this is not only misleading but may confer a sense of 'mathematical security' which is, in fact, quite absent.

(c) it leads to what might be called the 'border-line complex', i.e. the reluctance to place border-line cases rigidly in their correct categories. This leads, at the best, to a new intermediate category, and at the worst to the placing, albeit unconsciously, of a border-line case in that category which the observer would wish it to fall. It must be admitted that this criticism is invalid *if* a rigid adherence to section boundaries is observed.

(d) the placing of the boundaries is not always simple.

On the other hand, we can say of the numerical parameter method that:

(i) it is more precise, provided that the parameter chosen is a satisfactory representation of the function or situation being classified. From a sociological point of view, this is most important since one of the most basic differences between the natural and the human sciences is the ease with which the former can adequately express its variables numerically and the difficulty experienced by the latter in this same respect;

(ii) if a correlation is sought and, in particular, if a degree of confidence in this correlation is to be expressed, then the sectional division method falls lamentably short of what is required. To a natural scientist, one of the most serious defects of the human sciences is their apparent readiness to accept correlations based on non-numerical methods;

(iii) objective steps must be taken to ensure that the numerical data tells the story in the manner required. For example, if we seek only the height of a man, an Englishman and a Japanese each 5 ft 9 in high may be considered equally well represented by this one numeric; if, on the other hand, we wished to assess the likelihood with which each would fit a suit made for the average height of his nationality, we should have to acknowledge that the Japanese was some 10 per cent above average while the Englishman was probably no more than 1 per cent above average. The device of a dimensionless height (i.e., a man's height expressed as a ratio of the national average) answers this problem and would be the first thought of a physicist or engineer. It appears to an outsider, however, to be little practised in the human sciences except, perhaps, where they have been touched by Operational Research.

Turning now to the problem of classifying manufacturing situations, the method adopted in the South Essex studies was that of dividing firms into categories, and as will have been realized the problems encountered were intrinsic to that method. Moreover, from a sociological point of view it is doubtful whether the very broad spectrum of human behaviour observed could be correlated with such a limited technological division.

It was felt therefore that the second way of classifying might be of more value. When we arrange the conventional 'scales of production' in ascending order, viz., unit, job, batch, mass, we think of increasing rates of production, i.e., shorter time between the completion of one component and the completion of the next. Flow production is not listed since it refers to a type of production and hence a manufacturing situation is either of the flow type or it is not. Thus, we might use, as a tentative numeric for a manufacturing situation, either the production rate or the unit time, i.e., the time between completing one component and completing the next. (It should be noted that either of these is the reciprocal of the other, speaking mathematically.)

A moment's reflection, however, shows us that we are back to our

Englishman/Japanese difficulty; an automobile factory producing 800 vehicles per day is working at quite a high production rate but a tobacco company which made only 800 cigarettes per day would soon be out of business.

What we seek, then, is to give a more generalized meaning to production rate or unit time, i.e. a meaning which will enable us to compare quite different manufacturing situations. It is the thesis of this Appendix that the manufacturing time is the means by which this day be done. Manufacturing time would normally be taken to mean the complete time for the component or other article to be manufactured, but, in some cases, it might be desirable to assess the different parts of manufacture separately, e.g. production of sub-assemblies and final assembly. We may now define a production rate index (R) in terms of the manufacturing time (t_1) and either the production rate (p) or the unit time (t_2) viz., $R = \dfrac{t_1}{t_2} = t_1\,p$. It is mathematically more homogeneous to think of the ratio of two times but it makes no difference to the final answer how we calculate R.

Clearly the lowest value which R can take is unity corresponding to unit production, when the manufacturing time and unit time are equal. There is no theoretical upper limit to R, high values of R indicating either that the manufacturing time is long or, what is more likely in practice, that the unit time is very short. It seems reasonable to accept as comparable, all situations which yield the same value of R although the individual values of t_1 and t_2 may differ greatly.

This then provides us with a numeric which, on the argument proposed above, is representative of the rate of production and applicable to a wide range of industries. It was suggested, however, that this might not be the complete picture and that there might be differences between situations which yield the same value of R—not technical differences which would invalidate the argument presented above, but differences in behaviour patterns discernible by the sociologist.

Consideration was then given to other possible parameters. When this problem was first posed it was felt that there might be some correlation between R and the capital investment necessary to achieve it, i.e. the higher production rates would require more expensive, special-purpose machinery (the fact that this might reduce the unit manufacturing cost of the component is not relevant to the present argument). It was not expected that a 100 per cent correlation would exist—indeed, the main hope was that differing deviations from the perfect correlation would coincide with differences which the sociologist was able to discern in situations yielding the same value of R.

The use of capital investment was not favoured since, once again, it does not lend itself to comparing one industry with another, or one country with another. It was felt, however, that financial management practice was probably sufficiently the same to permit the time for recovering capital expenditure to be used as a criterion. This time, which we shall denote by T, is not readily disclosed by companies but there are some indirect ways by means of which it may be estimated.

Companies working on a contract basis usually know the period of time for which they will be making a specified component and it may reasonably be assumed that they will adjust their capital expenditure to accord with this. In some industries there are fixed periods at which capital costs recur, e.g. wallpaper where the season's new designs call for heavy expenditure on engraving of rolls, etc. In many consumer goods industries, products must be re-designed at intervals to maintain sales rates and, in the face of competition, it is reasonable to suppose that this period is usually the shortest which will recoup the capital invested. This period is fairly readily disclosed by companies since it is not difficult, but only tedious, to obtain it by other methods, e.g., searching advertisements over the years.

A pilot study was carried out to see if it was possible to get the kind of information required to identify R and T. Although a broad range of industries was covered, the time available limited the number of situations studied. More work is obviously required if any comprehensive conclusions are to be drawn but one or two observations can be made on the more limited results which are available.

Fig. 29 shows all the results in the form of the ratio R plotted against the time T. There was reason to suppose that situation H1 (a medium sized bakery) was not operating efficiently and, if we ignore it for the moment, the fact that there is some correlation between R and T is confirmed inasmuch as the situations plotted fall inside a definite band although the width of the band is rather large. As pointed out in a previous paragraph, one would not expect 100 per cent correlation but the presence of a trend tends to confirm that the argument put forward is not completely without foundation.

It may well be that the 'band' or correlation in Fig. 29 does not mean a great deal *per se*, and that many individual correlations exist between similar manufacturing situations, e.g., situations A1, A2, and A3 pertain to the manufacture of radio valves, situations B1, B2, and B3. to factories manufacturing cathode-ray tubes, and E1, E2, and E3 to the manufacture of motor-cars. The individual correlation for these three types of manufacturing are much higher than the overall correlation (Fig. 30). Obviously, the sample is absurdly small by statistical standards, but there is the negative satisfaction that, at least, the few existing points are not themselves randomly scattered over the diagrams.

Furthermore, there is some support for the suggestion that the width

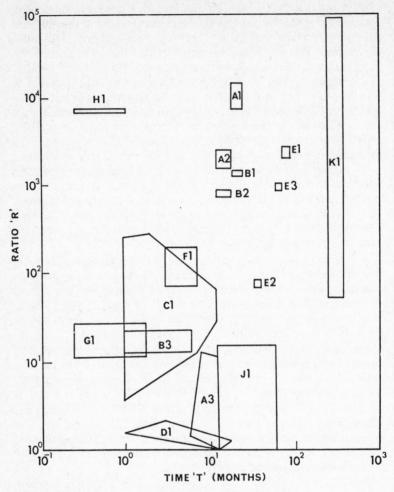

Fig. 29. Classification of technology by product density and order time

of the band in Fig. 29 is due more to the nature of individual correlations than deviations from one overall correlation, since the slopes of the lines for the three families A, B, and E in Fig. 30 are quite different. The 'A' line is the steepest indicating that a great increase in R can be achieved with quite a small increase in the time required to recoup capital investment. Output can be increased greatly (by mechanization or automation) without the need to maintain the sale of substantially the same model over a comparatively long period of time. For the same

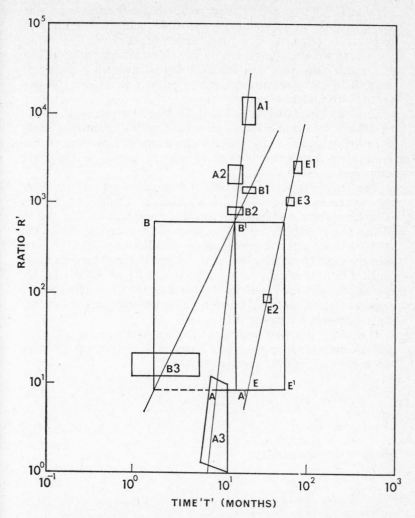

Fig. 30. Classification of three selected industries (from Fig. 29)

increase in R, the times over which the capital expenditure would be recovered are indicated by lines AA' (for valves), BB' (for cathode-ray tubes), and EE' (for motor-cars).

It will be evident also that the size of the area plotted for each company gives an indication of the diversity of its activities and one would expect that the unit, job and batch producers would show the largest areas. This is borne out in Fig. 29 with the exception of situation K. This pertains to a large crude oil refinery producing a wide range of fuels and the area is attributable more to uncertainty in assessing the magnitude of T than diversity of activities.

In many factories, the production of individual components will be on a batch basis while final assembly may be classified as mass production. In such circumstances, it may be more valuable to plot two separate areas joined by a line.

Summarizing, it may be said that the argument proposed and the information contained in Fig. 29 are not in conflict with anything which is qualitatively known and, subject to more complete investigation, the quantitative information of Fig. 29 may be helpful in classifying manufacturing situations.

There is, of course, the argument of simplicity to support the use of the value R alone as a method of classification; it certainly possesses the advantages which the 'numerical parameter' approach has over that of 'division into sections' and there seems little reason to doubt the adequacy with which it represents the situations studied. However, only the second axis in Fig. 29 (T) shows any difference between many pairs of situations. E.g., A2 and E1, G1 and B3, or A3 and J1. No sociologist could have much doubt that there were real differences in organization and behaviour between a factory making radio valves (A2) and a large motor company (E1).

It would thus appear helpful to use the concepts of Fig. 29 where possible but to bear in mind the advantages of using R alone in cases where it is difficult to evaluate or estimate T.

Index